The Rock

Looking Into Australia's 'Heart Of Darkness' From The Edge Of Its Wild Frontier

Aaron Smith

16pt

MELBOURNE, AUSTRALIA
www.transitlounge.com.au

Copyright © 2020 Aaron Smith

First published 2020
Transit Lounge Publishing

This book is copyright. Apart from any fair dealing for the purpose of private study, research, criticism or review, as permitted under the Copyright Act, no part may be reproduced by any process without written permission. Inquiries should be made to the publisher.

Cover design: Peter Lo
Front cover image: Glen Mackie, who is also known as Kei Kalak. He has been at the forefront of the Torres Strait Islander print movement since the 1990s.

Printed in Australia by McPherson's Printing Group

A cataloguing entry is available from the
National Library of Australia

TABLE OF CONTENTS

The Four Axioms of the Bush	ii
A FORE (LETTER) WORD	v
CHAPTER 1: THE WILD FRONTIER	1
CHAPTER 2: GOING STRAIT	13
CHAPTER 3: A WAR OF WORDS	32
CHAPTER 4: ON THE ROCKS	48
CHAPTER 5: MURALAG MOONSHINE	80
CHAPTER 6: ON THE LIGHTER SIDE	99
CHAPTER 7: DIRE STRAITS	124
CHAPTER 8: BIRDS OF A FEATHER	151
CHAPTER 9: SHIP OF FOOLS	169
CHAPTER 10: GOING NATIVE	187
CHAPTER 11: THIRSTY ISLAND	207
CHAPTER 12: A DOG ACT	219
CHAPTER 13: FLOWERS FOR A WATERY GRAVE	237
CHAPTER 14: SOUTH OF THE BORDER	248
CHAPTER 15: HANDSHAKES AND POISONOUS SNAKES	262
CHAPTER 16: MIND THE GAP	282
CHAPTER 17: THE ZOO	304
CHAPTER 18: WHITEWASHING AND BLACK CLADDING	318
CHAPTER 19: LORE OF THE LAND	344
CHAPTER 20: ALL THE KING'S HORSES	378
CHAPTER 21: TRICK OR TREATY	400
CHAPTER 22: WHERE THE WIND TURNS	418
CHAPTER 23: IN BLACK AND WHITE	452
CHAPTER 24: THE ROCK	469
ESSOS AND ACKNOWLEDGEMENTS	487
BIBLIOGRAPHY	491

i

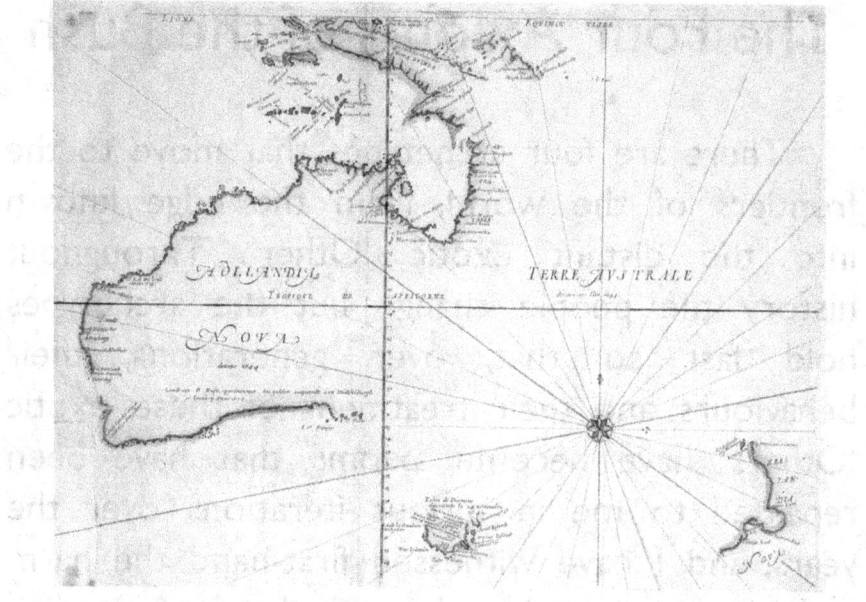

The Four Axioms of the Bush

There are four archetypes that move to the frontiers of the world, from the edge known into the distant exotic 'Other'. Throughout history the people change but the archetypes hold fast so that, over generations, their behaviours and their treatment of these exotic 'Others' have become axioms that have been repeated to me in various iterations over the years, and I have witnessed first-hand the harm and devastation they have had on Australia's Traditional Owners. These archetypes are:

I. The Missionaries: These come in many forms, from the original zealots who arrived into the unknown world clutching bibles and with the desire to thrash the wickedness out of the noble savage, to the many generations of great white saviours who arrive from the metropolitan centres and simply know what's best for their disenfranchised brown-skinned brethren.

II. The Murderers and Madmen: These are the stowaways, draft dodgers, drifters, convicts on the run, hermits and fringe dwellers who reject the ways of modern society, and while they

	have changed little over the last two centuries, they are a dying breed.
III.	The Misfits: They are the people who cannot get a job in their own world so come to the frontier, the inept middle-management and bureaucrats enshrined by mediocrity.
IV.	The Mercenaries: Since the birth of the corporation when the East India Company plundered the New World, the Mercenaries have been the most ruthless of all the archetypes. They are also the most honest. Morally bankrupt, but honest in that they only ever profess to be there for the money. Whether they brandish cutlasses, pith helmets, flash Italian suits, or high-vis vests and steel-capped boots, the Mercenaries have not changed one iota throughout the course of history.

Let no one say the past is dead.
The past is all about us and within.

OODGEROO NOONUCCAL

A FORE (LETTER) WORD

Fuck you.

With all due respect, fuck you – yes, you, dear reader of this page.

Fuck you, Australia, lost in the Great Forgetting, the Great Unknowing, the Great Denial of your bloody heart of darkness. We are all of us drowning in the modern era of narcissism, in the rising tide of bigotry and intolerance at the arse end of times.

Fuck you, the eighty-five percent who live in the metropolises, drip-fed an augmented reality by your smartphone and wide-screen TV, swallowed up by suburbia – each quarter-acre cut off from the vast expanse of the Country by a five-foot paling fence. That's Country with a capital C, which rolls across hundreds of nations in this great southern land, our ancient island home – this beautiful desolate rock cast adrift in Oceania.

With all due respect, fuck you, North Shore Sydney, with your blue-eyed, blonde-bobbed, intergenerational over-privileged perfect-tanned nip and tuck; fuck you, St Kilda, with your deconstructed lattes and your simpering inner-city neoliberal sensibilities; fuck you, Fremantle, with your laissezfaire, sun-bleached, mineral-leached

Great White surfie grin, which conceals your true nature lurking just beneath the undercurrent; fuck you, South Bank Brisbane, with your buffed bodies in snarky suits and bougainvillea-dripping walkways to nowhere; fuck you, Adelaide, and your silver-balled Rundle Mall, your wine bars and marijuana mansions; fuck you, Hobart, with your nature porn and your own Guggenheim in the burbs, the MONA groan white noise of art-wank prattle; and fuck you, Canberra, in the middle of a paddock in the middle of nowhere, with your giant Hills hoist crowning the Parliament, where politicians' banal rhetoric is lost in the bleating of a million surrounding sheep – who, like their constituents, are lambs for slaughter.

Also – of course, with all due respect – fuck you, akubra-wearing rural Australia too, and the farmers who may or may not know their hands are bloodied by the atrocities of their grandfathers, both to the land and to the people who were there before them.

Fuck you, oligarchs and plutocrats of democracy, the mining magnates and media moguls and the rest of the corporate mongrels guzzling Penfolds Grange and tearing the carcass of our country apart. And fuck you, army of bureaucrats in public servitude who deliver the death of a thousand paper cuts.

The truth of the birth of *Terra Australis Incognita* is yet to be understood and owned by all Australians.

Until it is embraced as part of our nation's story, we will never be united – we will never reach our full potential. Until we do, we will never heal our past, our people, our seas, our reef, our dirt – our souls. Until we do, this disconnection from our Country will continue to plunge us towards our communal demise. We gorge on the fat of a fragile land, whose ancient spirits glow illuminated by the Southern Cross, the footprint of the cosmic emu, bleached out by city lights and the bluish hue of ten million tiny digital screens.

So with all due respect, fuck you, all of you, white-bread Australia, and fuck me, too. Born a prisoner of Her Majesty, son of one of the last ten-pound Poms, I am as placeless and baseless as the rest of us. Fuck us all, the bastard sons and daughters of bastard sons and daughters, the bastards we are and the bastards we have been. It's time to wake up and be the better beasts that deep in our selfish, blackened hearts we know we truly can, and should, and desperately need to be.

A house divided against itself cannot stand, so I reckon we should all learn to sing the songlines, shake a leg, share the yarns and stand as one on this sunburnt Country or Countries with a capital C.

So it's with the greatest respect and humility and gratitude I say: fuck you, Australia.

Yours with absolute sincerity,

The Author.

CHAPTER 1

THE WILD FRONTIER

17 June 2015

As he grins, Captain Magic's few remaining rotten teeth glisten cherry red with narcotic betel nut juice. Salt shimmers on his Melanesian complexion, trapped in smile wrinkles and crow's feet. Narrowing his gaze through the sea spray, he picks a line and deftly manoeuvres our banana boat through the molasses-coloured Arafura Sea, which pounds the remote coast of Papua New Guinea's Western Province.

Also pounding are my temples, as we punch through the tempestuous waters at first light. I'm suffering the aftermath of a week of drinking into the wee hours. We would neck Bundy Rum, whisky and whatever else we could get our hands on in desperate abandon in the fenced-in compound of the Crow's Nest Hotel.

A vermin-infested shithole with rising damp and peeling paint, with dengue and malaria lurking in every dark corner – where every mozzie bite was a spin of Russian roulette – the Crow's Nest is the upmarket digs on Daru.

This island outpost is the only semblance of civilisation in the whole province.

A province riddled with corruption and lawlessness.

Anyone on Daru knows it's a lousy time of year for the annual delegation of multi-governmental agencies from Australia and PNG to be visiting the thirteen isolated Torres Strait Treaty Villages along the Western Province coast, which can only be reached by small boat or helicopter. A couple of months earlier the doldrums would've provided calmer waters and gentler winds.

Daru, a 14-square-kilometre mudflat a nautical mile south of the PNG mainland, is an anarchic shantytown that has the region's only hospital, airport, supermarket, running water and electricity – and pub. It's the epicentre for villagers scattered up and down the coast who scratch an existence that's changed little since the Pleistocene. They come to trade their subsistence crops and fish for enough kina to buy basic supplies. It's also a den for drug and gun runners, wildlife poachers, the occasional people smuggler, and illegal Chinese fishing boats filled with shanghaied slaves.

With the only bank in the region, Daru is also where tribal Traditional Owners converge to get their meagre monthly royalty cheque from the open-cut copper mine Ok Tedi, the country's biggest and dirtiest revenue raiser. Each day it dumps tens of thousands of tonnes of tailings into the Fly River, where they flow out to sea and are carried on the current along the Western Province coast.

Around 20,000 people – 30,000 on royalty payday – are crammed into lean-tos or live in the muddy marina, where rubbish and raw sewage form a cesspit around the many outrigger canoes at low tide. Gangs of machete-wielding raskols maraud the potholed streets stained red with a patchwork of dried betel-nut spit. The malevolence is palpable. Life is cheap here. Murder, rape and corruption are rife; dengue, malaria, HIV and drug-resistant TB are rampant, while witchcraft and sorcery are trusted more than Western medicine.

Daru is one of the few islands of the Torres Strait not to fall under Australia's territorial claim. It's a different world to that enjoyed by Australian citizens. This wild frontier is only a few kilometres' dinghy ride from our porous border, which its residents legally cross, up to 50,000 times a year, due to a unique treaty that shares traditional fishing territory and acknowledges family ties severed by PNG's independence in 1975.

After independence, PNG became a nation of villages, wrangling together 700 tribes, and more than 800 language groups. It became part of the Commonwealth, under the British monarchy, funded by Australia, which remains its largest supplier of foreign aid. A troubled young country wrought with inter-tribal war, violence, disease and corruption – thrust under a sovereign not of its choosing, which imposed a political and judicial system incongruent with tribal lore.

For the thirty-year anniversary of the Torres Strait Treaty, I am invited by the Department of Foreign Affairs and Trade (DFAT) to accompany a delegation on its annual Treaty Village awareness visit, which aims to remind villagers about the rules of the treaty. The delegation includes representatives from the Australian and PNG high commissions, the Australian and PNG Foreign Offices, Australia's Border Force, the Australian Fisheries Management Authority, the Department of Agriculture and Fisheries, Queensland Health and a couple of CSIRO soil scientists. I am there as the editor of Australia's most northerly newspaper, the *Torres News* (I am also its photographer and paperboy), and the region's only resident journalist.

Apart from the soil scientists, the bureaucrats are a little nervous about having a journo in their ranks. This may be due to the periodical roasting their departments have received in the *Torres News*, which regularly gives their bumbling boondoggling a good airing. Despite its small circulation – a couple of thousand copies a week – the *Torres News* punches well above its weight, often pricking the ears of southern journalists and triggering flustered responses from state and federal ministers. It's the only voice from a region with twenty-one Indigenous communities spread across the tip of Cape York and throughout the archipelago of 274 islands scattered in the treacherous Torres Strait. It is the nation's most culturally diverse mix of Australian Aboriginal, Melanesian, Asiatic and European descendants, where English is a second language to Torres Strait Creole, as well as two native tongues. It is also nearly completely unknown to the majority of Australia.

It's the first time the government has invited a journalist on this trip. I like to think it's so the rest of the country can get an on-the-ground account of our only international frontier, on the thirty-year anniversary of our world-first treaty, which took into consideration the aspirations and needs of its Indigenous people. It later turns out that Australia has no interest in the treaty, the people it serves or the implications it has for the nation. It simply isn't sexy enough. My pitches of exclusives to news outlets across the country are met with complete silence.

Right on Australia's doorstep, our poor cousins in the Western Province are racked by poverty and pestilence, and as with most of Australia, the urbanite Bunnings weekend warriors of Australia's metropolitan heartland are largely oblivious to their plight. It's an ambivalence that echoes across the nation, from here at the frontier right into the Australia's colonial heart of darkness – our reluctance to reconcile our past or understand 'Country' beyond a lip-service preamble of acknowledging 'Elders past and present'.

Ray, DFAT's Treaty Liaison Officer, had to fight hard to get approval for my inclusion on the trip, but I suspect the main reason I was invited was he knows I can hold my liquor, respect off-the-record and love to live a little dangerously – like him.

Ray, mid-forties, short, pudgy, with a hypertensive glow and a shock of greying blond hair, sports a permanent white mark around his eyes where his sunglasses have shaded his otherwise sun-kissed face. Ray loves a drink and he needs a wingman.

Ray and I met on Thursday Island, the Torres Strait's administrative hub and its biggest community. We bonded at boozy dinner parties, where despite our scowling wives, we were always the last to leave, sharing raucous tales from our youth or comparing our sketchiest near-death travel stories from when we were younger, wilder men.

Ray's PNG field trip out of Daru is six days of predawn starts, crossing turbulent seas in dinghies to visit communities where he is never sure if we will be welcomed with flower wreaths or machete-wielding mobs. We have to grit through wind and rain, wade through pestilence and observe abject poverty and suffering before punching back through the terrible weather to Daru at sunset. We then retreat to the compound of the Crow's Nest Hotel, safe behind barbed wire and armed guards. Overflowing with the visceral throb of the frontier, we soak our brains in drink to decompress, with total disregard for the following morning's early start.

On the last morning, Ray tells there is not enough room in the specially equipped DFAT-funded Ranger boats, so I have to ride with Captain Magic in his banana boat. The three Ranger boats, a gift to PNG, cost some $70,000 dollars each: they are supposedly unsinkable and have all the state-of-the-art GPS and safety gear.

'Sorry, mate, we have an extra person from the High Commission, so your seat got bumped. Government staff are only allowed to travel in approved vessels. It's for safety reasons.' Ray pats me reassuringly on the back as we walk down the pier at Daru marina.

Clammy sweat clings to me as my hungover temples throb. Clouds bluster across the morning sun, spitting rain and blotting out the horizon. White caps start to break on the waves out at sea. A squall rumbles towards us along the Western Province coast, which is being engulfed by an ominous grey haze.

A tall, wiry Papuan man approaches. He could be either thirty-five or fifty, and is smoking a handmade 'spear', a bush tobacco cigarette rolled in newspaper. His dark eyes sparkle. He spits out his betel nut, smiles, and thrusts out an open palm.

'Meet Captain Magic – he's the best banana boat skipper on Daru,' Ray says. 'He's called Captain Magic as he can get you out of any situation, and no matter how rough it is he will keep you safe and dry. You're in good hands.' Ray pushes a life jacket into my chest and walks away.

The slender, 6-metre-long fibre-glass banana boat slices smoothly through choppy seas. There is no built-in floatation, so if the outboard cuts out and waves swamp the hull, it will sink like a stone.

An hour later the delegation's three Ranger boats are labouring in a spearhead formation. They plough through waves, airborne over the crest of one only to have the next break over the bow, drenching everyone on board. It is a spine-jarring grind, everyone holding fast with the same grim expression I had the day before. Everyone but Ray, that is, who is sitting up in the bow taking the full brunt of the vessel's heave-ho, sodden but grinning at the sublime madness of it.

Meanwhile Captain Magic glides between the waves, surfing the edge of one and darting through the valley of another. There is barely a splash on me, but when the occasional one does, fearing his reputation is on the line, he wails an apology over the roar of the elements and the Yamaha Enduro 60 two-stroke.

Hugging a coastline swallowed up by untouched jungle, we skim across a sea the colour of chocolate milk. It's the sediment washing out of the Fly River from the Ok Tedi mine in the highlands. Apart from some paltry payouts to Traditional Owners, the only 'trickledown effect' is the silt: it chokes the villages downstream, muddies the water and decimates the barramundi, their main source of protein. The villages claw a foothold in occasional gaps in the mangroves. The inhabitants stand where the land meets the sea, with one foot in their world and one in ours. They stare at us in wonder and desperation as we hurtle past. Here petrol is at a premium, and our big delegation is a spectacle in a place where twenty villagers squeeze into one banana boat, the gunnels only inches above the waterline, to make the rare and perilous trip to Daru. Those who cannot afford the fuel take giant outrigger canoes with sails made of rags, crewed by the whole family on a trip that can take days. They tend small camp fires on the bow, cooking whatever subsistence they catch en route. Raptors circle above, awaiting ill fortune.

Feeling both fearful and exhilarated, I can't help but smile like a crazed Dennis Hopper in *Apocalypse Now*, which was based on Joseph Conrad's *Heart of Darkness*. Conrad's novel explored the psyche of European colonialism in the African Congo: good and evil, black and white, sanity and insanity. Just as Conrad's tale ventured deep into the emptiness at the core of Western modernity, we too pressed on, past the edge of the modern world.

We entered still, uncharted waters where no Australian border patrol ever goes – as insiders will admit after a couple of beers. This is the back door for raskols in banana boats loaded with contraband, people desperately seeking asylum, fishermen after a good catch of lobster or bêche-de-mer. They do the run with no GPS, navigating using the night sky, skimming over shallow water at full throttle, dodging exposed reef using smell, with nothing more than a drum of fuel, ancient knowledge and a big set of stones.

On the surface Ray plays the iconic Aussie larrikin. He seems to know and be tolerated by people across political, racial and cultural divides, and it's easy to forget he is actually a representative of the colonial overseer.

The harsh realities of life for the Traditional Owners of this land are all too apparent and serve as a stark reminder of our own nation's failing in our own backyard to close the gap, reconcile our colonial past and understand the first custodians of the great southern land.

The work of Missionaries, Mad Men, Misfits and Mercenaries, and our little delegation was no exception.

Balancing in a squat, I manage to steady myself as if I'm surfing a long-board into oblivion as Captain Magic performs his miracles. Two DSLR cameras swing around my neck as the taste of last night's rum rises and sours the back of my throat. I swallow and breathe through my teeth as I try to photograph the edge of this frontier.

Between Captain Magic's dips and graceful turns in an angry sea, I find a moment of stillness to frame and shoot Ray, who is grinning back at me as his boat bursts through the top of a wave, capturing his sublimity in the elemental mayhem and chaos.

I chuckle to myself. 'The horror, the horror.'

CHAPTER 2

GOING STRAIT

Two years earlier...

30 May 2013, first day on the job.

As we fly over Cape York, I press my nose against the egg-shaped perspex window and stare past the whirl of the Dash 8's propeller. My gaze fixes on the wild terrain as we hurtle towards Australia's most northerly community – one of the world's most remote. (Everyone thinks the tip of Cape York is the most northerly point of Australia, but it's not – there's another 150 kilometres of country, Sea Country, which falls under our flag.)

It's the last leg of a two-day trip across the continent, from Bass Strait to Torres Strait, and I feel a flutter of trepidation.

I've left behind my friends and family. I won't see my wife and toddler daughter for three months. Like most Australians, I don't know a damn thing about the Torres Strait, its people, its culture or its history, but I am about to become the region's newspaper editor. Am I mad? This is one of the country's last frontiers, with crocs and sharks ... and Queenslanders.

But the thing that terrifies me is that I'm about to start a job I blagged my way into. It is actually my first 'real' full-time job, with superannuation, holiday pay, the whole nine yards.

I have previously done just about everything to get by. I've been a musician, an actor, a playwright and guerrilla filmmaker. I've been a dishpig, driven trucks, picked fruit, weeded gardens, painted houses, laboured on construction sites and even worked briefly as a telemarketer until I couldn't take being hung up on or told to fuck off anymore. I once had a job interviewing gay men about their condom use, back when I was young and nubile, straight out of university with a science degree I would never use. My very camp boss suggested I hit the sauna clubs to find likely subjects. I went to gay nightclubs instead and persisted till I got the job done.

I've never had a predilection for being the hamster in the wheel, running the unwinnable, never-ending rat race. But things change – I'm forty-three now and it's time to go straight, or should I say Strait.

I partied very hard in the extended puberty of my twenties and some of my thirties, first in the grunge/metal scene and then in the rave scene, until it became mind-numbingly boring. I look back at it now as my ten-year weekend. I spent the second half of my thirties traipsing around the globe trying to work out who the hell I was, until I fell into travel writing.

I returned to Australia in 2009 with a Brazilian fiancée and three maxed-out credit cards. We retreated to my childhood home in Hobart and crashed on Mum and Dad's couch ... for eighteen months.

I figured it was time to leave home (again) once my wife got pregnant.

Now that I was a father and a husband, my wife decided I should get my proverbials together. She was probably right – annoyingly, she usually is. I thought I could just write the great Australian novel and swan around in a silk bathrobe and drink single malt for breakfast while the royalties rolled in. But either despite of, or due to, my Hunter-esque tendencies, I realised my book work wasn't going to feed my new family, so I started writing freelance for glossy travel and adventure sports mags, and wherever else I could successfully pitch my copy to. I did most of it via the phone or email from my kitchen table, usually in nothing but my underwear. I was a bottom feeder, jostling for contracts from magazine editors and digging around for leads on juicy stories.

In between freelance contracts I scratched out an existence as a handyman, which kept me at the level of poverty to which I had grown accustomed.

Then one Monday morning I saw a job online for the editor of a newspaper in a remote Indigenous community. It said they wanted someone with three to four years' newspaper-editing experience – I had none. So I wrote an unconventional application letter, which began, 'To be frank, I would chew my right arm off for this job', followed by an offer to work at half-pay for three months while I worked out the ropes. I then showed off my investigative journalism skills by digging out my future employer's name and finding his private email, where I sent my application.

Two days later I got a phone call to say I had the job. Serendipity or just luck?

In an era when the newspaper is dying, when redundant journos scramble for whatever soul-destroying PR jobs they can find, I decide to become a newspaperman. Or more to the point, my new employer decides to throw an old dog a bone.

A fortnight later and I'm on a Dash 8 flying into an uncertain future. I'm coming out of the wilderness of freelancing and into the wilderness of the Torres Strait.

The plane drops towards a patched-up bitumen runway on Horn Island, the only one of the islands big enough and flat enough to have a landing strip. The first thing I notice is nothing: there is so much of it. Scraggly scrub interspersed with 3-metre-high termite mounds. Stepping off the plane and crossing the tarmac, I read a large sign on a cyclone fence telling me I am in *Kaurareg Country*.

I become acutely aware of being suburban Caucasian. I'm now the minority, and I will be for the foreseeable future. I can feel eyes burning into me — more likely, it's just my uncomfortableness at being somewhere unknown and unfamiliar. Welcome to the real Australia, the one we all pretend to have affiliations with (just like Crocodile Dundee) but only from the safety of our lounge rooms. Nobody actually gives me a second glance.

Horn Island is called Narupai in Kaurareg language. I soon learn that all of the eighteen inhabited islands of the Torres Strait have two names, an Indigenous and a European.

Since World War II, when the Horn Island allied airfield was bombed nine times, making it the second most bombed Australian territory in the war (after Darwin), the island has been pretty much left alone.

As I walk into the dry heat outside the terminal, I fantasise that I have stepped into a spaghetti western, me the grizzled protagonist on the edge of nowhere, a desperado.

The air-conditioned courtesy bus that takes us to the ferry for Thursday Island interrupts my dusty desert fantasy. All the Indigenous kids are fiddling with their iPads and smartphones, while a widescreen TV bolted above the driver belts out 'Stayin' Alive' from the Bee Gees' comeback tour. For the first time since I set out on this odyssey, I think I might be able to do just that.

After a fifteen-minute ride on the *Australia Fair*, a former Sydney Harbour ferry, I am at my new home. At less than four square kilometres and with a population of around 3000, Thursday Island is the administrative hub of the Strait, and has almost half the region's population. It also has the only hospital, police station, bank, courthouse, post office, all the federal and state government departments and Australia's most northerly Army battalion, known as the Sarpeyes, Creole for 'sharp eyes': 'the eyes and ears of the north'.

A couple of Sarpeye soldiers are on the ferry in full camo fatigues – and thongs. It's bloody hot, after all.

Serendipitously, I have arrived at Thursday Island on a Thursday.

The name Thursday is derived from Thor, the Proto-Germanic god of thunder. How apt an angry rumbling sky would have been; instead, it is slightly overcast with a touch of drizzle, which I later discover is called the 'mango rains', a last vestige of the Wet season already in remission. It's just enough to moisten the roots of the mango trees for one last crop of fruit before the Dry takes hold.

The Kaurareg Traditional Owners call it *Waiben*, which I think sounds much nicer. It means 'no water'.

I step off the ferry and the gusty south-easterly buffets me down the pier past an old Islander lady sitting on a milk crate fishing with a handline; she has a bucket with half-a-dozen small bluish-coloured fish. On one of the island's two hills, two wind turbines slowly turn – apparently the first in Australia. I drag two suitcases of everything I thought I would need (one of them six years later is still under the bed full of everything I actually didn't need, which is basically everything other than board shorts, T-shirts and thongs). In slacks and a long shirt, I'm completely drenched with sweat by the time I reach the seating area in the car park where I wait to meet my boss for the first time.

I didn't change into short sleeves that morning as I thought it better that all my old punk tattoos were covered up for first impressions. An Islander family sitting in the shade look nonchalant as they swish flies away with small flannel 'sweaters' and pat down their brows. A sweater is a small hand towel printed with frangipani flowers, fringed with lace. There are also frangipanis on the ladies' traditional laced-fringed floral dresses, on the men's shirts and growing on a bush in the far corner of the car park.

They laugh and talk among themselves, in Creole, or Yumplatok (meaning loosely *you lot talk*), the lingua franca of the region and one of four languages spoken, of which English is at best a second, if not third.

Smiling awkwardly, as one does in a foreign country where you don't speak the lingo, I squirm. How the fuck did I not know English is not the first language here? Torres Strait Creole and the similar Kriole, spoken across the northern part of the country are uniquely Australian languages. It has thousands of speakers and is the second most widely spoken language across Northern Australia. But I, like most white-bread Aussies, didn't have a clue of this until I find myself sitting like a gormless fool listening to them laugh and chide, perhaps at me. It then really strikes me how little I know of the people I am about to write a newspaper for, how little I know of all First Nations cultures in the country I call home. But I am no more pig-ignorant than most of mainstream Australia. How many of us know there were well over 500 First Nations clan groups that at the time of the arrival of the First Fleet spoke more than 250 different languages and 800 dialects? A quiet sense of shame undermines me. I, like many urban Australians, have travelled extensively around the world; I have spent time with Indigenous groups in South and Central America, I have sat with Buddhist monks in Thailand and China and Sadhu holy men in India, but I know so little about my own backyard. Is it not just our cultural cringe that makes us such prolific travellers, but also our shame of our unreconciled history with this land's first inhabitants? Either way it's now my job to become their voice, editing a newspaper whose readership they predominate.

 I sit there waiting for my boss. Among the perks that come with the job are a house and a company car. Everyone seems to drive around in Landcruisers, a respectable, tough-as-nails car to suit a frontiersman's wet dream. I wonder which one will be mine as they roll into the car park to drop off or pick up passengers.

 My heart sinks when I see a tiny Hyundai Getz hatchback pull up and Corey, my boss, jumps out. About my age, laconic, lanky with blond hair in a surfie cut, he's casually dressed in short chinos and a T-shirt. We shake hands and he helps me squeeze my bags in the back. I wonder how I will ever be taken seriously in this little symbol of impotence. With us both at six foot plus, I feel like we are squeezing into a clown car.

It's a short drive to the house, as all drives are on the island. The two-bedroom ground-floor apartment sits right on the beach. The back door opens onto a 4-metre deep sun-bleached lawn fringed with a few shrubs stunted by the constant salty sea breeze and the occasional king tide that comes up to the back door. The newsroom is a broom-closet-sized home office annexed off from the apartment. It's a graceless building, clad in cement board with a corrugated Colorbond roof and rusting C-section steel framing, but the seafront position is nothing short of spectacular.

Despite his relaxed demeanour, I sense Corey has a short fuse and little tolerance for bullshit. He speaks disdainfully of my predecessor, who was sacked so quickly it seems he left in a hurry. Corey has a couple of decades' experience as journalist, having worked for newspapers in South-East Asia before making a sea change in 2002 and buying *Torres News* with his father, Mark, who I soon learn everyone calls Senior.

He has half a century in the journo game. Between them they've built a small media empire, Regional and Remote Newspapers. They have three other community newspapers, two more in the Cape and one in Arnhem Land in the Northern Territory, and represent the only independent and local voice for the region.

When I sign my two-year contract, I tell Corey I'd be happy to do three; I figure I need at least that long to make my résumé remotely viable in an industry that is imploding.

'We'll see how we go – newspapers are dying all around the world, there's a good chance they won't really exist in five years,' he says with neither lament nor irony – he's just bluntly saying it how it is.

By the end of the day my white-collar attire slowly slides to shorts and a T-shirt as I slip into my role as the next barefoot editor and Island – or *Ailan* – journo.

Unpacking one of my suitcases, Corey eyes off my suit.

'You won't be needing that, not unless you're going to an Elder's funeral,' he said dryly.

'Or maybe if an important politician came to the island?' I ask.

'An Elder's funeral for sure, but not a politician – I make a point of wearing shorts, T-shirt and thongs.'

I make a mental note to do the same.

The first two days of the job are overwhelming. Corey constantly tells me how to do things at a frenetic pace, as I madly take notes. Scraps of paper covered in my desperate illegible scrawl blow round the office like confetti each time the door opens and the sea breeze barrels in. I know I will never read them: even if I could make out my own handwriting, I realise I will simply never get the time.

Corey rattles off the names of VIPs I should know, loons I should avoid, Indigenous protocols to remember, faux pas to never make. I forget it all as fast as he tells me. All that runs through my mind is the children's song *I'm a little tea pot short and stout, here is my handle and here is my spout.* It has always just jumped into my head at times of heightened stress, like some little pressure valve that pops when it all becomes too much.

This place is a rat's nest of who's who and what's what, and for a newbie these can be turbulent waters. Everybody knows everybody — everybody, that is, but me.

In between all the really important and really complex technical things I must know but forget, it's his asides that stay in my mind.

'Be careful going out on a Friday night – the young blokes like to punch out whitefellas, but it's fine during the day.'

'Watch out for the Papuans, they are all tribal, you don't want to get on the wrong side of them.'

'Be really careful about printing names, it's a small island, and you will have a family here after all.'

Right, that I remember.

These comments are usually followed with 'but it's a really nice place'.

It *is* a really nice place but just under the surface bubble tensions and unresolved issues, feuds and fallings-out, but they all have to live together on this small island isolated from the rest of the world by hundreds of miles of croc and shark-infested waters.

I am relieved Corey is going to be around for a week so I can really get a handle on all the things he's told me that I've forgotten or written down on notes whisked away by the constant south-easterly.

The next day, he's gone.

Abruptly, he says after breakfast: 'I think you'll be fine, no need for me to hang around.' He grabs his carry-on, leaves me half a bag of boutique Gold Coast coffee beans, half a carton of Four X beer in the fridge and takes the afternoon flight back south, back to the big smoke, to all the trimmings and pleasantries of the urban world: real coffee, fancy restaurants and all the other stuff I thought I wanted to escape but now realise I'll miss.

As he clambers out of the Getz at the jetty, he leans in through the car window and smiles. 'If you treat this job like you are the blackfella's little white lackey, you'll do fine.'

Flying solo on my first big story I go down to ANZAC Park on Mabo Day, 3 June 2013, which commemorates the date the High Court passed its decision on the case of *Mabo v Queensland* in 1992, which made history when the state lost. I make reams of notes of impassioned speeches by community leaders, whose names and faces are all new and unknown to me. Eddie Koiki Mabo is revered here as the national hero he rightly should be, and I don't want to cock this up on my first edition.

The Mabo case lead to the dismissal of *terra nullius*, a legal fiction in British law that the continent was not inhabited prior to European arrival, and challenged the existing assumption by the Australian legal system that Aboriginal and Torres Strait Islander peoples had no concept of land ownership before the arrival of British penal colonisers in 1788. It represented the end of a ten-year fight for Eddie Mabo and the five plaintiffs, which Mabo and three of the plaintiffs did not live to see. Five months prior Mabo had died of cancer at the age of fifty-five.

The Mabo case was the continuation of earlier failed attempts to overthrow *terra nullius* by Indigenous activists since the 1970s and is now considered a landmark case in Indigenous rights around the world. While Mabo and the five plaintiffs were fighting for recognition of land ownership on their home of Murray Island – Mer, as it is called in their Meriam language – the result had ramifications for the nation and the world.

As a newbie to the region and the history of land rights, I assumed it was a black and white case, good versus bad, David versus Goliath, but it marked the beginning of my understanding of 'black politics', a journey through smoke and mirrors where every truth often has a counter-truth, preempting the mainstream post-truth political era the world now endures. As the region's newly appointed journo, I soon came to realise that peeling back these onion skins was fraught with dangerously differing opinions, as I tried to navigate different tribes' 'truths' and not become the conduit for clan spats going back generations.

The Mabo case was no exception.

Prior to the 1992 High Court decision, the Queensland Supreme Court was convinced to convene on Mer on 23 May 1989 to consider evidence of the existence of family garden plots from sixteen witnesses too old and frail to travel. Justice Martin Moynihan said he '...doubted [whether] the Court has ever sat further north or perhaps further east.'

Two of the five plaintiffs were pressured to withdraw their support (but later again gave it), and the Queensland government tried to exploit differences of opinion on boundaries and ownership of some of the Mer garden plots that were the basis of the case. In a three-volume report a year later Justice Moynihan rejected all of Mabo's claims and most of the claims of the other two plaintiffs, but acknowledged a couple of garden blocks were traditionally owned under Meriam law. While the Queensland government saw it as a victory, it was the foot in the door that allowed the second part of Mabo's case against Queensland to successfully prove that Meriam customs and laws are fundamental to their traditional system of ownership, and hence eventually broke down *terra nullius.*

The niggling disputes of garden bed boundaries on Mer that formed the basis of the Mabo case ultimately united Indigenous Australia and set a precedent for Indigenous peoples' rights across the globe.

Three years after his death Eddie Mabo's grave in Townsville had a traditional tombstone unveiling ceremony; that night vandals desecrated it with red spray-painted swastikas and the word 'Abo'. The bronze bas-relief portrait of him was removed. The act both galvanised his family's decision to return his body to Mer, where he was buried with a tribal Meriam ceremony, and officially crowned Mer the cradle of native rights.

I am blissfully unaware of the shades of grey in black politics during the commemoration of Mabo Day in ANZAC Park that sun-drenched afternoon in 2013. It's a comment from an Elder, Noel Bon, which gives me my first clue. In a *lava lava* (traditional Islander sarong) and a dark brown fedora, Noel looks frail with his slight and stooping frame, but he has the mischievous glint in his eye of a young boy.

'I was a branch manager at IBIS (the local supermarket) on Mer when Koiki smashed *terra nullius*. But nobody was supporting him back then — now we celebrate, but the truth needs to come out. We need to stand together, respect one another, not just here, but the whole world.'

Feeling out of place, still acutely aware of my outsider white minority status, I sense my photographing people is an intrusion – but it's something I need to do to fill column space.

I know it may make some wince when I say 'white' and 'black' people – perhaps I shouldn't be differentiating between the two. A cute outlook from the urban heartland where all but a few blackfellas endure, where as a Caucasian you are never confronted with the reality of being a minority on the outside of a race, culture and language of what is ultimately the 'real' original Australia. So suck it up, buttercup, I know I have to.

I turn and frame up an Islander man in my camera's viewfinder.

In his early thirties, tall and barrel-chested with shoulder-length manicured dreadlocks and a trimmed beard, he gives me a salubrious smile which I shoot.

As soon as I do his smile drops away and he looks at me sternly. 'In our culture we believe a photograph steals our soul.'

After a pregnant pause, when I'm no doubt looking utterly mortified at my crime, Frazier Nai, a councillor from the outer island community of Masig (York Island) puts me out of my misery.

'Nah, all good, *bala* (brother), just kidding,' he says as the grin returns.

It's my second lesson of the day. Nothing is straightforward in the Straits, and it seems there is also a good self-deprecating sense of humour in *Ailan* ways.

Over the ensuing days I start to meet people and learn names. A couple of times I hear, 'It's a beautiful place here, really friendly. Have you been threatened yet?'

It's the *yet* that makes my heart palpitate. *Yet* has an inevitability about it that doesn't rest easy, unclear if it's a warning or another joke.

Then another Elder tells me to let him know if I am threatened in any way, that they will get it worked out, and it jars my sense of tropical island ease a little.

As I start to sort out the office I find some traditional hunting spears, so I mount them on the wall. In the storeroom I find a Louisville Slugger, but I know there is no baseball on the island. It's aptly named 'The Ambassador'. I put it within easy reach of the front door. In a drawer by the back door I find a Brazilian Tramontina, the best-quality machete money can buy. Maybe that's just for the coconut tree in the garden. I keep it by the back door for good measure.

If this is life in the slow lane, it's starting to feel a little racy.

CHAPTER 3

A WAR OF WORDS

3 July 2019

The words of Councillor Gabriel Bani, on Mabo Day 2019 at Thursday Island's high school, revealed how much further we have to go in healing our nation.

'Just what did happen to this country that has led to this turmoil? To understand that we need to look at how this country was first formed,' he said.

'Looking at Captain Cook's journal from the *Endeavour*, seven words can teach us more than a mountain of bodies that left us deep issues we today fight to resolve and continue to be dreadfully impacted by. These injustices make our fire burn strong.

'The first four of those seven words: *A musket was fired.*'

'In 1770 this is the first encounter the British had with First Nations people, when they fired their muskets to scare them away.

'Cook's crew then went through their houses, looking through their possessions and taking a spear back to their boat.

'It was a violent and forced entry on day one of our relationship and in the initial founding of Australia as we know it today, and this has come down through the corridors of time.

'The last three words are: *I took possession*.'

On 22 August 1770 Cook noted that they went ashore on Possession Island and claimed the entire east coast all the way down to Victoria.

'The consequence of this for us was dispossession — this was the single biggest damage. Not only the loss of land, but it triggered a chain of further losses, a loss of livelihood and culture, a loss of language which became forbidden to speak.

'A musket and possession — that is Australia's beginning.

'For true justice we must remove the lies and allow the truth to be revealed — we need a shift in the paradigm back to zero and build it again.

'As Mabo said, it's not really about the land, it's about the people.'

Like many white suburban Australians, I grew up with the cliché of the woomera-holding Aboriginal warrior, balancing on one foot and leaning on a spear, which appeared on TV shows — and on people's lawns, 3-foot-high, cast in plaster, next to a white-painted tyre swan or a

Romanesque concrete birdbath. I had no contact with Indigenous Australians or their cultures. Their history and cultures went largely unmentioned when I was at school in the seventies and eighties, a period that was distinctly prejudiced in favour of Britannia, before *terra nullius* was dismissed by Mabo.

We were taught a whitewashed version of Australian history, with stories of stoic squatters and bushmen and their conquest of an unforgiving landscape. Explorers were often tragic, such as Burke and Wills, who sacrificed their lives to map the unknown frontier, and were memorialised with a statue on Melbourne's Swanson Street. Our penal colony beginnings were romanticised like a Disney-gentrified *Oliver Twist* – and we all played bushrangers in the playground.

In Tasmania, where I grew up, the Palawa people, made up of eight tribes, had been decimated by Europeans. All I learned of their culture and demise occurred briefly at primary school: our textbooks contained a few nineteenth-century sketches of 'noble savages' wrapped in wallaby skins and some scant references to their 'inferiority' to mainland Aboriginals due to their 'inability to make fire'. We learned more about the extinction of the

Tasmanian tiger than we did of the plight of the Palawa.

Growing up in this era and being raised by counterculture, anti-establishment parents, I had a view of Aboriginality that, while empathetic, was equally naive. In my romanticised view, Aboriginality meant having almost mythical intuition and powers drawn from the land. Truganini's story, which we learned about at school, seemed akin to a Greek tragedy.

Truganini was born in 1812 on Bruny Island, and by 1829 she had lost her family: her mother killed by sailors, her uncle shot by a soldier, her sister abducted by sealers, and her fiancé brutally murdered by timber cutters, who then repeatedly raped Truganini. Bruny, where my family has a shack, is now a sleepy weekender island getaway forty minutes' drive and a ferry ride away from Hobart. But in Truganini's time, whaling was a boom industry where thousands of southern right whales were slaughtered and cut up at eight whaling stations based there. It's hard to imagine the gentle rolling surf and white sands stained red with blood, and the brutality that Truganini's family suffered.

By 1830 Truganini was forcibly relocated to Flinders Island in Bass Strait with the last surviving hundred or so Palawa, most of whom succumbed to diseases such as influenza. In 1838 she was taken to Port Philip Bay in Victoria to form a settlement for Aboriginal people. There she, Palawa resistance fighter Tunnerminnerwait and three other Tasmanian Aborigines became outlaws, robbing and shooting at settlers, triggering a long pursuit by the redcoats.

After being captured and surviving a gunshot wound to the head, Truganini was returned to Flinders Island. In 1856, she and the few surviving Palawa were moved to a settlement at Oyster Cove, south of Hobart. By 1873 she was the sole survivor; she died three years later.

Despite her request that her ashes be scattered in the D'Entrecasteaux Channel, she was buried in a convict graveyard, and then two years later her skeleton was exhumed by the Royal Society of Tasmania and put on display. A hundred years after her death, her remains were finally cremated and scattered on her Country.

On the edge of Hobart, near the house my hippie, arty parents built in the early seventies, a small bronze plaque was erected in 1976, a century after her death. Bolted to a rock, inches from the ground in the middle of the bush, it literally has to be stumbled over to be found. It sits at the top of Truganini Track on Mount Nelson, a vantage point that looks over D'Entrecasteaux Channel down to Truganini's home of Bruny Island. The switchback trail cuts down to Taroona, the suburb that fringes the channel. The plaque reads bluntly and without explanation: *Truganini died 8 May 1876, Truganini Park 8 May 1976. Dedicated to Tasmanian Aboriginals and their descendants.*

Traipsing around this bushland, lost in my boyhood fantasises of bushrangers or catching blue-tongue lizards or chasing my tamed pet cockatoos, I would often visit the strangely oval-shaped monument. Sometimes overgrown, the green-tarnished bronze looked like a sad, solitary, unseeing eye facing the vista of the D'Entrecasteaux Channel, shackled to the low-lying rock. It was often desecrated, smeared with dog shit or stinking of piss, and it represented my first tactile encounter with our nation's brutal past and unreconciled present.

Because of this monument, or perhaps in spite of it, the bushland backcountry of Mount Nelson imbued a sense of Truginini's spirit throughout my childhood. The clinking of currawongs and black cockatoos, the mists of low-hanging clouds drifting through the peppermint and ribbon gums like spectres, and the cool, dark, moss-covered gullies all fed my childhood imagination and gave me, an immigrant, an ancient, ethereal sense of place.

Truganini's husband, William Lanne, known as King Billy (1835–1869), the last 'full-blood'

Palawa man, has no shit-encrusted monument. The native Tasmanian tree that was named after him is renowned for the durability of its timber and its resistance to rot and parasites. Yet due to droughts and bushfires driven by climate change, and the clear-felling of old-growth forests, the King Billy pine is verging on extinction.

Lanne's short life was spent first in an orphanage and then working on a whaling ship until his death from cholera and dysentery. His body, too, was dismembered in the name of nineteenth-century science, and the Royal College of Surgeons of England and the Royal Society of Tasmania squabbled over his remains. His skull and skin were stolen by one the college's surgeons from the morgue, so the Royal Society of Tasmania cut off his hands and feet before an unceremonious burial.

It was rumoured that he died at the Dog and Partridge Hotel in Hobart, which in the eighties and nineties was called the Doghouse Hotel, a dark and seedy punk rock venue with sticky, threadbare carpet, clouded in cigarette and bushweed smoke, where bikers, punks, hippies and other misfits would brawl out their differences around the pool tables.

Sitting upstairs in the squalid rooms drinking and tuning our guitars before thrashing out another set of angry distorted noise, our brand of homegrown grunge, I often wondered which room King Billy had died in and what his ghost made of our loud, youthful, suburban bucking of the system.

It wasn't until researching this book nearly thirty years later that I realised the brutality and totality of the Palawa's genocide and Tasmania's Black War, contradicting the claims in my schoolbooks that generations of Palawa just died out or faded away, a curio of history. The truth of the Frontier Wars is only now percolating to the surface of the nation's psyche, despite it having been there in plain sight the whole time, with place names like Murdering Point, or Butcher's Creek and multiple journal entries by early pastoralists who use the euphemism of 'dispersing the natives' for the genocide they inflicted by 'bait or bullet'. Bait referring to the strychnine-laced flour and blankets given to communities.

Torture, gang-rape and murder of children were order of the day. But the First Nations People didn't go down without a fight and there were many bloody battles, from Tasmania to the Torres Strait and from New South Wales to way out west.

In 1852 colonial missionary Reverend John West, who was later editor of the *Sydney Morning Herald*, described this sentiment of the war saying,

'...every white man was a guerrilla and every black an assassin.'

Some colonists pickled the ears of their victims, others cut the cocks off Aboriginal men for fun to watch them run off in agony. The depths of the depravity turned the colonists into dogs of war.

Just as the shame of having a convict ancestor shifted to pride around the time of Australia's bicentenary in 1988, so now there is an acceptance that the First Australians did not go quietly into that good night – or 'mutely die', as 1930s anthropologist Raymond Firth described. While there is little doubt much of the Indigenous population was decimated by disease, including the common cold, flu, measles, venereal diseases, tuberculosis and smallpox, we are still coming to terms with the massacres committed against Aboriginal people by pastoralists and the tenacious resistance they responded with.

The massacres started within months of the First Fleet's arrival and spread throughout the colonies, and continued right up into the early twentieth century.

Early estimates put the pre-European Aboriginal population at somewhere between 700,000 and one million people. Within a hundred years of the arrival of the First Fleet in 1788, the population of Indigenous Australians was reduced to around 100,000. In the 2016 census that number was 649,171. However, a conversation with ecologist Professor Corey Bradshaw in July 2020 revealed the extent of the genocide might have been much more extreme, where he has new models suggesting that the pre-European Aboriginal population could have been potentially as high as six million people.

'Six million is the upper limit of the ecological carrying capacity of the continent when people first entered Australia, but as there are no real data from the time, the numbers represent an upper limit rather than a true population estimate,' Corey tells me over the phone in July 2020.

'You have to remember we are dealing in timeframes that make the heyday of the ancient Egyptians look like yesterday – it even makes the last Ice Age look young.

'The population would have waxed and waned over those 65,000 odd years, especially when Australia was the super-continent Sahul, which included Tasmania and New Guinea, so there was a lot more viable land than there is today.

'I do think that there was a lot of downplaying of the abundance of Indigenous populations, as an ethical justification to subjugate them under colonisation, so I think these early estimates of Indigenous populations were formulated with an element of racism.'

But is it any surprise the presence First Nations peoples and their communities, and the Frontier Wars that followed the arrival of Britannia, have been whitewashed from the collective consciousness of mainstream Australia? It's important to remember the Union Jack, or the 'butcher's apron', has been bloodied by Britain's incursions into the fifty-seven countries claimed by the empire on which the sun never sets. It was complicit in the death of many millions of people from the Irish Famine and the Opium Wars with China of the mid-nineteenth century, to the many atrocities in the twentieth century, including famines in India and Bengal; the partition of India and Pakistan; the Boer War concentration camps and the Kenyan Gulags; and the Malayan Emergency after World War II. But these blemishes are never remembered, only the zeal of the Allied victory and post war optimism with its sanitised history, despite the fact the Empire's death count exceeds that of the Third Reich's Holocaust.

My grandfather, a career soldier for the British Army was twice shot to pieces in World War II, for which he was awarded a Distinguished Service Order and got to get drunk with Winston Churchill. At the end of his career he fought the guerrillas in the Malayan jungles, dragging his wife and five army brat kids with him from one incursion on the empire to the next. My mum, born in the WWII ruins of Berlin, remembers having to be driven to primary school in a tank.

As a young man I tracked him down – long-shunned by most of the family, he'd had a string of affairs and broken marriages. I turned up on his doorstep in 1999, a small cottage near Ashdown Forest, home of Winnie the Pooh. We ended up on a three-day whisky bender together where he confessed, 'I've killed hundreds of people – any other time I would be jailed for being a mass murderer, instead I am called a hero. I remember the last person I killed – it was a young woman, a communist guerrilla in the jungle. After that I just vomited and knew I couldn't do it anymore.'

'Fuck the whole Queen and Empire thing,' he told me, 'it's a load of old bollocks.'

White Australia's national myth-making from the bloody slaughter of our ANZACs at Gallipoli to the stoicism of Weary Dunlop with 'Lest We Forget', has canonised our core values of mateship and the tenacity of the underdog Aussie battler. But when it comes to the Frontier Wars, First Nations People are told to 'just get over it'. Where are the epitaphs for Kebisu – the king of the canoes, or Tunnerminnerwait, Maulboyheenner, Pemulwuy, Musquito, Windradyne, Yagan, Jandamarra and Tarenorerer? Never heard of these names? Well then, perhaps, dear reader, it's time for you to dig a little deeper.

Tony McAvoy from the Wiri mob was the first Indigenous person ever to be appointed a Senior Council ('silk') in Australia's judicial system in 2015. Tony told me at a 2019 forum about Torres Strait regional autonomy the day before the federal election: 'I am sure many country folk, when they sit around after a few beers amongst themselves, that they talk of the box of bones buried in the barn.' He said, 'They are scared to face their part of history. Our country really needs a healing, we need a truth council not just for the victims but also for the perpetrators as well.'

The suppression, or at best downplaying, of the bloodiest parts of our history has become the battlefields of the Culture Wars, or History Wars, over the last two decades, as historians and politicians have questioned whether or not the country was invaded or colonised.

Seven months after the landmark 1992 High Court decision had recognised native title and ruled the doctrine of *terra nullius* had no basis, Prime Minister Paul Keating delivered his *Redfern*

Speech to a predominantly Indigenous crowd, in which he said: 'We committed the murders. We took the children from their mothers. We practised discrimination and exclusion. It was our ignorance and our prejudice.'

At the time largely ignored by the media, the *Redfern Speech* is considered by many to be one of the greatest Australian speeches.

Prime Minister John Howard said in his 1996 *Sir Robert Menzies Lecture* that the 'balance sheet of Australian history' had come to be misrepresented:

The 'black armband' view of our history reflects a belief that most Australian history since 1788 has been little more than a disgraceful story of imperialism, exploitation, racism, sexism and other forms of discrimination.... I believe that the balance sheet of our history is one of heroic achievement and that we have achieved much more as a nation of which we can be proud than of which we should be ashamed.

Following the release of the 1998 *Bringing Them Home Report* by the National Inquiry into the Separation of Aboriginal and Torres Strait Islander Children from Their Families – the Stolen Generations who were removed from their families by the Australian federal and state government agencies and church missions – Howard passed a Parliamentary *Motion of*

Reconciliation. He described treatment of Aborigines as the 'most blemished chapter' in Australian history. However, he refused to make a Parliamentary apology, arguing it was inappropriate as it would imply 'intergeneration guilt'. It was that intergenerational guilt Prime Minister Kevin Rudd claimed for the nation when he made his famous *Apology to the Stolen Generations* in 2008, after his 2007 landslide election victory.

At the time I was largely oblivious to Rudd's apology, living in South America and immersing myself into the culture of Amazonian Indians. I was too busy chasing my spiritual El Dorado by trying to define my own mythology contextualised by Indigenous knowledge from a distant land. I knew vaguely that Rudd apologised, but wasn't sure why, or interested for what exactly, I figured it was just a general sorry for us being such monumental bastards. It never occurred to me then to look any deeper. It wasn't until I started researching this book, pulling at a thread of cotton that I began to understand the limited context of the apology, of the importance of Keating's *Redfern Speech*, and the extent of the Frontier Wars.

The apology represented the national zeitgeist: hundreds of thousands of Australians watched it on screens erected in public squares in the major cities, and millions more on their TVs. Many Aboriginal and Torres Strait Islanders wore black T-shirts emblazoned with one word: *Thanks*.

But I can't help but think now that it's the rest of the nation that should be saying thanks, and not just sorry. Lest we forget.

CHAPTER 4

ON THE ROCKS

Sometime in the afternoon, 31 December 1987

I had just turned eighteen when I first met an Indigenous Australian. It was the day after award-winning Australian writer, lauded poet and political activist Kath Walker changed her name to Oodgeroo Noonuccal and gave back her MBE to the Queen. It was also the day before the 'celebration of a nation', where the government-funded TV jingle sung by a bunch of white TV personalities in front of Uluru hoped to encouraged us to rejoice the bicentennial year of Captain Arthur Phillip's arrival with the eleven ships of the First Fleet in Sydney Harbour.

Noonuccal's 30 December article in *The Age* newspaper, 'Why I am now Oodgeroo Noonuccal', announced her name change to that of her North Stradbroke Island tribal heritage of the Noonuccal people, and explained why she had returned the MBE she received in 1970. She expressed her frustration that the parliaments of England and Australia had not attempted to: ... *rectify the terrible damage done to the Australian Aborigines. The forbidding us our tribal language, the murders, the poisoning, the scalping, the denial of land custodianship, especially our spiritual sacred sites, the destruction of our sacred places ... 1988, to me marks 200 years of rape and carnage, all these terrible things that the Aboriginal tribes of Australia have suffered ... what is there to celebrate?*

Emerging from the bowels of Central Station with throngs of other New Year's Eve revellers heading to the Rocks and Sydney's waterfront, I inadvertently made eye contact with a small group of derelicts and drifters in Belmore Park, an enclave for the homeless, drunks, junkies and other detritus of the city.

An older looking weather-beaten man with rotten teeth, a nicotine-stained beard and knotted frizzy hair gestured for me to come and join them. He had an approachable smile so I crossed the street and sat down with him.

'Drink some flagon with a blackfella?' the old man asked as he passed me a brown paper bag concealing a large bottle of port. He exuded the sickly sweet, unwashed odour of someone who had been drinking steadily for a long time. I was not struck by his Aboriginality but more by his browbeaten yet friendly demeanour.

The idea of rubbing shoulders with society's disenfranchised appealed to my young, punk rock and hippie hybrid sensibilities, so I shared a drink with him. The crowds on the street thickened and transformed into a protest march of young political activists angrily chanting, 'Don't celebrate 88'. A smattering of socialist uni students in John Lennon spectacles had converged with a throng of Aboriginal youth brandishing black, red and yellow flags. Their sentiment appealed more than drinking from a flagon on the sidelines, so I joined them in a march that dissipated not long after it started. I too was angry, not entirely sure at what or why, but a rage festered deep inside my white-bread suburban soul that would take me a lifetime to understand.

The brutality of our young country's history is always seething just below the surface, deflected by our laconic, ironic sense of humour, mocking the wowser, 'taking the piss', and our 'no worries' attitude – but it's palpable and can explode at any moment. That hair trigger is usually a couple of drinks, and New Year's Eve in Sydney had come to represent the antithesis of the 'fair go', 'true blue' spirit we desperately try to embody, revealing the raw beast that lies beneath.

From the age of fifteen, when I first staggered around Hobart's waterfront, I saw in each New Year with binge-drinking in the streets, tongue-kissing and groping strangers and copping the occasional king hit punch for no reason. I thought nothing of it then, to go down swinging

– it was all just part of the landscape of our national identity.

Since white Australia was an embryonic colony, the bastard of the empire built by its outcast criminals and paid for in blackfellas' blood and cheap Bengali rum, alcohol and drunkenness have been in the underbelly of our national psyche, ready to become violent at any moment. From the days of the First Fleet, the New South Wales Rum Corps, to Prime Minister Bob Hawke's record for sculling the yard glass – 'the drink' has been seen as the great equaliser of classes, the glue of 'mateship', and subconsciously deified as part of our disregard of the empire who dumped us at the end of the earth. It has both defined and decimated us as a nation.

The fact that the blighted Governor Bligh was dragged from under his bed in the Rum Rebellion on the same day exactly twenty years after the arrival of the First Fleet on 26 January 1808, the only successful armed takeover of government in Australian history, perhaps echoes a truer of the spirit of our nation – a date we have since 1994 celebrated as Australia Day, a day on which drunkenness and patriotism, and denial, go hand in hand. The drink has helped drown our cultural cringe and to forget our bloody past.

In the eighties 'the drink' was the way I grew up understanding how to bond with my countrymen, 'black, white and brindle'. Howling at the moon, flipping the middle finger salute to the world on Sydney's waterfront that night of the bicentennial came to represent the start of a watershed for me. I had left my childhood home, come of age and stuck my thumb out at the side of the road seeking adventure. Hitchhiking up the east coast of Australia was not only a pilgrimage, a necessity to reach manhood, my rites of passage, but also when I first developed a sense of place and a sense of being an Australian in all its paradox.

I got as far as Byron Bay before my funds dried up, a month after leaving Sydney. I stuck out my thumb again and ended up in regional Victoria, outside the town of Shepparton near the Goulburn River, picking Packham pears on the farm of Dundas Simpson.

On the farm there was a constant flux of drifters and nomads who worked the fruit seasons as a way of life. The pickers never fraternised with the workers of the packing shed, who were predominantly white locals living in town. Picking fruit was backbreaking work and the play afterwards roughhouse, drinking cask wine and beer around camp fires and sharing tales of the road.

After one Friday-night bender I woke up dew-sodden and hung-over next to the dying embers of a fire ringed with old silver goon bags and empty bottles. A Scot with a thick red beard and long wavy hair had passed out next to me, his leg lying in the fire. I lifted it out: welts and blisters hissed and steamed as I gently placed it in the wet grass. Bandaged from ankle to knee he was back working on Monday morning, grinning with a mad glint in his eye. His quiet teenage hippie girlfriend, a decade his junior, also toiled among the trees, a baby strapped to her back.

Misfits made up the ranks of pickers, like the young guy who had obviously fallen through the cracks of the system and joined society's detritus on the backroads. During the day he would wander through the fruit trees mumbling to himself as he tried to tune in to the cosmos, one hand clamped over his ear, another holding a stick as an antenna skywards, then in the middle of the night – in the tent next to mine – he would have screaming rows with one of his multiple personalities. This was life on the farm.

One of the permanent fixtures of the farm was Johnny Speedy. He might have been in his forties but he looked older: wizened and elfin, sun-leathered, skin and bones, with a cowlick of peppered black hair. The guy worked harder and faster than anyone else. He would pick five tonnes of pears a day, filling ten pallet-sized wooden crates. In my prime I struggled to fill four in a ten-hour day. We got $14 dollars a crate.

Johnny was a blackfella, a term he used to describe himself with neither pride nor shame. He liked country music, hand-rolled cigarettes, and a cold beer or twelve each night after work. I would cadge a couple off him as we cooked our dinner in the kitchen quarters. He was always dressed immaculately, rhinestone cowboy shirt tucked into blue jeans with a big belt buckle, folded up at the ankles to reveal tanned-coloured boots. He was a man of few words and the ones he spoke were neither profound nor memorable, yet our nightly ritual around the frypans left an indelible mark on me. We shared an unspoken affection, and when I moved on a few weeks later it felt like I was leaving behind a much-loved uncle.

I never thought to ask him about his Aboriginal heritage, so I had no idea whether he was a local Yorta Yorta man. A decade later in 1999, Federal Court Judge Howard Olney would say that the 'tide of history' had 'washed away' this clan's traditional laws and customs, and so dismissed their native title claim. This claim would go on to lose at appeal, and again in the Supreme Court in 2002.

I also befriended scraggly-haired, lean but tough Charlie, who at seventeen was sick of living in an old school bus with his mum, stepdad and two siblings. He had done four laps of the continent, rolling from country town to country town working the seasons. We bonded over beers, swimming in the dam and hunting yabbies. Angry at the world, Charlie picked a fight with the farm boss over our exploitative work conditions. A visit by the unions followed, then a slight improvement for the workers, as well as Charlie's dismissal. I was fired for being his mate.

Charlie bought a clapped-out 1968 HR Holden sedan from the wreckers. It was sun-faded sky blue with a peeling cream-coloured vinyl roof. Charlie dropped in a secondhand gearbox, pushed AC/DC's *TNT* into the cassette player and left his childhood in his wake. He was heading north, to nowhere in particular, so I joined him in what would become an iconic Australian road trip – the iconic road trip that laid the foundation of much of my adult psyche.

The orchards of the Goulburn Valley disappeared behind us, then the dry wheat belts and sheep stations of the interior gave way to the edge of the continent. Skirting around the outskirts of Sydney and Brisbane, we chased the Pacific Highway blacktop ever northwards, keeping the cobalt blue ocean that disappeared on the eastern horizon always to our right. Within a couple of weeks we reached Bundaberg, with its rambling Queenslander houses on stilts, just south of the Tropic of Capricorn.

Catching up with two mates from Dundas Simpson who had returned home, we camped on the beaches, tore around the mangroves in flat-tray tinnies, caught prawns and mud crabs, skinny-dipped in the lagoons and played cricket on low tide beaches. Before continuing northwards we stopped at what looked like a fuel depot next to the Bundaberg Rum distillery: it sold cheap fortified wine and rum by the litre from a bowser. It kept me in drink while Charlie drove.

I have little memory of reaching the outskirts of Cairns a couple of days later, or of the redneck party we crashed where I instigated a street brawl for being called a hippie. I copped a good ole-fashioned north Queensland pounding, saved only by Charlie driving the car into the centre of the fray, dragging my unconscious body in through the car door while fists kept punching through the broken sunroof as we were pelted with beer cans and rocks.

I liked Cairns, the sticky heat, the humidity, the wildness of the rainforest just on the outskirts, seeing saltwater crocs in storm drains, sharing joints at traffic lights with random long-haired strangers in the next lane, the palpitating fear of the next fight, chewing magic mushrooms plucked from sugarcane fields – it all galvanised my armour of Australiana.

We were eventually run out of town by the police, so we retreated to Townsville and turned back to the interior. Luscious green rolling hills quickly fell away to long, flat, dry and dusty as we crossed the barren Barkly Tableland on the A2, through Cloncurry, past the monument for Burke and Wills and on to the Northern Territory, where the browns turned to reds, and the cracked blacktop, belted by the midday sun, disappeared into the horizon shimmering under the unforgiving desert sky.

Great expanses of nothing – there was no life except termite mounds, saltbush and snakes. The road was punctuated with the tread of truck tyres spat to the roadside like giant black banana skins and the occasional bloated carcass of roadkill you could smell before you saw it. Intermittently the road trains roared past us: the world's largest and heaviest multi-trailer trucks, often more than 50 metres long, weighing over 150 tonnes and travelling faster than 100ks an hour. They'd appear on the horizon in a haze, kicking up a plume of red dust that would grow larger and more ominous until the truck thundered past, shaking and shuddering our chassis, buffeting us in its wake as everything disappeared in a turbulent vortex of grit. It felt like we were driving off the end of the earth and straight into George Miller's *Mad Max 2* in all its dystopian post-apocalyptic glory.

Territorians have the world's highest rate of alcohol consumption. After we hit Three Ways, the insidious reach of the drink became more starkly apparent. The Three Ways intersection is where the Barkly Highway from Queensland crashes into the Stuart Highway, which bisects the country from north to south. There's a roadhouse, bar and service station at the centre of a huge plain of gravel where the road trains converge.

The all-male clientele dressed in shorts and wife-beater singlets stretched taut over sweaty beer bellies eyed us suspiciously as we pushed open the squeaky flyscreen door. The first thing I saw was a large sign above the bar. Crudely drawn, it depicted a very short woman and a trucker who rested his VB beer can on her head while thrusting his cock, up to the hilt, down her throat. Scrawled above this were the words *The perfect woman, three-foot high with a flat head.*

Alcohol's depravity only worsened as we travelled up the Stuart Highway. As we passed through the town of Katherine in the middle of the day, a group of middle-aged Aboriginal men and women in a drunken stupor brawled, vomited, leered and hurled abuse and empty cans at us from the kerb.

We pressed on north 300 more clicks to the end of the road where we ventured into the notorious Hotel Victoria, in Darwin's CBD, a huge sign above the bar plainly outlined the pub's etiquette: *If you cannot fight it is recommended you do not drink at this establishment.* Beneath this sign the clientele thronged two-deep at the bar: Vietnam vet bikers trying to drown their PTSD, stockmen in from the remote cattle stations trying to quell an unquenchable thirst, criminals on the run, and all the other misfits the Territory had lured to its bosom, with its lax laws and limited police resources. Dressed in sarongs with knotted long hair, and me still a little bruised from my Cairns bashing, we only braved a couple of bevvies before leaving town.

The raw unruliness was palpable.

We spent a month languishing in a caravan park in Casuarina on Darwin's outskirts, smoking pot and hanging out with NT's constant flotsam and jetsam of transients. With no more north left to travel, we decided to press on east into

Kakadu National Park on the Arnhem Highway. The car became more and more dilapidated the further we ventured: the sunroof had long since been taken out by a rock shot up by a passing road train; the starter motor died in the desert, which meant we had to push-start the car; the radiator leaked water; the cracked sump, oil, and we were never sure when one of the twenty buck retreads, softened by the sun-boiled bitumen, would peel away from a tyre.

We pushed that old HR onwards, through croc-infested river crossings and over scrubland. We explored wetlands and slept in the car, pulled in off the roadside. We continued to hurtle east until the Arnhem Highway blacktop thinned out and the sun-bleached white centre line petered out onto a red dirt road. A road sign informed us we had entered Arnhem Land and that tribal law applied from there on in. We neither knew anything of what tribal law meant nor that we had just entered Yolngu Country.

The Yolngu's bark petitions to the Federal Government in 1963 were the first formal proclamation of native title, and even though it failed it was the beginning of a tide of descent building up to the 1967 Referendum. It continued until 16 August 1975 when Prime Minister Gough Whitlam poured a handful of red dirt into the palms of Gurindji Elder Vincent Lingiari at Wattie

Creek, in the lead-up to the passing of the *Aboriginal Land Rights Act* of 1976.

'Shit, tribal law? I think that means they can spear you,' Charlie said as he pulled over, the headlights making the road sign glow in the dying twilight.

The road sign, the elongating shadows as daylight retreated into the scrub, the real fear of the brutality of life in the Northern Territory mixed with the fear generated by our ignorance and our imaginations.

'Right, so fuck that,' I said.

Charlie turned the HR around and we retreated southwest on the Kakadu Highway and back to the Stuart Highway.

I, like many Australians, was oblivious to these seismic shifts in our recent political history, and of the ongoing fight First Nations People were battling in 1988, and that later the same year Prime Minister Bob Hawke would come to the NT with the government's promise of Treaty – a promise, still yet to be delivered.

That road sign represented a social backlash by Aboriginal groups in the early 1980s who had returned to traditional lands to escape the grog and petrol sniffing and to maintain traditional customs; today it remains one of the most culturally intact and separate regions in the country. It was known as the 'Outstation Movement'.

Heading southwest out of the National Park on the Kakadu Highway, we stopped to look at the rock art painting of a tall ship at Nanguluwur, which marks one the first known interactions of Aboriginal people with Europeans from the sixteenth century. It pre-empted their eventual encroachment and colonisation.

We also passed the controversial Ranger yellowcake uranium mine near Jabiru, which in its thirty-year history has had more than 200 leaks of radioactive waste and was built against the wishes of the Mirarr people, Traditional Owners of the World Heritage area.

We ended up in Tennant Creek, some 25 kilometres south of Three Ways. It represented the end of the road for us. We had run out of money – between us we had sixty cents, and it would be a couple of weeks before the dole office gave us a cheque. We both squirmed at the idea of looking for work at Australia's third largest gold mine, around which the town had built up since the 1930s, when it was known as Australia's last great gold rush. We had little fuel and no food, so we parked on a dry river flat on the outskirts of town and contemplated our options. Not long afterwards an old station wagon pulled up near us and a group of

Aboriginal men fell out, all drunk and raucous and shouting. My heart sank as I anticipated another beating.

The alpha of the group, Eddie Plummer, a Warumungu man some twelve years my senior, had a strong stocky build, thick black hair, bright eyes and a full set of teeth that shone white when he grinned. He approached our car. On hearing of our plight, Eddie first gave us a beer, then refuge in his home.

Working in community health care, Eddie had a steady job and a nice two-bedroom bungalow on the edge of town. The house was a new brick veneer and sat on a freshly laid bitumen road, with a concrete kerb and footpath — a slice of suburbia that could have been anywhere in Australia, except it was on the edge of a remote mining town in the country's red centre. Across the street, driveway entrances punctuated the footpath but led only into the desert, unchanged for aeons, whose restless red sand was already starting to creep onto the road.

Eddie's place was a local epicentre for mob to converge, and every night scores of blackfellas would roll up in cars more clapped-out than ours, or appear out of the haze of the desert's edge. Small throngs of skinny teenage girls would giggle and mutter about me and Charlie with their hands over their mouths, while their menfolk clowned around, talking half in English and half in Warymungu. All the while rivers of grog flowed, until the chill of the desert night was pushed back by the blaze of the new dawn. In every room and in the shade around outside of the house, drunken snoring rattled the walls and the air filled with scent of alcohol and sweat. But no matter what time we'd kicked on to, Eddie was always up, showered, shaved and out the door for work on time while we slept it off.

The drinking and horseplay were always good-natured, even the time one of the old fellas, with too much drink under his belt, started dancing around me on his toes, fists raised like a boxer. It was like something just clicked inside: one moment we were rambling on, arms flopped over each other's shoulders, the next he was prancing around with eyes glazed over in a trance.

One of the men laughed out loud. 'Oh no, old fella's back in the tent again, look out for his right hook!'

Old Fella had spent his prime as a fighter on the tent boxing's circuit, roughhouse carnies who would travel from town to town across the back country and fight each other, and the occasional local, under the big top.

It offered a chance for young Indigenous men to get off the missions and make a quid when there was little to no work, at a time when not having some coin in your pocket could land you in the slammer for vagrancy.

Something had snapped in the old fella dancing like a butterfly around me in Eddie's lounge that night. I could almost hear the *ding-ding* of the boxing tent's ringside bell as he stepped back into his days of life on the road when he was in his prime.

I never saw the roundhouse that stung me on the chin and catapulted me over the dining table into the wall. I only remember shaking the black stars from my vision and the metallic taste of blood in my mouth as a laughing mob helped me back on my feet, brushing me off and pushing a fresh drink in my hand while I checked if I still had all my teeth. Old Fella had snapped out of it and was again a languid old man, unaware of his flashback into the ring.

Three decades later while doing a story for *Australian Geographic*, I was sitting on a ship on the Great Barrier Reef, sipping beer with a young good-looking rooster, Duane Fraser.

'Shit, I reckon that could have been my pops that punched you out,' Duane said laughing after I told him the story.

At 31 and with looks somewhere between actors Aaron Pedersen and Errol Flynn, Duane sits on multiple boards and committees giving advice to ministers, prime ministers and the UN. A Wulgurukaba and Bidjara man, I'd wager Duane could be Australia's first Indigenous Prime Minister in coming years.

Not sure whether Duane was just winding me up, I chuckle back 'Cool, I'll wear that as a badge of honour, mate.'

During some of those nights in Tenant Creek, we would run out of grog – or 'charge', as Eddie called it – before everyone had run out of steam. So Eddie would commandeer either me or Charlie to go out 'chasin' charge' in our car – Eddie couldn't or didn't drive.

We would bounce around back roads or often no roads, bashing our way through spinifex into camps with small concrete huts and corrugated tin lean-tos. The living conditions were appalling, my first taste of the Third World and in my own backyard. Eddie laughed it off: 'They build them nice wooden houses first, but they just pulled them down for firewood, so now they're concrete.'

Scattered around the camps were late-model Landcruisers, all bushwhacked and buggered, missing doors, wheelless on bricks, with their windscreens smashed in.

'The miners gave them those, royalty payoff for putting a pipeline across our land.'

Little did I know at the time that Eddie's people, the Warumungu, were ten years into the nation's longest and hardest-fought land-rights claim, a claim that would be won, on paper, weeks after I had moved on. It took another eight years after winning their claim in the High Court in July 1988 for the Warumungu to get most of their land back. They were still fighting for parcels of it as late as 2007.

One time Eddie detoured to the town's dam, showing how it had developed a large crack, which according to him happened the day construction was completed.

'That's 'cause the Rainbow Serpent was angry, they never got permission from Elders to build it,' he said, pointing at the crack. 'That night a big storm blew in and it rained so hard all the excavators and bulldozers were washed into the bottom of the dam – they're still down there.'

I was never sure if this was a lashing of blackfella bullshit to put the wind up an earnest wide-eyed whitefella, but it was a good example of their discontent nonetheless.

Some nights chasing charge we'd fall through the doorless entrance of a derelict home, where a large mob would be sitting on the floor playing cards, the rules of which I could never work out. Betting was involved but it didn't seem to matter if the player threw in a handful of coins or a handful of notes as cards were quickly put down and picked up. Sleeping dogs, and young children on a mother's nipple would fringe the ring of gambling men, as Eddie worked his way around trying cajole a goon bag or a couple of beers.

Eddie explained there was a loose system when someone had a pay cheque or pension payout – everyone would go round and bleed them dry, and that was reciprocated on the next person's payday.

As long as I stayed in Eddie's company I was tolerated with a bemused ambivalence. On one occasion I strayed too far from his side and a young drunk man, fists clenched and a seething look in his eye, demanded I give him money for food – but having none, I just pulled out my empty pockets and shrugged. Eddie returned just in time to defuse a fray that would not have gone my way. Another time I was eyed off with lusty appetite by a large, toothless older woman sitting in the dirt too drunk to talk. She grunted at me, waving the half-chewed roasted goanna in her hand to signal me to come over. In the other hand she clenched a near-drained silver goon bag. She leaned to one side, projectile-vomited white wine and goanna meat into the dirt, wiped her mouth clean on her sleeve and grunted and grinned at me again.

Eddie and the young men he was talking to laughed at me. 'Aunty likes ya, mate, says she wants to have your babies,' Eddie said, grinning.

Terrified, I sank into the driver's seat till I was out of view, praying she didn't find her legs so she could walk over and drag me off to her humpy to make a meal of me.

Occasionally I was told to wait in the car while Eddie skirted around the back of a camp on a raiding mission, a snatch and run. One of these didn't go our way. It was late one night, Eddie had navigated me off road, bumbling over the desert, with not a distinguishable landmark (to me) in sight. We were driving with no headlights to avoid detection, until he instructed me to stop.

Knowing the starter motor didn't work, he whispered 'Keep the motor running' as he disappeared into the darkness, faintly illuminated by the Milky Way on the moonless night. Moments later he returned, jumping in the car panting.

'We better go, these fellas are a bit cheeky.'

'What d'ya mean cheeky?' I asked, unaware of any sense of urgency.

In the starlight, figures started to appear around the car.

'Go,' Eddie said, his voice starting to quiver. 'Go, go, GO. GO NOW.'

Finally sensing foreboding, I clunked the car into reverse and floored it, no idea where we were going, over undulations of the desert and through termite mounds and saltbush until the adrenaline subsided and we were far enough away to grind into a forward gear and find the road.

After a while Eddie said, 'Shouldn't have gone there. They were doing men's business – circumcision. Yeah, they could have got cheeky.'

I just turned and looked at Eddie, whose face glowed green in the dash lights.

'When they knew you were a whitefella, they wanted to spear ya.'

As well as driving Eddie around chasing charge, we also cooked many a feed for him and his mates, a contribution for the free lodgings and keep. One night Eddie pulled out a bag of beef steaks. They were slimy and green and had long since turned, forgotten in a recess of the refrigerator. The stench assaulted me when I opened the bag.

'Eddie, this meat is rotten, mate.'

'Nah, it'll be right, us blackfellas got guts made of iron. Cook 'er up, it'll be good tucker.'

All the other walk-ins murmured in agreement. I cooked it with as much garlic and birdseye chilli as I dared, protesting my concern as I served it up, refusing a portion myself.

Too tired to join them on the drink, I turned in early and awoke to the sounds of them all chundering and dry-retching around the outside of the house. Quietly smug, I rolled over in bed knowing there'd be no midnight charge run.

Living with Eddie and partying with his people, I nearly always felt safe and welcomed. The pub on a Friday or Saturday night, however, was a different story. The Tennant Creek Hotel was built in the 1930s and had an art deco frontage. It had two bars, one for blacks and one for whites – it was pub apartheid. Unlike the bar for the whites, which had barstools, carpet and wood-veneer finishings, the bar that Eddie and his mob drank in had concrete tables and benches bolted to the floor and the ambience of a gas chamber. The one and only time we drank there, Eddie insisted we go back home at 9p.m., in the minibus with the women and children. He was afraid we would be like lambs to the slaughter as the night slipped into drunken mayhem and violence.

The Stuart Highway tears through the main drag of Tennant Creek, at the centre of which sits the hotel. One Saturday morning, just before leaving Tennant Creek, I walked past the pub. A trail of broken glass and splatters of blood fanned out on the footpath in both directions. The town transsexual anaemic, skinny, middle-aged in a tattered summer frock, was sweeping the splinters of carnage from the front of her little bric-a-brac shop.

Aware of my presence as I stood by awkwardly watching, she said, matter-of-fact and without looking up at me, 'It's like this every weekend.'

I never asked how long she'd lived in Tennant Creek or why, but I sensed a resilience and tenacity in her unassuming demeanour, like a gnarled desert flower.

Charlie and I left Tennant Creek shortly afterwards. Our relationship had frayed – too much time in close quarters. He sold the car to Eddie's mates and we hitched to Alice Springs, where I managed to get a dole cheque. I bought a train ticket on the Ghan to Adelaide then hitched to Melbourne as I retreated from our nation's red centre and back into the dark heart of its urbanity. Tennant Creek was to be my last encounter with Aboriginal Australia before I was subsumed back into suburbia and then consumed by the metropolis, and it would be a quarter of century before I was to live in an Indigenous community again.

Three decades after staying with Eddie in Tennant Creek, I tried to track him down to yarn for this book. I was six years too late: Eddie died in 2011 at fifty-four years old.

But I managed to find his sister Rosemary Plummer, who still lives in Tennant Creek, and who I yabbered at, talking too much while she quietly listened. When I stopped, Rosemary, a poet and award-winning writer, grandmother, great-grandmother, Elder and teacher of Warumungu culture and language, told me of the struggles of the Warumunga land rights claim she was involved in, and of how Eddie, third oldest of seven, was the son of famous stockman Teddy Plummer.

'Dad owned two horses,' she said – it was apparently quite an achievement in his day. 'But he had to sell them when he got sick.'

'I'm really sorry I didn't call six years earlier, Rosemary. I would've liked to have said thanks to Eddie, for – well, for everything.'

She sighed and with a quivering voice said, 'Diabetes is such a terrible disease.'

The great divide between us became painfully apparent, and in those few words I sensed the suffering and loss Rosemary had endured, the burden she carried as an Aboriginal woman, while I had enjoyed the very best of what our society could offer a white man in the city. I asked if she remembered me and Charlie in 1988. She must have sensed how much my time with her brother had meant to me. In a tone I imagined she used doting over her great-grandchildren, she gently murmured a nurturing white lie.

'I think so, I think I remember you now.'

Not long after talking to Rosemary in 2017, I had a serendipitous conversation on TI with Rahm Adamedes. Rahm was filming a documentary commissioned by an Islander community group. He was a government youth worker in 2006 at the Aboriginal community Mutitjulu, which sits in the shadow of Uluru.

Rahm, who had been running a counselling and substance abuse prevention program in the community, said his department had breached confidence by exposing some specific case files to the ABC's *Lateline*. It became the basis of the infamous broadcast in May 2006, about sexual slavery and paedophile rings in Mutitjulu. *Lateline* aired the statements of an 'anonymous youth worker' who had lived in the community for nine months. His blacked-out cowboy-hat-wearing silhouette and digitised voice, purportedly hiding his identity for 'safety reasons', claimed that children were traded between communities as sex slaves and were paid for sex with petrol to sniff.

This 'anonymous youth worker' turned out to be Gregory Andrews, an adviser of the Federal Minister for Indigenous Affairs, Mal

Brough. He had never set foot in Mutitjulu – nor, it turned out, did *Lateline*, which used old stock footage of other communities to cobble together the story.

Rahm told me he feared for his life after the *Lateline* story aired and he was run out of the community – they thought it was him on TV. At the time he wore a similar cowboy hat.

Rahm looks at me quietly while sipping his coffee. Tall with a slight build, he has an intense stare that I sense can burn through any bullshit. In his early forties he seems an old soul.

'The government strategically used the media as a Trojan Horse to label all Aboriginal people as paedophiles, murderers, rapists and drug dealers to justify the Intervention,' he says.

The Intervention or the *Northern Territory National Emergency Response Act* was a raft of laws introduced by the Howard government. It received bipartisan support and was maintained by successive governments and extended until 2022.

The Intervention introduced a one-size-fits-all approach across seventy-five remote Aboriginal communities, including alcohol prohibition, welfare cards and mandatory land handovers. Racial discrimination laws, land-rights laws and native-title laws were suspended to implement it, and the army was sent into communities to enforce it. It is also in direct violation of the *Universal Declaration of Human Rights*. But it was based on fundamental lies drawn from the *Little Children Are Sacred* report that was a result of the falsified *Lateline* story, the details of which ended up in the Supreme Court. However, within weeks of publication the federal government stepped in, overrode the territory government and implemented the Intervention.

'Rivers of grog' became a catchcry of the media and one Minister Brough used to push the agenda of the Intervention. It was used to manipulate public sentiment of 'nuisance drinking' by Aboriginals in the urban centres of Tennant Creek, Katherine and Darwin. Binge-drinking culture, regardless of background, flowed much more freely in urban centres than in most of the Aboriginal communities that were dry from self-imposed bans, as part of the Outstation Movement. But no politician in their right mind would propose an alcohol ban in the towns, so instead blamed the bush. The Intervention took that self-determination away from Aboriginal people and replaced it with a sense of shame and hopelessness.

Rahm smiles. 'We talk about the overt and the covert curriculum. The covert curriculum (of the Intervention) was really about the suspension of the *Racial Discrimination Act*, it was about the imposing of martial law and it was about the forced acquisition of seventy-five Indigenous councils, most of who were already run effectively.

'So what we saw was an erosion of the last thirty years of land rights, of independent governance. So you had entire nations of people with no registered organisation or instruments to represent them, they didn't have bank accounts, all the computers and offices were taken over by the government and no independent entities could operate in the community without federal or state government permission. It stripped away all community control.'

Millions of dollars were spent as part of the Intervention to build hundreds of houses for the white administrative staff, who had little or no experience working in Aboriginal communities.

'At the same time this was going on, they were trying to establish a nuclear waste dump, trying to regionalise the seventy-five communities into twenty-five urban centres while adjusting native title land laws to allow external white enterprise to run the businesses and manage the towns and communities,' Rahm says.

'So basically they are trying to move people off the land and at the same time they were trying to stop English as a second language being taught at school. Basically it's paramount to cultural genocide.'

Research by Monash University in 2011 found that suicide, domestic violence and incarceration rates soared after the Intervention was implemented, yet there had not been a single arrest for child sexual abuse.

The Intervention was criticised for the lack of proper consultation with Aboriginal communities. Rahm said that the government officials that dealt with these communities are referred to by them as 'white cockies' – because 'they fly in, squawk a lot, shit on you and then fly out again'.

Rahm's name for this is a little more colourful. 'I call it white cunt syndrome, as in communities they say there are three types of them: the mercenaries, the missionaries, and the misfits,' he says.

Rahm recites to me his version of the Axioms of the Bush: 'First there were the missionaries, who helped steal a generation of children away from their families. Then there's the misfits, the mid-level bureaucrats that couldn't get a job anywhere else, and there's the mercenaries, the ones there to exploit the multi-billion-dollar industry that provides the services for these communities.'

But Rahm thinks there is another Axiom of the Bush emerging, a new generation coming through: 'Those who have a cultural awareness, who honour the cultural law and the values of the land, and the Elders. They are genuine people who will listen and are truly trying to facilitate positive change in the communities – I guess you could call them the magicians.'

'Is that you, is that us?' I ask.

'The road to hell is paved with good intentions,' he says, smiling.

CHAPTER 5

MURALAG MOONSHINE

27 January 2014

Since becoming the editor of *Torres News*, I now constantly hunt for the next front-page story. It's like a drug, nothing else matters, then as soon I find it and it's laid it out for the printer with all the other pages, there's just enough time for a post-coital beer and an *ah* of self-satisfaction before it starts again. The chase, it rises up my hackles as the muscles at the back of my neck tighten and my temples throb with the realisation that I have nothing for the next edition – the next front page. It's a cycle that rolls for fifty weeks a year (we shut down for Christmas).

Even though it's a small regional newspaper in a remote location many hundreds of kilometres away from a metropolitan area, I've found myself oddly at the centre of a hub of activity.

It's very different to my time in the wilderness of freelance journalism in a city.

Within weeks of starting in the job I discover I am one of the players, in a position of influence in this small community spread over an immense area on Australia's only border with another country a stone's throw away. My only lifeline is my boss Senior, Corey's dad, who is over 2000 kilometres away on the Gold Coast. We have never met, but we talk daily on the phone and by email: his dulcet tones are always calming and the peppering of expletives never jars. Pushing seventy, he's like a surrogate father figure, or as my wife describes him, like Charlie, the disembodied voice of John Forsythe from the 1970s American TV show *Charlie's Angels*, but with a broad Queensland accent.

Old-school, Senior never studied journalism at uni but learned on the job, spending a lot of time developing sources and finding stories by hanging around racecourses and pubs, despite being a teetotaller. After half a century in the game, Senior's address book is never short of a contact who can pry open the truth behind some government media release or what actually happened in a story covered by 'that southern media', as he describes anything south of Cape York.

I am occasionally courted by the same 'southern media', including national newspapers and TV channels who want to get on-the-ground intel out of me.

I discover over the following years that it's TV people who are the worst. Print media usually only call frantically around election time to ask some stupid questions, the dumbest yet being if the Torres Strait was part of Australia. But the TV mob seems to think they're doing you a favour intruding into your life and sprinkling a little stardust around. First it's the location scouts looking for ideas and characters. They call and chew up an hour of my time, and they all seem to have the same hackneyed ideas. Rarely do they plan to stay more than a few days hoping to drill down into the essence of the Torres Strait, but invariably that doesn't include leaving TI. Then when they get on the ground the director ignores you, as does the show's host, unless you have an on-camera soundbite or they're posing for a selfie with a fan. It's the producers who gush and fawn while they need you, promising 'beer tax', but they will drop you without a moment's thought as they follow a new whim. Then they up and leave as abruptly as they arrived, with not so much as a note on the bedside table.

Senior has little regard for them either – he always says, 'Tell the bastards nothing, they never do anything for us.'

Age and declining health are the only reasons Senior is not living on Thursday Island doing my job. He's had a love for the place and its people since they took over the paper in 2002.

As part of my weekly routine I frequently have breakfast with the ageing white elite of the Parish Hall Restoration Committee or Rotary. I often have a coffee with the police inspector, talk with the region's Indigenous leaders and have candid phone calls with federal politicians. The mayor leaves messages on my answering machine.

I've met premiers and prime ministers, governors and governors-general, drunk beer with the Chief of Army, jogged with Robert de Castella, swum with Lisa Curry, talked gardening with ABC's Dirt Girl, got to hold the NRL trophy – and even posed for a selfie with the US National Basketball Association trophy, when 2014 champions San Antonio Spurs star player and TI boy Patrick Mills did a homecoming tour. The trophy was set down on a lawn and the whole community feasted and danced around it in celebration. It's a far cry from my punk rock twenties, when my circles were struggling musicians and artists, seedy small-time criminals, drug dealers, working girls, acid freaks and junkies.

Actually more important than reporting on politics from the big end of town, I'm expected to attend the many local community events, sports carnivals, school activities and church fetes, as well as the occasional funeral, birthday and wedding.

TI has a distinct temporal dissonance that many tropical islands have, and it's not always conducive to writing newspapers. TI time, or *Ailan* (Island) time, is the lackadaisical, maybe-today, maybe-tomorrow attitude to deadlines, appointments and getting things done.

I had an electrical issue the other day and the electrician who 'would turn up within the hour', as I was told, arrived the next day, after I had resolved the issue myself and cancelled his appointment.

It's 'all good', the common expression here – it's all on Island time.

That is, except for me: my weekly deadline is unrelenting.

I should mention I am also the chief of staff, photographer, senior journalist, office administrator and paperboy, the reality of the collapsing newspaper industry with an ever shrinking bottom line – so my frenetic little world is in constant juxtaposition to sleepy TI time. The papers take four days to arrive from Cairns by barge, weather permitting, and they smell like bananas – always packed on the same pallet as the supermarket's stock.

This is a sleepy place. Ibises forage at the rubbish tip rather than seagulls, and cockatoos play on the beach. The large black and white Torres Strait pigeons coo in the tops of the beach almond trees in the afternoons, then at dusk screeching rainbow lorikeets dart and weave in formation through the canopy. When the sun drops blood red and orange into the sea, the night sky thickens with fruit bats hunting moths. In the mornings, blue-winged kookaburras croak and cackle in the she-oaks along the foreshore, whose branches hum hauntingly in the incoming sea breeze. Then as the sun climbs to its zenith again, schools of chestnut finches bounce through the long grass while indolent lizards look at you as if to say 'Why hurry?' before they reluctantly slide off the sun-cracked footpath to let you pass.

It's a good question. So much of the modern world suffers from the 'hurry disease', where our lives are justified by how increasingly busy we are, and in the interim life passes us by. On balmy starlit nights in the dry season, teenagers wander the streets with R'n'B blasting from their phones, and the occasional beach Bundy Rum binge ends in a 'daybreaker', where they are still howling and hooting at sunrise. In the wet season, kids fish squid off the beaches, as schools of them dart along the edge of the beach in the still waters of the doldrums.

The community have a love-hate relationship with me: everyone has an agenda and no one wants to be crucified by the press, especially in a small island community. But to your face it's always a smile. It's part of maintaining that polite exterior under which often lies the frustration of isolation, racial vilification, domestic violence and the 'gap' between Indigenous and non-Indigenous, not to mention family feuds that may date back generations. But overall *Ailan* folk are a happy, God-fearing, conservative bunch.

Some days I work from 8a.m. to 11p.m. straight, but other days I knock off early and go fishing, as I try to instil as much TI time in my life as is possible for a newspaper man. Ironically, it's often in that slow time I get some of my best story leads, when someone has a quiet word in my ear as I linger at the fruit and veg stand at the supermarket, fish on the pier, or have a quiet knock-off beer at the Torres Hotel, the country's most northerly, a rambling Queenslander shaded by strangler vines that calls itself 'Australia's Top Pub'.

One evening as I was flinging my handline off the pier hoping to snag a 'whitefish', or giant trevally, an Islander explained the *Ailan* way to me while showing me the correct way to cast.

'*Bala,* sometimes the politics and fights go back generations, but on the surface we're all nice to each other, it be *Ailan* way,' Solomon says as he flicks my handline a good twenty metres into the murky night waters.

He winds the line back in slowly, occasionally tugging quickly.

'We all got to live together, we see each other every day at events, supermarket, post office, so we can't be fighting all the time.'

Solomon hands me the line, corrects my positioning of the spool so it faces the water, then nods for me to cast. It makes a respectable ten metres and I catch my first fish, something Solomon's kids call a 'monkeyfish', a small mudskipper-looking thing that's obviously low on the evolutionary ladder and apparently not an eater.

I release the slimy critter to a snicker of laughter from the others on the pier, and Solomon pats me on the shoulder.

'When we fish, we fish for the whole village, so if I catch twenty fish, when I walk home past everyone's house, I give each a fish, so when I get home I might only have one fish.'

Determined to prove my mettle, I keep fishing as everyone else ebbs away, back to their homes. I don't notice the couple of nice whitefish Solomon has left in my bucket.

It's another three weeks before I master the art of casting and jigging, and one evening I land a couple of respectable whitefish and a coral trout. At first I think I will take them home and cook them, a nice boon for the weekly grocery bill, but then something clicks inside, an aha moment.

By the time I get to the end of the pier on my way home, I have given the fish away to the old ladies who have watched me for weeks tangle lines and loose lures into the deep blue. My bucket is empty but my heart is full. It's my first understanding of the custom of reciprocity, which I first encountered in the Central Desert with Eddie's mob a quarter of a century before. It's a way of life that has sustained and endured, and it is so incongruous in the take-no-prisoners, every-man-for-himself capitalist economy that is driving the world into an abyss.

For me, as an outsider trying to make sense of it all, it is like Alice going down the rabbit hole, but in a tropical paradise.

Senior warned me though: 'Doesn't matter how long you live there, you will never become true friends with Islanders. They will be friendly, but you will never be part of their social circle – they've seen it all bloody before, people come up from down south, stay a couple of years then bugger off – they just don't want to invest emotionally with you. They just like to keep to their own – and how you can blame them really?'

There is a steady stream of characters through the door of my poky office. Aunty Wasie Tardent often stops by for advice about how to operate Facebook on her smartphone. Limping with a walking stick, blind in one eye, she is always dressed beautifully in a traditional floral dress with her white hair tied back and pinned with a frangipani. A retired primary school teacher, she was one of the first Islanders to become qualified in the state. When her seventieth birthday party, which was attended by a huge contingent of the community, was on the front page, it ended up selling more copies than any other edition I edited. I had to restock outlets halfway through the week, it was so popular.

Bishop Saibo Mabo from Mer (Murray Island), cousin to Eddie Mabo, often drops in early in the week wanting me to transcribe the lengthy fire-and-brimstone sermon delivered to his flock on the Sunday, to be printed as a column. The first Islander Anglican bishop in Australia, he is one of the sharpest dressers around, his ceremonial gown and mitre the colours of the Torres Strait flag – greens, blue and black in crushed velvet – with a gold ring flashing on his pinky and an impeccable white toothy grin. Apparently a wild man in his younger days, he always has a mischievous grin for me and my heathen non-churchgoing ways.

'Maybe we will see you next Sunday, my son,' he'll chuckle as an afterthought as he leaves my office, knowing full well he wouldn't.

Then there's Brian Millit, who is pushing ninety but looks to be in his mid-seventies, who comes in every second day trying to get me to investigate the disgrace of the ATM not working on pension day, or delays with the postal service, power outages or the outrageous price of milk. Brian used to work for the bookies on the Sydney racetracks, collecting the winnings of high rollers. 'I remember one time I had to collect £38,000 – that was a lot of money in the fifties. I couldn't fit it in all my pockets so I had to go to the toilets, take off my singlet and wrap it in that,' he grizzles to me one day, in between hacking, phlegmy coughs – early onset emphysema, he reckons, despite not smoking since the seventies.

Brian came up to Thursday Island in the late sixties to work for a prawn fisherman, who went broke within days of his arrival. Brian bounced around the Cape doing odd jobs before buying a dinghy and diving for lobster. 'I've dived around all these islands,' he says, pointing out my office window to the visible archipelago surrounding TI. A dinghy hurtles past, a lean young Islander standing tall in the middle, legs wide like he's on a surfboard as he smashes across the chop. He pulls tight on a rope tied to the bow for balance, while steering and controlling the throttle with a metre of PVC pipe jammed on the end of the arm of the outboard. Another young Islander stands on the bow, leaning into the waist-high steel balustrade that's bolted on to help hunt turtle and dugong.

'I had no idea what I was doing, but I did okay.'

Brian then became a self-taught mechanic and ended up marrying an Islander lady and having a couple of daughters, as well as raising a couple more that weren't his. Despite his gruff demeanour he has a nice smile, a good heart and, although he'd never admit it, a gentle soul.

He only ever wears a pair of shorts and thongs, goes shirtless everywhere. The bank manager has always lamented to me about Brian's tirades in the paper about the failing ATM, until one day he breaks up a fight in the bank and throws the two lads out on their ears. After that the bank manager swoons about her shirtless knight in shining armour.

Robert 'Bongo' Sagigi, a mountain of a man in his fifties with hands the size of dinner plates, often stoops through my doorway. A formidable but friendly fellow, he must have cast quite a shadow in his prime. He bellows in a baritone deeper than Barry White's his disdain of 'those bloody coconuts, they are worse than the government, they get on the payroll and forget about our people'. Bongo is usually clutching a piece of paper, a letter to the editor highlighting the failings of the government and the frustrations of First Nations people. He's constantly trying to rally the discontent into action.

Then there's C'Zarke Maza, half Dutch and half Murray Islander, who is named after an infamous Islander sorcerer, or *zogo le*. A barrister who manages the government-funded Aboriginal and Torres Strait Islander Legal Service, C'Zarke Maza has the office adjacent to mine.

He often stops by for a coffee and to discuss possible weekend fishing trips, springing through my door unannounced like Kramer from *Seinfeld*. For a lifelong vegetarian his bloodlust for fishing is a little unnerving. Despite his being a teetotal legal eagle and me a boozy newshound with a shady past, we clicked. C'Zarke's dad, Bob Maza, was a political activist, actor and playwright who in the seventies addressed the UN, describing the Third World conditions his people endured; in 1972 he was part of the original Tent Embassy protest on the lawns of Parliament House in Canberra. He also helped establish an Australian chapter of the Black Panthers. His worked earned him an Order of Australia in 1993, as well as a spot on the same ASIO file as Eddie Mabo.

Sometimes Islander fishermen pull up to sell me coral trout from the ice-filled boot of a car, or come by dinghy to sell me Spanish mackerel by the metre, or they ask me at the local lobster packing shed if they can trade a bag of tails for my old newspaper returns, to use as wrapping to keep their product frozen on the flight south to Cairns.

Then there's Raph, who's in his early forties: a rough-hewn Queenslander softened by his French/Iranian heritage, who bakes the region's famous crayfish pies. He soaks up my aircon to escape the afternoon heat of the bakery ovens while sharing a glass of spiced rum and hatching plans to retire early by trading cryptocurrencies.

If it isn't people then it will be Boss and Boika, a couple of town dogs, a mongrel mix of every mutt on the island – TI thoroughbred, as Raph would call them. After cadging a feed off me they scratch at my door wanting to sleep it off in my airconed office. Over the years we've also adopted a stray Siamese cat, a three-legged fox terrier and even a wild rainbow lorikeet with anxiety issues my daughter brought home and named Andy. Andy, who couldn't or didn't want to fly, took sanctuary in my office for a couple of months, shitting on everything and screeching so much I had to relocate to the kitchen until it decided to take to the wing.

Sometimes when I'm on deadline drowning in unwritten copy and I see Brian's or Bishop Mabo's car pull up out my office, I hide under my desk. Sometimes I just can't afford the time for a yarn.

Then there are the regulars who phone in and hold my ear often longer than I can spare, despite how entertaining they usually are. Alf Wilson, our long-term freelance sports journo, calls periodically to get a feel for what's happening. A self-proclaimed 'old fat bastard', he's old-school like Senior and has a prolific output. In his sixties, Alf is a walking copywriting machine, and with his signature terry-towelling hat he's renowned and revered from mining towns in Tasmania to the Indigenous communities of the Cape and the Torres Strait. Senior said once: 'I've taken the bloke out to lunch, and on the way back from the toilet he tells me he's written two sports stories on a napkin – met one guy in the pisser and another walking past the bar. He bloody well knows everybody.'

Some of Alf's yarns are legendary.

'You could make good money as a freelance back in the day, hey,' he rasps down the phone to me. 'I used to do the photos for the home girls in *Picture* magazine. I got four hundred bucks for every photo I got of a girl flashing her tits, as long as they signed a release form. One time I was passed out drunk in my car in a pub cark park, and all these girls kept knocking on my window wanting their photo taken – I made nearly five grand that night. But I don't think my wife really liked it so I gave that one up.'

Alf's most famous freelance story involved him snapping a photo of INXS singer Michael Hutchence with Paula Yates, then wife of British pop star Bob Geldof.

'He punched me in the nose but I got thirty grand for that photo, so it was worth it.'

Another of my ring-ins is Larry James, the high school English teacher nearing retirement. Wizened, weathered by four decades of salt, sea and sun, white-haired with a foot-long beard, Larry lives on Muralag, or Prince of Wales Island. At 79 square kilometres of wild hilly scrubland and secret waterfalls, Muralag is the largest island in the Strait. It also has one of the smallest communities, with fewer than 100 people, who live in shacks without running water, sewerage or power, and whose only access to the outside world is by dinghy. I can see it from my back door, separated by probably the most tempestuous and turbulent narrow stretch of water in the whole region. Nicknamed the Washing Machine, it often boils and spits with wild eddies and currents, buffeted by seasonal winds, where the Arafura and Coral seas collide and jostle in an eternal battle of one-upmanship. It's treacherous for dinghies crossing it, and Larry is haunted by the drownings of students there many years ago.

Larry will walk straight past me on the street; I don't think he even knows who I am — either that or he ignores me. It's nothing personal, more just the *Ailan* way. Living in such a small, closed community we all tend to ignore each other from time to time, otherwise we would have to say hi and make small talk with the same person several times a day.

Larry moved to the Torres Strait right after finishing his teaching degree and never left. He got married here and raised a family, who have all since moved on, leaving him alone — now he is married to the Strait. With a predilection for the drink, Larry calls in the early evening. With his voice slurred from a bottle of red and Wagner belting out in the background, he laments the loss of the love of language. Fluent in Yumplatok, Larry is passionate about literacy and has tried teaching the kids Shakespeare. Sometimes he sends me handwritten letters in elegant cursive, and includes a poem. The latest was Dylan Thomas's 'Do not go gentle into that good night'.

In the accompanying letter, Larry laments at the loss of the *Queensland Tide Book,* a publication printed by the state government. It had been decided under the penny-pinching Premier Campbell Newman that it will no longer be printed. For Larry, a pious man, the tide book is his bible, as it allows him to charter safe passage to and from his shack. The Department of Transport and Main Roads says it will still be available online to download and print, but many in the island communities lack access to the internet. Given how perilous it can be not having the tide times on hand, I am able to apply pressure.

I keep it on the front page for a couple of weeks, even describing Larry adrift in his dinghy on a dark and stormy night clutching loose-leaf A4 printouts of the *Tide Book* as the wind and rain whip them from his grasp while he tries to navigate to a safe harbour. Eventually the state backs down and the *Tide Book* is again printed. It's my first small victory as editor.

The next time I check my post office box I find a small parcel. Inside is a note from Larry that just says, *May your automatic bilge pump or self-draining floor do you justice in the weather.*

Also included is a small opaque bottle of Muralag moonshine, a homebrew of coconut water, brandy and rum. The bottle has a quote by Oliver Goldsmith stuck on the back: *Let schoolmasters puzzle their brain with grammar, and nonsense, and learning. Good liquor, I stoutly maintain, gives genius a better discerning.*

However, Larry still ignores me when we pass in the street.

CHAPTER 6

ON THE LIGHTER SIDE

1 July 2013

It's not every day I get to see a white man on his knees pleading for his life as an Indigenous man stands over him with a spear raised ready to strike. Not in Australia – well, not in the twenty-first century, at least. To make the moment even more delicious, the white man is a federal politician with nothing more than a Bible between himself and the spear point. But the sweetness of the moment soon fades – this is nothing more than politicking in the lead-up to an impending federal election, on a day that celebrates the syncretism of tribal spirituality with Christianity, when the missionaries first took hold back in 1871. It's now a regional bank holiday known as the Coming of the Light.

Warren Entsch, the federal Liberal National Party Member for Leichhardt, the electorate that covers the Torres Strait and Cape York, is an indomitable character. Although he has the air of a used car salesman or the Barry Humphries character Sir Les Patterson, Warren is also quite personable. The Strait is a traditional Labor stronghold, despite which Warren makes regular appearances in the region at strategic times, like today – it may be why he has held the seat for five terms.

Later in the year, after Warren wins his sixth term, he invites me to Christmas drinks. Feeling incongruent with all his party faithful, I ask him his stance on Indonesia's occupation of Western Papua. He slurps on his glass of claret, drips of which have stained the protruding belly of his tieless ruffled white shirt, unbuttoned to chest hair. Without flinching he says: 'Did I ever tell you how I became good mates with the Dalai Lama?'

The segue is flawless – left of field, but flawless. On another occasion, at the opening of a community health program, a senior Queensland Health executive sidles up to us to make small talk about what he did the night before. Again, without missing a beat and completely deadpan, Warren said: 'I was at the Torres Hotel drinking cocktails with this bloke,' – nodding to me – 'we were dancing to ABBA under the mirror ball until way past the lockout.'

The bureaucrat looks at me, incredulous, and I just nod quietly in agreement. We both just leave it hanging.

Despite my disdain for politicians across the spectrum, I can't help but like the guy, even though he's not being much of a believer in climate change. Warren is a bit of a maverick in the LNP: he has been outspoken about supporting gay marriage and medical marijuana, and addressing the chronic tuberculosis crisis in PNG. He was also behind the first attempted leadership spill of Prime Minister Tony Abbott in February 2015. He called early in the morning of 15 September that year, all slurry and sweary, saying how he'd been up all night in the party war room after the successful toppling of Abbott by Turnbull the night before – no doubt many a bottle of Penfolds Grange the collateral damage. Shooting from the hip, it was Warren at his best.

Always knowing how to exploit an appearance to his advantage and ever the showman, Warren on his knees in the sand on Thursday Island's esplanade is him at his finest. Dressed immaculately in white slacks and shirt with a cream panama hat, Warren is taking part in a re-enactment of the London Missionary Society (LMS) first delivering the word of God to the Torres Strait on 1 July 1871.

Raised a strict atheist in a household where the 'G' word was a dirty one, I squirm a little when I hear of the work of missionaries 'saving the savages'. That said, it is largely accepted in the region that conversion to Christianity allowed a peace to endure, providing regional stability, putting an end to inter-island raiding and headhunting, and unifying the region. That is, they were converted to the light of Christianity to bring them out of the 'darkness' of their heathenism. The whole thing sticks in my craw, like the sense of quiet shame I feel attending Australia Day celebrations, where like everyone else I murmur lip service to a national anthem, embarrassed not because I don't know the words but by the national denial it represents.

However, the saving grace of the Coming of the Light is only a half-truth that on its own denigrates the old Islander way of life. In the three or four decades prior to the missionaries gaining a foothold in the region in 1871, one they saw as a stepping stone to get the Lord's word across to PNG, the Islanders had been increasingly worn down by incursions of lawless European and South Sea Islander crews, who were lured first by bêchede-mer (sea cucumbers), trochus shell, then pearl shell. Crews raided communities, raping the women and kidnapping the men to work as enslaved divers. They also desecrated holy sites, raided gardens and stripped islands of timber, causing havoc to the Islanders' way of life. On Masig in the central islands, it's reputed that whenever a European vessel appeared on the horizon the women were buried in the sand with only their nostrils showing.

With an increasing number of outsiders arriving due to the rise of the pearling industry, soon to become the world's biggest, Islanders were becoming a dwindling minority.

The Islanders fought back for a long time from the raiding parties of European fishermen and the region was feared for the brutality they would reciprocate. Unlike Australian Aboriginal peoples, the Islanders were never dispossessed from their lands. Yet as more and more boats came, and spear and arrow increasingly lost to cutlass and musket, despite the braveness of their warriors, some communities were deserted as Islander populations and morale declined.

So the ways of the white man were well familiar to the residents of Erub when Reverend Samuel Macfarlane, a Scottish engineer turned evangelist, and Reverend Archibald Murray of the London Missionary Society (LMS), along with eight New Caledonian missionary teachers, hove to in their vessel the *Surprise* in Treacherous Bay in the early evening of Saturday, 1 July 1871.

Aware of the lawlessness just beyond its jurisdiction, the Queensland Government encouraged the missionaries to move in, as this offered a way of administering the region and provided them with a process of colonisation. It pre-empted the government's move a year later to pass the 'Kidnapping Act', to try and regulate the region's labour trade, as well as lay the foundation for changing the colony's border to include all the islands of the Torres Strait, which came into effect in 1879 with the *Queensland Coast Islands Act*. It was essentially just a way for the Queensland government to claim territory and the pearling industry it came with.

The easy uptake of Christianity throughout the Strait seems to have been assisted by its similarities to the Malo cult, which originated in the Mer but had influence throughout the region. The myth concerns Bomai and his nephew, Malo. Malo arrives on Mer looking for Bomai; the narrative has parallels with Jesus and God the Father.

Bomai, the pinnacle of sacred power, is so sacred that no ordinary mortal can call that name. Meriam people today compare the sacredness of Bomai's name with the Old Testament rule *Thou shalt not take the name of the Lord thy god in vain*.

There is also a parallel with the New Testament's Devil in Waiat, who came to Mer from Mabuiag. He went to the opposite side of the island than Malo had done, where he became the head of an evil cult.

So Christianity may have been accepted more as a changing of the guard than a complete abandonment of pre-Christian belief systems –

and maybe the Coming of the Light was a rebirth, in which the Islanders were born again as Christian. I guess learning of the original sin, guilt and the shame of nudity was a small price to pay for peace and stability. By the time influential Cambridge anthropologist and ethnologist Alfred Cort Haddon arrived in 1898 to lead an exploration that spent a year documenting Torres Strait Islander culture in six volumes, it was already in decline. Haddon gathered a collection of more than 1200 artefacts.

While it seems the early European missionaries may have had a liberal view of some of the old ways, the newly arrived South Sea missionaries were sticklers for the Good Book, which was later perpetuated by Islander men of the cloth. Clothing was mandatory, especially the neck-to-ankle Mother Hubbard dresses on the women, popular throughout the Pacific with the zealots and still worn in the Straits today. Traditional songs and dance were suppressed and many artefacts destroyed. Punishment for disobedience or sin was delivered by the lash. However, the use of the traditional drum called a *warup* and singing hymns in their language became tolerated.

What sacred objects were left were hidden away, and what rituals of the earlier Malo cult remained were done in secret in what today survives as *puri puri*, usually delivered as black magic in the form of hexes, illness, and misfortune. Although nobody admits to practising it today, everyone knows someone who has been afflicted by it. Bottles filled with coconut oil hang from Islander porches, a *puri puri* protection from hexes, and even the police have told me of a mysterious blacked-out *puri puri* Commodore that frightens residents as it tears around the neighbourhood late at night, driverless, in and out of the ether like an apparition.

'You see all those graves?' Kenny Bedford says smiling, as we drive along a narrow concrete causeway fringed with coconut trees that dissects the village on Erub.

I'm covering the 2016 Recognise Campaign — the push to change the Constitution to recognise First Australians. Kenny, son of an Erubian mother and legendary fisherman, Bluey Bedford, has the presence of a giant. A wry grin behind a bushranger's salt-and-pepper beard and a knowing gaze allows him to navigate the treacherous seas of Indigenous politics deftly and intelligently, always maintaining a grace under fire. Kenny knows everybody — from Daru, where we've spent a couple of rum-soaked nights together, to Canberra — and seems to spend half his time in the air flying between various political powwows.

Kenny and I struck up a unique friendship early in my tenure after my boss told me to take him out to lunch to make sure this political powerbroker was an ally. After the lunch he texted me saying *thanks for the lynching*, I didn't understand until I read my previous text to him, where my phone had autocorrected *Want to meet for a lunch?* to *Want to meet for a lynching?*

Kenny nods to the ornately decorated headstones of graves that adorn the front gardens of homes as we drive slowly past.

He smiles. 'Yes, we like to keep our family close here on Erub.'

Erubians have a ritual, *takarr*, of mummifying the remains of prominent tribal members.

As we drive past the derelict All Saints church, the region's first LMS church, I ponder how this pre-missionary custom has managed to hang on.

Life for Islanders changed quickly after the Coming of the Light. A system of administrative control was in place by the turn of the twentieth century, as missionaries had become established and the Queensland government acquired the territory extending right up to the coast of the Western Province of PNG. A *mamoose*, or chief, was appointed to work with the police to maintain law and order in each island community. This was replaced in 1936 with a system of Island

Councils, each of which had a limited amount of autonomy, administration and judicial control for minor crimes. It was the system of local government until 2008 when each island council was amalgamated into the Torres Strait Island Regional Council.

Milton Savage, who is the chair of the Kaurareg Native Title Prescribed Body Corporate (KNTAC), the Traditional Owners' formal representative entity for TI and inner islands, says the Coming of the Light leaves a bad taste in his mouth.

Milton, a stocky man in his fifties, has a silver goatee and dreadlocks tied back with a red bandana. A white cockatoo feather sticks up out of the ponytail. He smiles, revealing several missing teeth.

His soft voice and patient demeanor have delivered Welcome to Country ceremonies for the endless parade of dignitaries, including prime ministers and premiers, who come to his land.

'They come along and do their re-enactment – people don't want to come out of that, they feel a security from it. Really, it's a mockery for Indigenous people, the way the British put it forward that "you are a native, you are a savage".

'We only ever had one name – they made us take surnames, like mine. Savage is their name, not mine. Savage was given to my ancestors because a white man couldn't spell Puiyanga, which was our name, too hard for them so they just give us the name Savage.

'When you talk about identity, I'm Kaurareg, I'm Italaig, Gudang, Yadhaikana, Gomukudin, Kawaig man, that's my people's tribes, they are from all across Cape York. The word "Aborigine" or "Aboriginal" is a British word to define a group of people, but I'm not so comfortable with that word myself, I am a First Nations person.

'Then the missionaries came and said, "Oh, we give you the good news, a new belief system. But now when everybody's woken up and can actually read it, the Bible say *thou shall not kill,* the Bible say *thou shall not steal* – but how will our people understand that when we have seen the white man do the opposite? That's a problem.

'So now when *yumi* (you all) talk about magic, the interpretation today is *mayid,* or black magic *puri puri* that they use to kill each other because of jealousy. This is not our way – this was imposed, established by the whitefellas, this was the system of the government to claim and conquer this region. People will fear the sorcerer and the sorcerer will fear the gun, you see, so you have an order in place now – I call it the impact of colonisation.

'Today many of the people that work in the government here are Indigenous people, so they too have a culture and tradition they belong to. But sometimes they forget that and lean too much into the colonisation mindset. That's what causes destruction amongst ourselves – infighting, lateral violence, the "I, me" attitude.

'We can talk about our cultural lore, traditions and customs and what do you have? Nothing – as nobody is out there practising it. Why? Because we have become too exposed to this Westminster system.'

Milton's people, the Kaurareg, are unique in that they are Aboriginal and not Islander, but have a history of using canoes, bows and arrows. Milton tells me that not only did his people face prejudice from the White overseers, but he believes they have historically been looked down upon by the Islanders as well. The colonisation process also fractured the Kaurareg people into several factions that squabble and struggle to speak with one voice.

The Kaurareg Archipelago of forty-five islands and islets in the Straits around the tip of Cape York is called Kaiwalagal. In its Dreamtime story, Waubin, a giant mythical warrior from Australia's Central Desert, came to the island of Muralag in the Torres Strait, where he fought warriors including Badhanai, who was of very small stature.

In a battle, Badhanai darted underneath Waubin and sliced off his right leg with a bamboo knife. The blood from the wound flowed into the waterhole Rabau Nguki, whose creek carried the blood to the sea, where currents spread it throughout the waters surrounding the Prince of Wales (Kaiwalagal) group of islands.

Milton says the distance the blood spread became the territorial boundary of the Kaurareg. It included Muralag (Prince of Wales Island), Bedanug (Possession Island), Narupai (Horn Island), Kirriri (Hammond Island), Kudalagal (Tuesday Islets), Maururra (Wednesday Island), Waiben (Thursday Island) and Gealug (Friday Island), among others.

After the fight, Waubin sat down in the ocean north-east of Kirriri, where he turned to stone: now known as Hammond Rock. Today he protects the cluster, sending strong currents around Muralag: these treacherous currents, also known as the 'washing machine', buffet dinghies around like corks.

Milton says he can empathise with the Aboriginal people of New South Wales who were there when the First Fleet arrived.

Three months after Captain Cook first made landfall at Botany Bay on 29 April 1770, he sailed north up the east coast to Cape York. Cook, or so the history books claim, then landed at

Bedanug at the tip of Cape York, which he named Possession Island.

I now once more hoisted English Coulers and in the Name of His Majesty King George the Third took possession of the whole Eastern Coast, Cook wrote in his journal at the time.

Milton says: 'There wasn't any negotiation table put at the beach where we could say, "We can give you a bit of land." Nowadays you go to any country, you have to negotiate. But back then the British only perceived us as part of the flora and fauna, it was a degrading perception.

'There are many stories told by the Elders that there were people all along the hilltops and all along the foreshores watching what he was doing and they say he didn't set foot on the island, he just hoisted the flag on his ship. The other talk says he fired a canon with a flag wrapped around a cannonball to the island, because there were people all armed with spears and a few holding bows with bundles of arrows.'

To this day the Kaurareg and neighbouring tribes are still trying to gain the native title rights to Possession Island from the Australian Government.

As the Kaurareg people's Country included Horn Island and Thursday Island, the white administrative hub of the Torres Strait, they suffered the most extreme dislocation since the steady arrival of Europeans in the 1870s. They were massacred to near extinction after being wrongly accused of attacking and killing the crew of eight on the small cutter *Sperwer* on nearby Wednesday Island in April 1869.

Frank Jardine, the region's first police magistrate, ordered the execution of three Kaurareg men for the attack, who were discovered soon after to be not guilty; rather, it had been a tribe of Islanders from further east.

Thus began a series of retaliatory attacks in 1870 against the Kaurareg on Muralag. Milton says the oral history passed down told of how the police ambushed the Kaurareg in the middle of the night, 'while everyone was asleep'. When they 'opened fire on everyone in the village, they shot every man, women and children. For us here, we're the ones that survived from our ancestors camping out around the island. That was the main population of my people.' By the turn of the twentieth century the Kaurareg population was a few hundred people.

With the 1869 *Aboriginal Protection Act* coming into effect by 1871, the government controlled where First Nations Australians could live and work, what they could do and who they could meet and marry. It resulted in the forcible removal of people from their country, communities and families. 'Because of the establishment of the Act, our ancestors were forcibly removed at gunpoint from Muralag to Kirriri. The Act said we were not allowed to return without permission; we were kept away from Thursday Island, they didn't want us to mix with the whites,' Milton said.

In 1922 the Kaurareg population on Kirriri, which had dwindled to eighty people, was again relocated to the island of Moa, in the north of the Torres Strait, a place that was not their country.

In 1947 Kaurareg Elder Elikiam Tom, Milton's grandfather, attempted to move back to Kirriri, but he was told by the Catholic mission he could only stay if he converted to Catholicism. 'The Catholic missionary who told them that, "You can't come here because this is a Catholic community," and the old man got angry and was talking language: "Mate, your head's going to fly off here" – he was angry after experiencing that intergenerational trauma, he was still suffering from it, as we are still today,' Milton says.

'Then the Catholic missionary told him if they want to live here they had to become Catholic, and he said "bugger you", so he took his family to Horn Island, where they camped on the jetty, where he befriended some American soldiers based there, who gave him roofing iron. So he cut a few posts, did a bit of hard yakka there and built himself a house and established himself. Then others heard and they came too.'

In 1950 the Department of Native Affairs, which was responsible for enforcing the Act, tried to relocate the Kaurareg again, this time to the mainland, but they stood their ground.

'They didn't realise they breached the Act, but when they sent over the troopers with a boat, Granddad stood with all them other Elders, they pulled out all their machetes and spears and they said, "Our blood will spill here, this is our land, we'll cut off your heads, so come over." There was screaming and crying, you could see the hatred, they weren't going to move.

'When all them black troopers looked past them Elders, they saw the spirits of the fallen warriors, all painted up holding spears, so they backed off. In some ways this is one of the first successful native title fights won by standing our ground.'

The Kaurareg are still on Narupai today. It wasn't until 2001 that they successfully claimed native title of Narupai and Murulag.

However, the resistance shown by Milton's grandfather never really made it to the history books; ironically, it only appeared in records of the Anglican Church, which anthropologist Dr Nonie Sharp discovered when she spent 1978 to 2002 trying to piece together what happened to the Kaurareg.

I interviewed Sharp in 2018 when I was commissioned to write a piece about the frontier wars for CNN and my editor wanted to verify Milton's account.

'The Kaurareg were the closest geographically and socially and culturally to mainland Australian Aboriginal groups, and the white powers of the day regarded them as the "most backward", they were the forgotten people,' she told me. 'There was very little record of what actually happened … to them, other than what the missionaries then the Anglican Church had.'

Sharp spent thirty years visiting the region, collecting first-person accounts from Kaurareg Elders, including Milton's grandfather, and collating what scant records she could find, piecing together what had happened.

It troubled me that I had been asked to verify Milton's account with a white academic, who in turn got her story from first-person accounts which had been passed down orally.

The irony is not lost on Milton. 'But what is truth, what is true?' he says.

'Jardine, in the colonisation history, he was a good man, when the tourists come up and learn about what he established, but for us Indigenous people he was a murderer, he was a wicked man, and he died a very sinful death which was witnessed by everybody, a story that has been passed down from generation to generation. He died a cruel death, with maggots coming out of his body.' Frank Jardine died of leprosy in 1919.

'We heard stories of him riding on horseback, snatching babies from the mother's arms and bashing the head against a tree, but yet they name streets, rivers and hotels after him – that is an insult. People naming buildings and streets after the early settlers, I really think the early settlers, their names, their stories, their histories should be kept in a museum somewhere, not in the public places. The naming of the roads or buildings should come back to Traditional Owners, because this is our country, and the Australian people need to respect that.'

We sit on the porch of Milton's cement-board house on Thursday Island, shaded by a lush tropical garden he has nurtured since moving back to his traditional homeland in 2007. Milton is stripped to the waist above a pair of footy shorts. He sips green tea and puffs on a cigarette while two old dogs lie at his feet, wheezing in the monsoonal heat. In a lull between downpours, chickens scratch around the papaya and banana trees.

Milton chuckles through a haze of smoke as he waves a large brown envelope. It's correspondence from Cambridge University.

In 2002 Milton started collating all the historical documents about the Kaurareg people from as many archives that he could source. But he thinks many were destroyed by successive governments trying to hide the past.

In 2010 Milton was part of a group of Indigenous representatives from the region who went to the British Museum to repatriate nineteen items of ancestral remains that had been collected by Cambridge University anthropologist Alfred Haddon on his Torres Strait expeditions between 1894 and 1898.

'We had to negotiate with them to get them back, which they didn't want to do – they said they wanted to keep them for scientific reasons. And we said, "You do that with your people, not ours."'

The remains were returned to Australia but are still in Brisbane, as Milton and other Traditional Owners continue to negotiate for their return to Country.

'We are still trying to get them home, it makes me cry. People tell us we should just get over it, get over the past, but we need to understand these things, why they happened.'

Milton would be justified in being angry, but he is not; his people endure.

'We can't change the past but we can learn from the past and make sure nobody makes the same mistakes ever again. We are supposed to learn from the past and heal ourselves today so tomorrow we can all walk, not in front, not behind, but side by side with everyone, for a brighter, brand-new day, for a better future.'

But it's no wonder Milton dislikes the Coming of the Light, the ensuing colonisation and all it represents.

Although the consensus is that the arrival of the LMS had a unifying, positive impact, the loss of cultural practice and the entrenchment of colonisation need to be remembered; the Coming of the Light cast some shadow of its own.

Despite the suppression of ritual and dance, Islander culture survived. It was later in part revived, while coexisting with the now dominant Christian paradigm: today there are around a dozen different churches on TI alone. This cultural revival was spearheaded by the work of the late Ephraim Bani, a respected intellectual leader, Elder and traditional chief from Mabuiag. In the 1970s, Bani became known as a linguist and traditional language expert who had a wealth of traditional knowledge passed down from his uncles. He was passionate about restoring and preserving Torres Strait culture: his words, *Past must exist for Present to create the Future*, are engraved in the boardwalk of TI esplanade.

Considered a visionary, he initiated the biannual Torres Strait Cultural Festival in 1992 to claw back the missionaries' erosion of cultural practice. The festival has seen the resurrection pride in *Ailan Kastom* as well as several ritual dances.

A century after Haddon returned to England, Bani went to Europe on a cultural reconnaissance of his own. He went to Cambridge to view Haddon's collection, as well as others housed in museums in the UK and Europe. In a documentary about his journey he said:

(The missionaries) told us to abandon some of the practices and our culture was slowly declining ... then the anthropologists came.

We were the subject of Haddon's great scientific expedition. We had given up everything. Our eyesights were tested, our temperatures were taken, we gave our songs to be recorded on the wax cylinders, we gave our stories to be written down – what good did it do for us?

I have two opinions about him. Haddon in a way preserved our culture; in another way it was lost from the Torres Strait. Not to do anything about it is like a great silence in the history – no one will know.

Bani found the curators' reluctance to return sacred objects and ancestral remains disappointing and became disillusioned when he discovered artefacts had been sold to private collections. He thought museums should be a safe place for historical artefacts and contemporary Indigenous art to be kept, and it drove him to push for the establishment of the Gab Titui Cultural Centre on TI. *Gab,* interpreted as 'journey' in the eastern language dialect, and *Titui,* from the western dialect, meaning 'stars'; the name Gab Titui is translated as 'Journey of the Stars'. Bani passed away only months before the centre's official opening, in April 2004, but his vision of bringing his people's culture back into the light shines on as his legacy today.

Bani's son, Gabriel Bani, is both a very pious man and a traditional cultural adviser. One day he tells me, chuckling with a glint in his eye: 'Dad said the wisdom of the Elders is the firewood, and he said his job was to push the wood into the fire and fan the flames, and now he's gone that job now falls on our lap.'

'All the cultural practices at that time were seen as pagan, especially with the missionaries arriving and taking over. They got rid of the traditional meeting places, the sacred places, known as the *kwods,* and they put curfews on us at night.'

Gabriel says his culture is about connection: 'we connect everyone, it's about belonging in this world, to belong somewhere.

'The core of our culture is our family kinship structure, and there was a breakdown within those structures, so that's where the real work is now – it draws in the responsibilities of not only one father but many fathers, not one mother but many mothers. When you start talking about families and kinship structures then you start talking about land, these are the cornerstones of culture, family, land and language.'

But Gabriel says the value system has changed over the years. 'Now it's all to do with connecting to the global world, economic growth, and it's about the individual. That's all impacted on that traditional practice, as there are values that are conflicting with that.

'The biggest struggle is to try and get back to these original core values, that's what we're doing now. But the wheels are turning, and they have been turning for some time, and they are getting movement now, the fire is burning stronger. Now at the high school graduations, every student comes up, says, "My name is, my totem is, my wind is..." That's never happened before, I didn't do that at school, people are now being connected to their totemic relationships and people are starting to speak language now; we were never allowed to that before. Imagine the changes twenty years from now. This is like wow for me,' Gabriel says, grinning. 'It's about people infrastructure, not bricks and mortar, so culture is really important. Like Dad said, life without culture is life without life,' he says with a belly laugh. 'Too good.'

CHAPTER 7

DIRE STRAITS

6 September 2013

Just as the nation is about to go the polls on 7 September 2013, three ragtag yachts pull into Horn Island; one whose engine failed in its voyage up from Cairns is under tow. Calling themselves the Freedom Flotilla, they plan to voyage to Merauke, the closest West Papuan town to the PNG border, to let the world know about Indonesia's long list of ongoing human rights abuses in the region.

Foreign Minister Bob Carr describes the protesters as 'fringe activists' who are perpetrating a cruel hoax on the people of the Papuan provinces, by suggesting that Papuan independence is on the international agenda ... 'The world recognises Indonesian sovereignty over its Papuan provinces, as do both sides of Australian politics.'

The shadow foreign minister, Julie Bishop, provides a glimpse into how the incoming Abbott government will handle its foreign affairs when she said: 'If this Freedom Flotilla breaches Indonesia's territorial sovereignty, Indonesia is entitled to use whatever means it wishes to protect it.'

Meanwhile, Indonesian authorities have promised to meet the flotilla with the full brunt of their navy, and haven't ruled out using lethal force. Tension is mounting.

Apart from South Australian Aboriginal Elder and long-time environmentalist Kevin Buzzacott, who first had the idea of the flotilla, West Papuan refugees Jacob Rumbiak, Amos Wainggai and Ronny Kareni, and Melbourne rapper Izzy Brown, most of the twenty-odd crew reek of patchouli oil and pot. They sport nose rings, Thai fishermen's pants, old-skool punk rock T-shirts, Gaia tattoos and steampunk designer-dread haircuts.

One girl in her twenties tells me she flew up to be part of the flotilla, and came straight from a protest in an old-growth forest in Tasmania.

Looking out from Horn Island pier at a water police zodiac circling one of their yachts, she murmurs, 'Fuck the police, hey, brother?' looking back at me for support.

It turns out the police are just advising them where to berth safely, as the strong tides could drag them off their moorings and into the croc-infested mangroves.

I cringe when she describes the flotilla as 'peace pirates'.

I cringe because at her age, it could have been me.

I can't help but agree with Minister Carr's view that the Freedom Flotilla is fringe – possibly professional protesters – and I wonder what good will come of it all. Four community leaders in Merauke were already interrogated by Indonesian police a couple of weeks ago. They were charged with treason and face lengthy jail terms just for holding a church service to pray for the Freedom Flotilla.

In my tween years in Tasmania I channelled my anger into activism. The state was a battlefield over the proposed damming of the Franklin River in the state's south-west wilderness, which had been World Heritage listed in 1982. The iconic green triangle *NO DAMS* sticker could cop you a brick through your car window or a punch in the teeth in many back-country towns or even just the wrong pub.

All for a river that the Tasmanian Liberal premier of the day, Robin Gray, dismissed as: 'Nothing but a brown ditch, leech-ridden, unattractive to the majority of people.' A river that would later divide the nation and help Labor leader Bob Hawke sweep into power in 1983. It also galvanised the formation of the world's first political Greens Party, whose yet-to-be-elected senator Bob Brown said: 'Flooding the Franklin would be like putting a scratch across the *Mona Lisa*.'

On 3 February 1983, Liberal Prime Minister Malcolm Fraser called for a double dissolution and announced a snap federal election for 5 March. It was the same day Bob Hawke replaced Bill Hayden as Leader of the Opposition and voiced his support for saving the Franklin. The following day 20,000 people rallied in Hobart against the dam, the biggest protest there since the Vietnam War, while 15,000 people roared with approval as Bob Hawke's wife, Hazel, donned a par of *NO DAMS* earrings at a Melbourne protest.

At thirteen I was in the thick of it, inside a giant platypus made of tent poles and calico that became a mascot at the front of the Hobart march. Of the half a dozen inside the beast, I was responsible for the right rear leg. Carrying it down Davey Street en route to the site of the march at Franklin Square, a logging truck made a swerve across from the oncoming traffic, and the burly driver, ruddy with hypertension, blustered, 'Fucking greenies,' as he ran over the front leg of the platypus. We stoically continued to the rally with a limp.

In the months leading up to the rally I had insisted on joining my parents in a war-room meeting with Bob Brown and the Wilderness Society. I sat in the ring of chairs in a vacant office space in Hobart where plans were hatched to blockade the construction site of the dam. Premier Gray had already turned down $500 million to drop the project from Prime Minister Fraser and sent in the bulldozers. Anticipating protest, the premier passed a new law making it illegal to 'lurk, loiter or secrete' in riverside rainforests. Throughout the summer of 1982–83, the blockade drew more than 6000 supporters, of whom more than 1200 were arrested – including Mum and Dad. Nearly 500 were jailed after refusing bail conditions, filling to capacity the local prison. I was bitterly disappointed Mum wouldn't let me join the blockade.

Three decades later around one in eight voters are of green persuasion, and nearly all of those would support Indigenous rights and closing the gap. However, the feeling is often not mutual.

Demographically skewed to the higher income brackets in the inner suburbs of our urbane capitals, the Greens voter cliché of latte-sipping hipsters, mainly white atheists who send their kids to private schools, holds water – or perhaps more aptly, caffeine-infused soy milk. It is also the antithesis of the majority of

Indigenous Australians, who are more inclined to live regionally or remotely, tend to be God-fearing and suffer a lower standard of living – and who traditionally may have preferred a strong cup of Bushells tea.

Climate change sceptics relish pointing out the inconvenient truth that some of the first environmentalists were Hitler's Nazis: Nazi soldiers planted trees and made nature trails. As Hitler himself said: 'As in everything, nature is the best instructor.'

There is often a misinformed assumption that Indigenous Australians share the sentimentalities that environmentalists have, but the fact of the matter is they are often incongruent and have created moral dilemmas from the Kimberley in Western Australia to Cape York's wild rivers. In a National Press Club speech in 2012, former Kimberley Land Council CEO Wayne Bergmann said of the environmental movement: 'They value our culture only if we always say no to development. This attitude is an abandonment of their support for Aboriginal self-determination. This is wrong and insulting.'

Environmentalists are also seen as a threat to traditional hunting practices, in particular of dugong and turtles in the Torres Strait.

I like to think the softening of my political edges was not the clichéd middle-aged drag to greater conservatism, but rather a combination of pragmatism and a realisation that complex issues can't be reduced to slogans.

I've been thinking of printing my own bumper sticker: *I fish, I hunt and I vote Green.*

Days before the so-called 'climate change' election in 2019, which was hugely influenced by the redneck kneejerk reaction to talk of stopping the Adani coalmine, Tony McAvoy, Australia's first Indigenous silk, tells me that the gap between First Nations people and environmentalists has finally started to narrow, and that the Greens are becoming a lot more aligned with them in protecting Country. McAvoy is from the Wiri mob, whose Country includes the site of the Adani coalmine, which is right on top of the Great Artesian Basin, the country's largest system of rivers, ancient springs and aquifers.

Another issue dear to inner-city lefties' hearts (myself included) is Australia's treatment of asylum seekers. Again, it is presumptuous to assume that Indigenous Australians hold the same beliefs. After all, they have endured the arrival of boat people for over 200 years now, and all the comments I have heard about the trickle of refugees arriving in the Torres Strait have cast them as yet another unwanted incursion on their sea country.

The number of asylum seekers arriving in Australia by boat, hopscotching across the Indonesian archipelago in overcrowded unseaworthy hulks, quadrupled from 2011 to 2013. In the lead-up to the 2013 federal election, then Opposition Leader Tony Abbott locked his jaws onto the rising fervour about this issue. 'Stop the boats' became his mantra.

Flailing in the polls, Prime Minister Kevin Rudd announced on 19 July 2013 that he had come to a 'very hardline decision', namely the so-called 'PNG Solution', where refugees arriving in Australia by boat would be refused settlement in the country, and would instead be banished to a detention centre on Manus Island. Abbott initially supported the proposal but soon dropped the political hot potato, while protests against the policy were held in every major Australian city because of violations to human rights.

Indigenous leaders in the Torres Strait were also quick to criticise the idea; they had not been consulted about the impacts of the decision and feared it would allow asylum seekers to enter through the Torres Strait. Fred Gela, mayor of Torres Strait Island Regional Council from the outer island communities, said: 'We might as well start drawing up maps in a state of readiness to give to asylum seekers, showing them the way to George Street, Brisbane'. Gela feared it would allow the Torres Strait Treaty to be abused and become 'like an open-door policy' for asylum seekers.

However, Manus Island is a couple of hundred kilometres off the north-east coast of the PNG mainland. Getting from there to the Torres Strait would involve traversing the roadless PNG Central Highlands to the Western Province, which 'would be no easy thing', as a flustered Tony Burke, Minister for Immigration, told me on the phone from Canberra a week after I printed Gela's and other local leaders' concerns. 'This policy absolutely can't and won't affect the Torres Strait,' he said, after accusing the LNP and Warren Entsch of fearmongering to garner votes.

But the idea that the Torres Strait would be a back door for a new wave of asylum seekers gained traction. A week later I found myself on national television as an apparent expert in the region's asylum seeker issue, less than two months after I had started at *Torres News*. ABC's *7.30 Report* titled the story 'Dire Straits', and I was only wheeled in because they were short of content, unable to secure much in the way of on-the-ground comment.

So I became part of the hyperbole, my comments nicely snipped to add fuel to the political fire, where I talked about how 'regional leaders up here are concerned' and feared our 'porous border' could become 'a back door into the country'. My asides suggesting it was all a bit of a beat-up were left out.

Three days before the story went to air on 13 August, two well-dressed Somali men carrying a duffel bag, a backpack and US$1600 were detained on Boigu Island after paying a PNG villager to dash them across in a dinghy. They were joined in the Thursday Island police watch house by one West Papuan and one PNG national intercepted in a canoe the previous day, near Saibai Island. Mayor Fred Gela described it as 'the first wave of many more to come.'

Queensland LNP Premier Campbell Newman said it represented a 'launching pad' for a fresh wave of illegal migration into Queensland, a sentiment swiftly echoed by Warren Entsch and Shadow Immigration Minister Scott Morrison. Senator George Brandis said: 'Once you spring a leak, it's not very long before it's a torrent.'

By 14 August it had almost become a meme: Mr Abbott, while posing for photos with Premier Newman pointing at a map, described the Torres Strait as both a potential 'back door' and a 'front door' for 'people smugglers'. (It was two days after Mr Abbott's gorgeous gaffe to a room full of party faithful in Melbourne, when he said: 'No one, however smart, however well-educated, however experienced, is the *suppository* of all wisdom.')

The trickle of asylum seekers reported in the Torres Strait was ten in August 2013, the same as the year before. Hardly a flood instigated by organised crime syndicates; rather, it was the occasional desperado making an opportunistic dash.

While it was pitched under the guise of humanitarianism – the need to prevent illegal people smugglers risking the lives of refugees, after several boats and all hands had been lost at sea – the nation knew this was really appealing to something much baser.

At the coalface of this xenophobia were the swinging voters of Sydney's western suburbs. It dragged voters and the leadership of the country down to this bogan lowest common denominator. This same demographic of flag-wearing, boozed-up Caucasians rears its ugly head periodically, such as the Cronulla race riots eight years earlier, going right back to the foundational orgy on Sydney's Rocks, that historian Robert Hughes described in his 2003 book, *The Fatal Shore*, of the First Fleet's motely cruel disembarkment in Botany Bay, where 'couples rutted between the rocks, guts burning from the harsh Brazilian aguardiente, their clothes slimy with red clay.'

This issue struck right at the underbelly of white 'Straya'.

Mr Abbott used this stick well to whack the Rudd government, often misquoting how the 50,000 asylum seekers arriving by boat each year had ballooned under their soft leftie policies. It didn't matter that 50,000 was actually the number of total refugees to arrive since Rudd came to power in 2007, not each year, and that the annual count quadrupled with the outpouring of millions of Syrians escaping civil war, which represented the largest refugee crisis the world has ever seen.

None of that mattered. Abbott had successfully corralled the nation's prejudice and fear.

For a country whose First World status had been built following successive waves of immigrants since the First Fleet, we have become increasingly intolerant of the 'Other'. In the society we have created, we treat dogs far better than we treat some of our fellow human beings.

Just days before Abbott rode this wave of hysteria to power on 7 September, the Liberal candidate for the western Sydney bellwether seat of Lindsay, Fiona Scott, linked the trafficking of asylum seekers to outer-suburban traffic jams in her neighbourhood. '[Asylum seekers are] a hot topic here because our traffic is overcrowded,' she told the ABC's *Four Corners* program. 'Go sit on the M4, people see 50,000 people come in by boat – that's more than twice the population of [western Sydney suburb] Glenmore Park.'

Abbott liked the cut of her jibe, describing the future backbencher as having 'sex appeal'.

As the Stop the Boats hyperbole filled Abbott's sails and got him across the line, the Freedom Flotilla in the Torres Strait loitered at the edge of our sovereign waters. Dissuaded by the might of the Indonesian navy, the flotilla didn't dare cross the line; instead, it used subterfuge to send a contingent in a couple of dinghies to meet with Merauke political activists on an island near Australia's Boigu Island, in arm's reach of our territorial waters. There they shared a handshake and a photo op before a hasty retreat to their yachts and then withdrew to the safety of Australian territory, landing in Gove, Arnhem Land, on 14 September.

Meanwhile, on 25 September, seven of the Merauke political activists who met them arrived at Boigu in a dugout canoe appealing for asylum, but the newly elected federal government used the case to road-test its new stance on refugees. Immigration Minister Scott Morrison had just established the government's zero-tolerance posture towards illegal boat arrivals in Australia, in conjunction with mandatory detention. Operation Sovereign Borders – or Operation Sovereign Murders, in Mr Morrison's Freudian slip of the tongue – was the beginning of the Abbott government's 'see no evil, hear no evil, speak no evil' approach to asylum seekers. Morrison hired some ninety-five spin doctors at around $8 million a year to make sure his department said as little as possible about 'the boats'.

The seven Merauke asylum seekers were kept at a holding centre on Horn Island overnight before being flown to Port Moresby, where they were unceremoniously dumped by the Australian Government at the aptly named Hideaway Hotel, in a sketchy part of one of the world's sketchiest cities. Not only did Australia ditch all responsibility for these people, they also didn't pay the hotel bill – it was left to a Swiss NGO to pick up the tab.

While Immigration hoped the whole affair would not draw much attention, someone slipped one of the asylum seekers a mobile phone, and slipped me the number.

Yacob Mandabayan, twenty, fled West Papua with six members of his family, including his uncle, his brothers (one of whom was a ten-year-old boy), and his five-months pregnant sister, all of whom feared for their lives.

'We were being hunted by the Indonesian military and police intelligence had surrounded our houses, so we left to seek asylum in Australia,' Mandabayan said in a thick accent down the crackly line. 'We were told by the immigration people we needed medical tests so we could go to the Australian mainland. Then they put us on a plane at Horn Island airport. After the plane door was closed and locked, the immigration officer told us we were being flown to PNG. We were very scared and very disappointed. When we asked why they were sending us to PNG they said they were just doing their job.'

Not only did Australia breach its commitments to the UN Refugee Convention and to the Declaration on Human Rights, it also breached its 2003 memorandum of understanding with PNG, designed to prevent PNG being used as a transit country for asylum seekers hoping to make it to Australia. Under that agreement, Australia is only able to return asylum seekers to PNG if they have spent more than seven days in that country prior to their arrival, something the seven vehemently deny.

Mandabayan explained that they had been fearing for their safety in a stand-off with PNG immigration. They faced an ultimatum: to apply for political asylum in PNG or be sent back to

Indonesia – a potential death sentence. 'If we are sent back to Indonesia, we will be killed,' Mandabayan told me. If they refused to apply for refugee status in PNG, the government threatened to imprison them as illegal immigrants, despite the fact that they were dumped there by Australian authorities in the first place.

Mandabayan said PNG immigration demanded they make a formal application seeking asylum by 4 October, but they refused to sign any documents until they received legal counsel; they were then given an extension to 10 October, but were refused access to lawyers.

The last time I spoke to Mandabayan, he told me the group tried to lodge an application with Port Moresby Court on Friday 11 October due to be heard the following Monday, for a stay from being incarcerated, but 'police officers with M16 guns' took them by force to the airport the Sunday night before. The seven were then transported by the PNG government to a disused detention centre near the Indonesian border.

At around the same time, at a press conference in Jakarta, Prime Minister Abbott gloated over his government's actions: 'We are fair dinkum about doing what we can to help Indonesia in every way and you might be aware of the fact that there were some people who turned up in the Torres Strait last week wanting to grandstand about issues in Papua. Well, very swiftly ... they went back to PNG.'

It didn't seem to matter that he wrongly stated they'd been sent 'back' to PNG, when actually they came from West Papua, and as Warren Entsch said to me: 'I understand PNG doesn't treat the West Papuans very well.'

Guardian Australia managed to reach Mandabayan on his mobile one last time on 14 October at the camp near the border, when he said, 'We do not feel safe here because this place is not guarded by police or security guards.'

Nobody has ever heard from them again.

Pretty poor form from Scott Morrison, a Pentecostal happy clapper who in his 2018 maiden speech to Parliament said: 'So what values do I derive from my faith? My answer comes from Jeremiah, chapter 9:24: "I am the Lord who exercises loving kindness, justice and righteousness on earth; for I delight in these things, declares the Lord."'

However, I did get to remind then immigration minister Morrison of the asylum seekers' fate when I intercepted his boat at Thursday Island pier on 30 April 2014.

Despite a tip-off during happy hour at the Torres Hotel a week earlier that Morrison was heading to the Straits, no amount of phone calls or emails to his army of spin doctors requesting an interview garnered a response. Morrison's noreply modus operandi became such a norm we created a meme – a photo of him with bandaids photoshopped across his lips for his *no comment*. I had previously sparred with his captain of spin, the young Julian Leembruggen, about the Merauke asylum seekers after getting his personal mobile number, which I called relentlessly day and night, using different phones until I finally got through one Sunday morning. Caught off guard, he apologised that he had not got a response from the minister, saying, 'There was a problem with Telstra.'

Leembruggan was a greenhorn who had done a cadetship with community paper *Manly Daily* on Sydney's north shore before taking on the top comms job in Immigration. Since then my number had no doubt been added to a black list, so my last phone message said: 'Okay, Julian, I get it, you are avoiding me, but this is TI and I will know when you are coming, where you are staying and where you are going, so we can play it that way.'

In my most sublime moment in the job to date, while interviewing iconic marathon champion Rob de Castella on the foreshore, I notice a Customs zodiac streaking across the channel in the afternoon sun. I know Morrison has recently landed at Horn Island.

'Excuse me, Deeks, I just have to go and catch this story,' I say as I jog down to the pier.

The first person Morrison meets as he steps onto TI is me. We are toe to toe, his heels overhanging the shark and croc-infested waters as I deliver my questions about the fate of Yacob Mandabayan and his family, and the breaches of international law his department committed in exiling them.

When I ask him why he is visiting the region, he flusters a reply. 'I'm here to meet the troops, and go out to one of the islands.'

Leembruggen, who is jumping behind me like a jack rabbit, jabbers, 'You have to book an appointment to speak with the minister.'

Without turning around, and still photographing Morrison at point-blank range, I say: 'You must be Julian. Well, you are a very hard person to get hold of – you never return my calls or emails, so how can I book an appointment?'

'Okay, you can have an interview tomorrow,' the browbeaten Leembruggen replied.

The following day, more *Ailan* intel tips me off that when Morrison and his entourage flew out to Boigu Island 'to meet the troops', Traditional Owners forbade them to land, as the community was in 'sorry business' – in mourning. Of Morrison's ninety-five spin doctors, not one of them thought to ring someone on Boigu to see if a meeting was possible.

During my interview slot, as Morrison clambers around the Customs vessel, *Roebuck Bay*, I ask him how his visit to Boigu went, despite not being able to land.

He mutters almost inaudibly, shaking his head in disbelief, 'I couldn't understand that,' before gaining his composure and replying: 'It was good to fly around the island though and see how close it was to the PNG mainland.'

But Morrison's Boigu blunder is just a sideshow to the main circus, as Morrison has announced to *The Courier-Mail* overnight in an exclusive. Journalist Peter Michael wrote: 'Crime syndicates are using high-powered boats to exploit Australia's most porous border in a disturbing new trend of drugs (ice), guns and human trafficking in Torres Strait,' saying that Morrison 'plans to "plug the gap" and match the criminals with "flying squads" in a fleet of new tactical boats for high-speed pursuits up rivers and over reef systems'.

'This is Australia's blind spot,' Morrison was quoted as saying. 'It is our nation's most porous border and we have identified it as highly vulnerable. We need smaller, faster, more-agile craft to match the speed, draft and ability of the vessels used by these gangs.'

The article even went as far as comparing the region to 'Colombian cocaine cartels in Florida, Chinese triads in Hong Kong and Malacca Straits pirates using planes, helicopters and speedboats to evade the law.'

Morrison won't tell me which countries the West African gangs come from. 'I can confirm that there is an emergence of presence to our north, which presents a very concerning trend, and that's something we want to keep ahead of, not be behind of.'

Queensland Police Torres Strait Patrol Inspector David Lacey later tells me he has no knowledge of high-powered boats full of contraband crossing the Strait.

PNG Western Province Police Commander Chief Inspector Silva Sika, speaking to SBS, said that gun and drug smuggling were 'fairly rare incidents', but has no knowledge of drug syndicates involving West African gangs smuggling methamphetamines from PNG through the Torres Strait to Cape York, as Morrison claimed.

The Australian Crime Commission, which released its annual report the previous week, also makes no mention of these activities in the Torres Strait cross-border region with PNG.

A more insidious flood of illegal entries into the Torres Strait came not from the north but rather the south, stowed away on shipping containers. Cane toads, previously unheard of here, became a front-page story in 2013 when three were discovered in a backyard. Within a couple of years they spread across TI and Horn Island in their thousands.

The reporting of ice and people smugglers, gun runners and syndicated gangs was no doubt intended to add gravity to Morrison's announcement of six tactical speedboats, three of which are to be assigned to the Torres Strait. It is all part of the build-up for Morrison's announcement the following week of the formation of the Australian Border Force, which combines the departments of Immigration and Customs into a new, beefed-up, Gestapo-like department of 'border protection'.

While Mayor Fred Gela welcomes the news of the promised three tactical speedboats, he will later say of Morrison's beat-up: 'I think the minister should stop watching the TV show *The Straits,* it sounds like something from the script, it's just a real exaggeration.' He adds, 'We definitely do need shallow-water vessels that are capable of getting over the reefs and monitoring the regions that are currently unsurveyed, but as much for catching illegal fishers as anything.'

However, the fast-response boats will become a carrot on a stick, a reward always just out of reach. A year later, the day Border Force officially donned their new uniforms, I asked the Acting Queensland Regional Commander of Australian Border Force Rachel Houghton when these boats would arrive.

'I am fairly new to this position and I am not even aware that there were going to be new patrol boats,' she said.

I even asked Prime Minister Abbott himself a couple of weeks later, when he visited TI, 'Where's the boats, Tony?'

The word association pricked his ears and he stammered, 'Those patrol boats that Mr Morrison promised will be delivered, I don't have an exact timeline on it, but they certainly will get delivered.'

Another year later, in December 2016, I asked a Border Force Canberra boffin, another comms greenhorn wearing too much cologne and his first time in the field, the same question, which he too couldn't answer as it was the first he had heard of it. His email a week later said it would now be two fast-response boats, to be delivered sometime the following year. They finally arrived in March 2018, but with incompetent skippers hitting reefs they never ventured far from their moorings off TI – conveniently in front of my office window – and spent as much time out of the water for repairs as they did in it. By the start of 2019 the two boats were left in a storage shed, disgraced and forgotten at the back of a holding yard on Horn Island.

Border Force's ageing *Roebuck Bay* is stationed in the Strait, and the newer and larger Cape-class vessels are very limited in the area they can patrol. Due to the depth of their draft, they are restricted to major shipping channels. Smugglers from PNG know this and stick to skimming south in banana boats across Warrior Reef, which connects Daru to the Strait in a labyrinth of shallow reefs, sandbars and uninhabited islands, all outside the shipping channels. Much of this territory is uncharted and unsurveyed and no Australian vessels are allowed to enter due to safety concerns, including the water police and Australian Border Force. Everyone knows it's the smugglers' hotspot. It's the path they have always taken – Senior tells me the police always know when the PNG gold, the strong bushweed, has reached TI as the pubs are quiet and there are not as many fights. From all accounts it's never international syndicated gangs but rather some raskols following ancient clandestine trade routes to bring in a little contraband and the occasional opportunist asylum seekers, not that Morrison's successor, Peter Dutton, ever acknowledged it, even bragging on radio that the country had experienced over

1000 days without any asylum seekers arriving by boat on 27 August 2017, a week after six Chinese men arrived by boat at Saibai Island.

It is a claim he has made several times since taking on the ministerial role, where it seems Dutton only recognised the last boat arrival as a vessel containing 157 mostly Tamil asylum seekers from India that was intercepted by Australian authorities 27 kilometres from Christmas Island, on 7 July 2014.

The government at the time refused to confirm the existence, location or status of the boat, until the High Court placed an injunction on any attempt to return the passengers to Sri Lanka.

Yet in Dutton's 1000 boat-free days I had reported on three asylum seekers of Pakistani and Somali descent reaching Saibai in September 2014, and another on 4 August 2016. No doubt there had been other arrivals in the region that went unreported. When I pressed Border Force about it they responded: 'The Department does not report cohort numbers smaller than five,' and later admitted in a Senate estimates hearing that Operation Sovereign Borders did not include the Torres Strait.

Gela described the minister's comments as 'wishful thinking, that's the department trying to justify and evaluate their performance – no, that's not the case, we've had boats coming in.'

Stories of smugglers were nearly always tantalisingly off the record, such as the tale told to me at a bureaucrat's barbecue, where drinks had loosened lips. The crew of a trawler were awoken by a *tap-tap-tap* on the hull late one night. It was a couple of raskols in a banana boat with a lump of half-melteddown gold bullion the size of a bowling ball. They were willing to trade it for whatever the crew had. In exchange for a couple of drums of fuel and all the ship's petty cash, the skipper became the owner of a small fortune he was too scared to cash in, fearing potential legal repercussions. Legend has it the lump still sits on his desk as an overpriced paperweight.

A few drinks in one night in a dark corner of the Torres Hotel, a young knockabout Islander with a mischievous glint in his eye and the wildest of afros tells me about the smugglers' way. He would run the gauntlet in a banana boat from Daru south across Warrior Reef.

'*Bala*, we just take dinghy and two drum of fuel and follow the stars, no GPS, no compass – we just know to go to the top of that reef, then to that *ailan*, then that reef. Don't matter which way weather is turning.'

He sways, slopping half the Bundy Rum I just shouted him onto the floorboards. I'm not sure if it's just the drink or if he's puffed on the ice pipe. The subtle aggressive undertone has subsided and his repartee reveals the cheeky Islander demeanour. I can't help but like the guy, like some younger brother I never had.

'*Bala*, Daru is a wild town,' he slurs. 'One time on a run with the boys, walking down a laneway I see a fella fighting with his missus. She screams at him so he grabs his machete and hits her – cuts her good. The boys tell me, "Don't look, just keep walking or you'll be next."'

I ask him about the impact the new Border Force presence has had in the region.

He locks his elbow around my neck and pulls our noses together; I'm not sure if he will kiss me or headbutt me.

He intones his reply, dragging out the last word in the distinctive *Ailan* whine, the same one my daughter has picked up to complain about not getting her way. '*Bala*, it be the same, but now these new Border Force mob, they charge too much to let us pass, makes it too expensiv-v-v-v-e.'

CHAPTER 8

BIRDS OF A FEATHER

4 March 2019

It's a 'sky-high moment', Prime Minister Morrison says in March 2019 at the naming of Sydney's new airport after Australian aviation icon Nancy Bird Walton. 'Australia's biggest aviation project will honour one of the nation's trailblazing stars of the sky.' He's keen to exploit a good-news story two months out from a federal election. 'Australia's story is a tremendous one and it's the story of so many amazing women in our country,' he says.

'They have a real cheek ... using Nancy's name, considering the fact that our side of her family are not considered real Australians,' Cathy Bird, one of Nancy's nieces, tells me over the phone the following day.

I have struck up an unusual friendship over the last few months with Cathy and her sisters Mary-Anne and Vitoula, after Cathy had reached out to me while in hiding from Border Force, fearing deportation.

What I thought no more than a strange but cruel anomaly, resulting from the independence of PNG in 1975 that left the Bird sisters in a citizenship limbo, her story I soon discover is echoed across the country and had particularly nasty implications for many Aboriginal and Torres Strait Islanders, where even registered Traditional Owners have been held in detention centres for years on end and even deported.

Cathy is one of six children of decorated Australian World War II veteran John Bird, brother of Nancy Bird Walton, who from the age of fifteen served in both the US Army and on Australian merchant vessels during World War II in the South Pacific.

After the war Mr Bird married a Papuan woman and lived in Port Moresby. All of Mr Bird's children were born in Papua prior to PNG's independence in 1975, when it was still an Australian protectorate, which automatically granted them Australian citizenship at birth. All six siblings attended boarding school in Charters Towers, Queensland, and all have lived in Australia since.

Even though those who were born in Papua when it still was an Australian protectorate were automatically granted citizenship at birth, this became complicated after the PNG government changed the law in 1975 and subsequently. PNG lawmakers decided dual citizenship was not allowed, because 'no man, it is said, can stand in more than one canoe'.

Then the Australian Government created legislation in 1975 that removed Australian citizenship from anyone who became a PNG citizen on Independence Day, including Papuans living in Australia, who were not necessarily aware of the change. After 1975, these people were put on a Permanent Stay Visa, which after 1999 forbade travel out of Australia, but the government at the time didn't notify them of their shift from citizen to visa holder.

With Dutton starting to tighten down the screws on who can and can't be an Australian in 2014, his newly established Big Brother Department of Home Affairs started declining passport applications and revoking citizenship papers after these visa holders travelled overseas.

An aged-care nurse's assistant from Cairns, Cathy, sixty-two, is not a criminal or a terrorist, but went into hiding in November 2018 after a bridging visa expired and she was threatened with detention and deportation by the Department of Home Affairs.

Cathy has had an Australian passport since she was eighteen and was issued a certificate of Australian citizenship in 1985. She has been living in Australia since the age of six, but when Cathy asked why her passport renewal application was declined in 2017, she was told her citizenship had been revoked, for being 'incorrectly issued'. Immigration informed her she needed to apply for a Resident Return Visa (RRV) as a beginning process to get her citizenship. She refused, on the grounds that she has been an Australian citizen her whole life.

'I was absolutely gobsmacked. I have lived here for fifty-six years, this is my home I haven't lived anywhere else including PNG,' Cathy says.

Cathy says she was told by Immigration they might knock her door down, detain her and send her back to a country she has not been to since she was six years old.

'I've worked here, I've paid taxes here, I've voted here – I'm a good citizen, I've never even had a parking ticket. They said the department made a mistake and issued me a citizenship certificate wrongly. So somebody made a mistake, which I think *they* should fix – why should I have to fix it?'

Cathy was told she had to apply for an RRV but she refused, 'because I haven't returned from anywhere, I've been in Australia the whole time ... But they said I had to apply for that visa, and if I get it, apply for my citizenship, and if I don't get it then I have to go back to where I came from, but I don't come from anywhere but here – it's ridiculous. If I apply for that visa when I haven't returned from somewhere, then I am telling a big lie, so I don't want to do it.'

The day after I break Cathy's story on 31 October 2018, it goes viral and is picked up by multiple news outlets. Cathy's sister Mary-Anne, a single mum with three decades' service in the Army Reserves, who is also suffering citizenship woes, is on the front page of the *Sydney Morning Herald* the next day.

When I ask Warren Entsch about Cathy's situation he says he was aware of her case. 'Catherine Bird has been a pain in the arse,' he says. 'It's her God-given right to be gifted citizenship ... I've sent her the forms, all she has to do is fill them out. By her own admission she doesn't want to work with the department and now wonders why she finds herself in this situation ... she has just decided to say, "Up you, Jack" ... There is no reason this couldn't be resolved in a heartbeat, but there are requirements and there is no grey area in immigration.'

Dr Peter Prince, ANU law expert, has previously described Australians born in external territories such as Papua as having a 'second class status of Australian "citizens" is a reminder of the prejudiced attitudes of Australia's past, including the White Australia policy.'

Cathy's was not the first challenge to this immigration grey zone. An unsuccessful 2005 High Court case by a Mr Amos Bode Ame, Papuan-born Australian, prompted constitutional law expert Genevieve Ebbeck to say at the time: 'An Australian citizen has no constitutionally guaranteed right, deriving from his/her citizenship, to enter Australia ... If it is correct to say that an Australian citizen possesses no right to enter and remain within Australia, the fundamental worth of his or her citizenship becomes questionable.' The 2005 case has implications for Australian citizens with dual nationality and from the external territories of the Cocos (Keeling) Islands, Christmas Island and Norfolk Island.

Facing deportation for overstaying his visa, Mr Ame, born in 1967, argued that he was an Australian citizen by birth and had never lost this status. However, the High Court declared that people born in Papua were never 'full' or 'real' Australian citizens, and that their inferior form of Australian nationality disappeared when Papua and New Guinea became one independent nation in 1975.

Despite the unanimous vote against Mr Ame, one of the judges on the case, Justice Kirby, noted that nobody had asked Mr Ame if he wanted to give up his Australian citizenship. He said that at the time under Australian law he had lost this automatically on PNG independence 'without the specific knowledge or consent of the applicant, without renunciation or wrongdoing on his part, notice to him, due process or judicial or other proceedings, he was purportedly deprived of his Australian citizenship.'

Cathy ended up being granted Australian citizenship in December 2018 but is concerned that she will not be eligible for an Australian pension. 'I have been told that you are only eligible for a pension if you have been an Australian for ten years at least ... I don't know how they can get off making me an Australian from last year, it's mind-boggling ... While I now have my citizenship, they have robbed me of fifty-seven years, as they have made me a citizen as from December 2018, rather than when I arrived at six years old.'

Cathy's sister Vitoula Del Manso, who has held several Australian passports over the years, was heartbroken not to have made it to her uncle's funeral a month before Morrison announced the name of the Nancy Bird Walton Airport. Vitoula had her Australian passport confiscated at Cairns Airport while she was attempting to make a mercy dash to PNG to aid the family of her dying uncle. If the Nancy-Bird Walton Airport had been open on the day Morrison named it, Vitoula could not have used it to leave the country.

'I am now stateless in my own country, a country I have lived and paid taxes in my whole life ... Now that I have to apply for citizenship, will that impact that?' Vitoula tells me after her passport was confiscated. 'The Australian Government helped the Papua New Guinea government draft its Constitution. Both countries were fully aware of the impact a loss of Australian citizenship would have on Papuans born of Australian parents and brought up as Australians. Nothing was said or done ... The Australian government had ample time from 16 September 1975 to notify Australian citizens born in Papua of the change to their citizenship status ... so what's the excuse?' she says.

The story of the Bird sisters harks back to a remnant of racist White Australia Policy immigration law that was the crest of a tidal wave. After breaking a series of stories on the Bird sisters' struggle, I receive letters from people in similar situations from all over the country, including people who have become stranded and stateless overseas while trying to renew their passports, and even a woman who works for the Department of Foreign Affairs who was about to lose her job due to her loss of citizenship.

I have a dedicated file on my desktop called the 'Papuan Problem'.

The Permanent Stay Visa has also resulted in Australians being detained in detention centres and even deported. Amendments to the 501 Section of the *Citizenship Act* by Immigration Minister Peter Dutton in 2014 allow a person to have their visa revoked and for them to be deported on grounds of character if they have a total of twelve months' imprisonment on their criminal record. It was initially pitched as getting rid of all the 'bad apples', but it was snaring people with multiple traffic offences, minor drug charges and even public nuisance charges. It resulted in a huge spike of visa cancellations.

It also created a disturbing conundrum where recognised First Nations people were being detained and, in some cases, deported. Considering the gross over representation of First Nations people in the judicial system, the 501 amendments revealed a miscarriage of justice whose tendrils are far-reaching.

Torres Strait Islander Danny Gibuma, who is a registered native title holder of Boigu Island, called me after I broke Cathy Bird's story. Danny, a father of ten and grandfather to a lot more, has a chequered past. After completing a six-month jail sentence for an assault conviction in 2018, he was met by Border Force officials upon his release from Lotus Glen near Cairns and taken across the country to Western Australia's Yongah Hill Immigration Detention Centre, where I speak to him months later on the phone.

'I thought I'd done my time and that I was going home to my family in Edmonton in South Cairns, but they took me and brought me to Western Australia.' For the first five months of his detention, his wife and ten children did not know where he was. 'They didn't tell my wife what happened to me. I let her know,' he says. 'We've got no touch screens and no telephones, but I asked a guy here in detention to help me with a telephone and I called my wife. Luckily, I remembered her number. Then my daughter sent me a phone.'

Danny was born in Papua but was adopted by his uncle at age seven to live on Boigu. 'I lived there and never went back to PNG, (and I) met my wife and my children and lived in Australia until this day,' he tells me.

Danny thinks he is in the detention centre because authorities decided to make him finish his sentence rather than get out early on a good behaviour bond.

'*Bala*, you are in a detention centre, not jail – they are trying to deport you,' I tell him.

'I don't have a lawyer and I don't know what is happening,' Danny says. 'I feel like I am in double jeopardy here. If they deport me, where will I go? What will I do? I have only ever lived on Boigu.'

Danny's brother, Jerry Dau, was detained for two years on Christmas Island before being deported to PNG following eleven months in jail for sexual assault and other offences.

'I tried to fight it in court, but I didn't even have a lawyer,' Jerry tells me over a crackly line from Daru.

The more I picked at the scab of our ugly truth, the more cases came to me, such as that of another Torres Strait Islander, Daniel Charlie, who was deported to PNG in 2017 for a long criminal history. He became homeless and stateless while he successfully challenged the PNG government in the National Court, which agreed he should be a resident or citizen of Australia and was in fact stateless in PNG. Daniel made it back to Saibai by dinghy from Daru in May 2019, handed himself over to Border Force and demanded he be taken to a detention centre. There he was given one phone call, which he used to contact me. Daniel told me: 'I believe how this issue has been proceeding, everything is coming into the light – I think I now have a chance that my case may be heard. I was born an Australian citizen but I have been stuck in detention centres for years.' He had spent six years in Australian detention centres, including a year on Christmas Island.

Danny Gibuma was in Yongah with several other Torres Strait Islanders in the same situation.

Stephen Lawrence, a New South Wales barrister who regularly works on immigration cases, told me the situation is the direct result of Dutton's 'draconian' amendments. 'It is fair to say that this is an extraordinary use of immigration powers against immigrant communities that has never been seen before in Australia,' he said. 'The revocation of residency rights is becoming increasingly common and is having a massive effect in Islander and other immigrant communities in Australia. Tragically there are also reports that Indigenous families are being affected because of cross-border migration in the seventies that has left people caught up in the changes to citizenship law that followed PNG independence in 1975.'

When I queried the Department of Home Affairs about how a formally recognised Traditional Owner of Australian territory, listed on the Native Title Register, cannot be considered an Australian citizen and could be deported, I was told: 'A person's citizenship status is determined with reference to the *Australian Citizenship Act 2007* (the Act). A person's status under other legislation, such as that concerning native title, does not have the effect of making that person an Australian citizen.'

That didn't go down real well with the Indigenous community.

My exposure of Danny Gibuma's case leads to the PNG government saying they won't allow him to be deported to their country. It is not clear if the deportation of Jerry Dau and Daniel Charlie to PNG was with our sovereign neighbour's knowledge or consent.

PNG's Chief Immigration Officer, Solomon Kantha, tells me that: 'The Australian Department of Home Affairs has not contacted PNG Immigration and Citizenship Authority regarding these cases to verify the citizenship status of these individuals that were to be deported to PNG ... PNG's position remains that any person that will be deported from Australia to PNG including Australian PNG-born residents or Australians with PNG-heritage will not be allowed entry into PNG until PNG Immigration and Citizenship Authority verifies their citizenship status. Those that were already recognised as Australian citizens and were issued Australian passports and voted in Australian elections are no longer PNG citizens. They cannot be returned to PNG and they must apply for PNG citizenship if they meet the PNG citizenship requirements.'

When I confront Dutton's department with this inconvenient truth I'm told: 'Australia works with domestic agencies and international partners to remove non-citizens who have no lawful basis to remain in Australia.'

Expert in citizenship law Professor Kim Rubenstein tells me that the Australian Government's claim that they have been in communication with the PNG government about these deportations is echoed in the case of alleged Fijian national Neil Prakash in January 2019, where Fijian authorities were also not informed.

Rubenstein, believes the Australian Government may be in breach of its commitments under the *International Convention on Civil and Political Rights Article 12(4)*, which states that no one shall be arbitrarily deprived of the right to enter his or her own country

'If these people are not being recognised as Australian citizens and are being sent to a country that does not recognise them as citizens of that country, then Australia is in breach of the Convention on the Reduction of Statelessness,' Rubenstein tells me over the phone. 'Anything that has a chance of increasing people's statelessness is also totally inconsistent with other aspects of the *Citizenship Act*, which builds into it a protection against statelessness.'

Rubenstein claims that if 'a person's real and effective nationality is Australian by virtue of their life experience and Australia is the only place they have any real connection to, then the government should be looking at ways to use the Act to include them rather than exclude them.'

The thuggery of Dutton's Border Force bogan Gestapo is starting to feel like we're just a hop, skip and a goose step away from totalitarianism. Within weeks of Morrison's 2019 election victory, the affront to democracy ratchets up a notch when the Australian Federal Police rifle through News Corp journalist Annika Smethurst's undies drawer for seven hours and then raid the ABC, only cutting their hit list short due to all the bad press they received.

However Dutton's plans to deport Danny Gibuma, Daniel Charlie and others in their predicament faced a major hurdle the following year in February 2020 when the High Court ruled First Nations people cannot be considered 'aliens' under the constitution.

The case ruling prevented the deportation of PNG-born Daniel Love and New Zealand-born Brendan Thoms, who both had one Australian parent and identify as Indigenous. It set a precedent and a few weeks later many of these First Nations people were quietly released from detention, including Daniel Charlie and Danny Gibuma, but without any clarity over their citizenship status.

I meet Danny at his family home in Edmonton, south of Cairns after his return from Yongah Hill Detention Centre in WA.

'When I was locked up, Mum passed away in 2018. Then my brother passed away, then his son died soon after, and they wouldn't let me out for the funerals,' Danny tells me in a soft voice.

'Every day inside I would be thinking today they may come and take me and deport me.

'I saw how there were grabbing people from the centre, the Serco security that works for immigration.

'I would think tonight they will come into my room at 2am, 3am grab me and say "off you go," that's what they were doing.'

When Danny was finally released in April 2020, he received a single-page document from the Department of Home Affairs titled 'Statement of Identity' which had his full name, date of birth, his incarnation details and his citizenship listed as 'PNG National'.

'When I asked my Border Force case manager what my status was, or if I have a visa, and which visa I have, they just said I was the same as before and to stay out of trouble.'

Danny tells me he is scared if he returns to the Torres Strait and to work on his traditional fishing areas near the PNG border, that Border Force will refuse him access back to Australia, like his brother Jerry Dau, who is still in Daru.

'Border Force want to know everywhere I move and everything I do, if I change my phone number or address, they want me to tell them if I want to go back to Boigu. I have to tell them.

'I have to be very careful now; it feels like a trap. I feel like I have lost everything.

'It is like something being in house arrest.'

Incongruous or blatantly ambivalent to the treatment of those who have effectively become second-class citizens, our happy-clappy slogan bogan PM Morrison said that sunny Sydney day in March 2019, 'Nancy Bird Walton was an inspiring and natural choice ... Nancy Bird Walton is an Australian legend, a pioneer whose determination to take to the sky is an inspiration for generations who have followed.'

While Morrison's airport opener was lapped up by most of the country's media coverage as commemorating an iconic Australian, it was also an ironic reflection on the government's definition of who can be and who no longer is Australian.

The Bird sisters had all become incensed by the government's treatment of not only their situation but all those stateless in detention and deported. They championed the cause by organising protests outside Warren Entsch's office and creating online forums to raise awareness leading up to the 2019 election.

Cathy tells me the day after Morrison named the airport after her aunty, 'It would never've got this far if Nancy was still around – she would have spoken to whoever and said you have to do something about this ... She would have thought this is disgraceful and how dare they treat us like this.'

CHAPTER 9

SHIP OF FOOLS

26 January 1788

'Fuck off, we're full.' Is that what the Gadigal clan thought sitting on the high ground around Port Jackson Bay as streams of dirty boat people spilled out of the First Fleet and onto the beaches?

'You come to our country, you don't learn our language or make an effort to assimilate into our culture.' Is that what Arabanoo thought as he was cast in chains on New Year's Eve of that same year, the first Aboriginal forcibly abducted by the European settlers of the First Fleet at Port Jackson? Governor Arthur Phillip said Arabanoo's abduction 'was absolutely necessary' so they could 'attain their language ... and to reconcile them by showing the many advantages they would enjoy by mixing with us.' Arabanoo and an estimated 2000 of his tribe were dead the following year after a smallpox outbreak swept through the colony.

The arrival of boat people on the continent's shores was something Aboriginal people had been experiencing for at least a couple of centuries before the First Fleet came to Port Jackson.

Boats may have been arriving since as early as the 1500s, when the hundreds of Indonesian fishermen sailed each year from Makassar, on the island of Sulawesi, to the Arnhem Land coast of the Northern Territory. They came to trade with the Yolngu people for sea cucumber, and not to conquer. As well as commodities, knowledge was exchanged, and there were even intermarriages. Residues of Makassar language still survive in Arnhem Land, where the Yolngu word for money is *rupiah*.

The race to carve up the so-called New World started with the Portuguese and the Spanish. Then the envious English, French and Dutch all soon joined in. It's possible the Portuguese reached Australia first after they established an outpost in East Timor, 650 kilometres north, by 1515. Portuguese explorer Cristóvão de Mendonça's map *Jave La Grande* vaguely resembles part of Australia.

A century later Dutch explorer Willem Janszoon made landfall on the western coast of Cape York in 1606. Janszoon thought it was part of New Guinea, and after losing ten men in skirmishes with resident Aboriginal clans, and mapping 320 kilometres of mangrove swamp coastline, named it *Nieu Zeland* and left.

In May of the same year the three Spanish ships under the command of Pedro Fernandes de Queirós reached an island off Vanuatu, which they named *La Austrialia del Espíritu Santo*. Legends of *Terra Australis Incognita*, the great unknown southern land, had been proposed by the Romans and Aristotle before them, but had never been proven. This was what Queirós had been commissioned to find. After losing track of two of his vessels in a storm, Queiros, fearing a mutiny, retreated to Mexico. On one of the other two ships, his second-in-command, Luís Vaz de Torres, gave Queiros up as lost at sea and continued to sail west with the hope of reaching the Spice Islands on the outer edge of the known world. However the south-east trade winds and the treacherous tides of the Torres Strait pushed Torres's boats south, away from the mapped route along the northern coast of PNG. The trade winds, along with his compasses, deviated by the proximity of cutlass, cannons and muskets, led him into unknown seas and through the Torres Straits. Despite Torres's journey, most maps after 1680 still had PNG joined to *Terra Australis Incognita,* and some as late as 1750 also connected the coast and rivers of Vanuatu's Espírito Santo.

Torres is easily romanticised as an adventurous underdog, an accidental hero surviving against the odds, but it's important to remember he was as much a bastard as the rest of those early European explorers, where his crew shot Islander men for sport and took kidnapped girls for 'service of the crew and ship'. One of them, who was heavily pregnant, gave birth a few weeks later in one of the empty cannon bays. Most of the Islander and Papuan people he kidnapped en route died, but some ended up in a troupe of dwarfs and freaks for the court of the Spanish king.

The treachery of the Torres Strait, ribboned with uncharted reefs, shallow waters and strong tides and currents, all buffeted by powerful winds and swell, took its toll on venturing European colonisers. There are some 120 known wrecks in the region, and many others yet to be located. It may well be the final resting place of the ill-fated French explorer Jean-François de Galaup, comte de la Pérouse, commissioned by French king Louis XVI to try and outdo Cook's feats for the failing French empire. Louis XVI, on his way to the guillotine in 1793, supposedly asked his executioners: 'Is there news of La Pérouse?'

After arriving at Botany Bay just days after the First Fleet, La Pérouse witnessed the British begin the new colony before sulking off over the horizon and disappearing into history. That is until 2017, when Australian anthropologist Garrick

Hitchcock dredged up an Indian newspaper article from 1818 that revealed his likely demise. The article was about Indian shipwreck survivor Shaik Jumaul, who was picked up from Mer Island in the Torres Strait. He reported that he had seen swords and muskets, 'differently made from English', as well as a compass and a gold watch, spoils of another shipwreck thirty years earlier. Hitchcock suggests they had belonged to La Pérouse and his crew, who were most likely killed by the rightly suspicious Meriam Mer people. Thus La Pérouse began a heritage of 'boat people' passing through this territory, escaping ill fortune. There were rumours of caves on Mer hidden with treasures, the spoils of European shipwrecks.

I asked a young fisherman on Mer about the legends.

'*Wa bala*, those caves are real, but we never go inside them,' he says, flashing a toothy grin.

The treachery of the Torres Strait and its reputation of fearsome headhunting warriors must have also vexed Captain William Bligh, when a year later in June 1789 he floated through the Torres Strait, on his epic journey from Tahiti to Indonesia after the mutiny on the *Bounty*.

When Bligh returned to the region in 1792, recommissioned by the Royal Navy, he encountered Islander resistance on one of the

Central Islands, when they attacked Bligh's vessel. Bligh later named it Warrior Island (today Warraber Island). Matthew Flinders, who was Bligh's midshipman, described the Islanders as 'dextrous sailors and formidable warriors ... They could swim like dolphins, fight with the power of sharks and glide through the shallows with the ease of alligators...' and after the attack said from then on in the Torres Strait 'the marines were therefore kept under arms, the guns clear and the matches lighted'.

The dangers of the Torres Strait even made it into the pages of Jules Verne's classic *Twenty Thousand Leagues Under the Sea*, in which even the bold Captain Nemo hesitates to take the *Nautilus* through 'the world's most dangerous strait', which are 'obstructed by an incalculable number of islands, islets, breakers, and rocks that make it nearly impossible to navigate'.

This domineering imperial spirit still endures. While there are no more New World nations to claim, conquer and plunder, this aspiration continues in our efforts to one-up Mother Nature. Whether it is Hillary's first footstep at the top of Everest, Armstrong's on the moon, or Cameron's at the bottom of the Mariana Trench, there is still a desire to conquer the elements, and it's always some white guy.

On a smaller, more suburban scale, I saw them come and go during my stint as editor of the *Torres News*.

It's nearly always overprivileged white guys with more dollars than sense. They were either taut, lycra-skinned, middle-aged gen Xers trying to escape the confines of executive stress by kayaking or kitesurfing their way across the Strait and to get back their lost youth, or ageing baby boomers in yachts paid for with their golden handshakes as they sail off into the setting sun of their time on this mortal coil. Sometimes they make it, but sometimes they don't.

The south-east trade winds which Torres and later Cook used to pass through the Straits, which blow from the end of the Wet season in February to around November, often howl from 20 to 30 knots. These are what now bring these grey nomads of the sea.

They are the same winds that near finished off Barry Blackwood, sixty-two, a grizzled retired refrigeration mechanic and Vietnam vet. The engine of his 34-foot Nantucket sloop, *Shivoo*, failed as he was crossing the Endeavour Strait from the tip of Cape York to Thursday Island. The winds took him past Thursday Island and washed him onto a band of reef from which he had to be airlifted off.

He had already sailed through the Strait before this, clocking up some 25,000 nautical miles sailing around PNG and to India and back. He never radioed for help or triggered his distress beacon; he hoped to grit it out on the reef until the tide rose and washed him free, but a passing aircraft raised the alert. Prior to his grounding *Shivoo*, he'd lost a yacht in Cyclone Yasi in 2006. *Shivoo* was not just Barry's yacht but his home.

With his boat later salvaged by local water police and safely moored back at Horn Island for a month of repairs, Barry settled in at the Torres Hotel for a long stretch of drinking. An alcoholic with self-confessed PTSD, Barry took a liking to me, always calling me up for a liquid lunch as he delighted in yarns of my seedy past, and shared parts of his own, keen to connect us as birds of a feather.

Failed marriages and kids who didn't talk to him – I could tell Barry was on the run, most likely from himself. Barry had a white beard stained yellow by chain-smoking White Ox rollies, but his eyes were sad and his chuckling smoker's cackle didn't fool me for a minute.

'People like you and me, mate, we see the world differently, we see it how it is. Most people never have a clue their whole lives.' His gaze drifts off seawards as he slurps down the dregs of our third round.

Barry had signed up for the Australian navy at fifteen and by seventeen was serving in the Vietnam War, and as a result he now seemed most comfortable in calamity. While repairing his boat Barry flew down for a sojourn in Cairns, where he ended up in a bar fight. He rendered a man unconscious in a headlock, and when he dropped him to the floor, chipped his teeth and broke his jaw.

'He stole this woman's cigarettes, cunt had it coming, you don't steal, it's not bloody on.'

With a string of convictions, including a serious assault on police, Barry was nonchalant the next time we had a beer.

'I pleaded guilty to the charge, it's bullshit, I was just doing the right thing, I'm meant to go back for sentencing but the winds will change and I will be stuck here and I want to keep sailing to Indo, so stuff 'em.'

Barry had recruited a young offsider to help with the next leg of the voyage, but he had already changed his mind, telling me after Barry left that the drunken rages in the cabin put him off.

Barry sailed east to Mer Island on the edge of the continental shelf to catch up with a friend who was a pastor. After while there, he decided to go out fishing but was hit by a cyclone and was pushed out into the middle of the Coral Sea with no land in sight, no sail or engine. The currents carried an injured Barry towards PNG, where he signalled for help to a plane using a mirror, and was rescued off the coast near Port Moresby.

The day he was released from hospital he told PNG media he was looking forward to having 'a taste of PNG beer'.

I'd get the occasional phone call from Barry, promising to return to continue our beery confessionals, but he never came. He sank the *Shivoo* somewhere in Indonesia, he told me, but was planning to buy a new boat and start again.

Years later, in 2017, he finally faced court for the assault in Cairns. The judge acknowledged the impact of his time in Vietnam. 'You saw and did things which, like for so many others, has resulted in post-traumatic stress disorder,' Judge Morzone said. 'And like so many others in your situation have turned to drinking to cope with the demons that endure from that experience. I accept you are remorseful and regretful for your actions.'

Barry was sentenced to eighteen months with immediate parole.

The same trade winds washes five middle-aged Ukrainians onto the beach next to my office three years after Barry's first arrival. They have a six-metre inflatable rubber catamaran, which has no keel, no outboard engine, and no flares or distress beacon on board. They sit on a platform lashed between the two rubber hulls and plan to sail all the way to Merauke, the easternmost town in West Papua, some 200 nautical miles north-west.

A smiling, tall, bald and lanky man, Sergio Koralenkocap is the leader of the entourage. Sunburnt and somewhat crestfallen, he tells me because they had to stamp their exit of Australian territory on their passports on Thursday Island, Border Force banned them from making landfall on any islands en route to the PNG mainland. They had hoped to island-hop north to Saibai, one the most northerly of the Torres Strait islands in Australian territory and only four kilometres from the PNG mainland, then follow the coast of PNG west to Merauke, where they planned to deflate the boat and fly to Jakarta, then onwards home.

'This makes it very difficult for us, and this wind is pretty strong – if it was 15 knots we would be happier,' Sergio says in a thick accent. It's been howling 25 knots for a week.

When planning the voyage back in the Ukraine, Sergio just looked at a map over a bottle of Khortytsa vodka. 'It looked easy – we could just go from island to island, but when does this wind stop?'

'In a couple of months, then it's the doldrums, mate, and you won't be going anywhere,' I tell him.

I can't believe they're going to Merauke.

The easternmost city in Indonesia, not far from West Papua's border with PNG, Merauke is not a place people go to visit. It is rumoured to be rife with human rights violations and corruption, as the 'Merauke Five' case starkly illustrated, a term Senior coined for five unfortunate, middle-aged residents of Thursday Island. In 2009 they flew a light aircraft to Merauke for a weekend sojourn that became a nine-month ordeal. They were jailed for trumped-up visa violations, despite the air traffic controller assuring them they would be fine. It seemed to be a vendetta against the Australian Government for the treatment of Indonesian fishermen. With very little help from Australia their lawyers managed to get the charges overturned in the Indonesian judicial system and they were eventually released.

Sergio shrugs at this. 'We have been told it is okay, so it is okay.'

I couldn't figure out Sergio or his crew: they looked destitute, camping on the beach in cheap tents, living on sand-coated crackers and cream cheese. One of the crew is indolently adding a little more air to the catamaran's rubber hull with a foot pump you'd use on an air bed. He looked like a hobo but he was wearing a diamond-encrusted gold ring. The only woman of the crew was dripping with gold necklaces, sweating behind Dolce & Gabbana sunnies in an Armani top.

Sergio explains they are part of some well-heeled Ukrainian adventurers' club called the Shatun, which has been conducting similar adventures around the world since 2008, including sailing the coastlines of Finland, Thailand, the Philippines, Indonesia and northern PNG. They do this for a month before stepping back into their high-rolling Ukrainian lives.

'I think maybe we just sail anyway to Merauke,' Sergio says.

By the time I stop by the Thursday Island water police for my weekly chat, where they give me a round-up of search-and-rescues in the region, and to pilfer their jar of instant coffee, they've heard I met the Ukrainians on the beach.

Sergeant John Latham shakes his head in disbelief as I describe their plan. He says, 'I love the adventurous spirit, but this trip may just be a bit too adventurous.'

John is concerned the rough and windy conditions and the fact they have no outboard motor could end in disaster.

'Conditions in that open ocean can get pretty rough with big swell as well as the strong winds right now,' John says, sipping his coffee.

'What if they hit a reef or a tiger shark decides to have a bit of a nibble of their rubber hull?'

'So what are you going to do?' I ask.

'I'm not sure how to handle this, the Ukrainian embassy has contacted us to ask that we let them go, but if we do they could die, but if we don't it could be an international incident.'

'Why not try the good-cop approach, give them information about what they're facing, to scare them off,' I suggest.

So the police take Sergio and his crew out to Hammond Rock in a water police speedboat in a squall. Hammond Rock is where the Kaurareg god Waubin sat down in the ocean northeast of Kirriri after losing his leg in battle, and turned to stone. The blood from Waubin's wound still churns the waters with treacherous currents and the exposed location makes it the perfect spot to give them a taste of what the Torres Strait may dish up for them.

Sergio tells me afterwards, 'I think they really tried to scare us out there, turning the boat all over to make it very bumpy. I was okay, it didn't bother me, but one of the police guys looked a little pale.'

The police warned Sergio if they needed to be rescued it could cost them $20,000.

'The police wanted to bet me $1000 we would meet again. I wanted to take the bet but the others say it is too risky.'

So the crew deflate their boat, put it back in its suitcase and fly to Cairns with plans to fly to Indonesia, where they will try a fair weather sailing adventure.

Later one of the water coppers tells me, 'I think what might have broken them was when I said I reckoned it would be a 20-litre vodka run to make it to Merauke. They looked shocked, don't think they had that much on board.'

But the most endearing of these ageing Caucasian mad sea dogs I met was when I was only a month into the job.

Daniel Alary, a seventy-year-old retired philosophy teacher from the French Polynesian Tuamotu Island group, was exactly 100 days into a round-the-world voyage when he got into trouble in the Torres Strait, about 98 nautical miles north-east of Horn Island.

In the most quixotic of odysseys, Daniel had sailed from his home on the tiny Aratika atoll, where he had a shack which he called his sandcastle, in a homemade fibre-glass 8-foot yacht called *Poisson d'Avril,* a French expression for 'April fool'.

'The name was meant as a joke,' Daniel told me at Bernie's Kai Kai Bar, a café on Thursday Island's waterfront, as he munched on one of their signature crayfish pies.

As he brushed pastry crumbs out of his grey beard, his eyes sparkled like those of a deranged Santa Claus. He didn't speak a word of English, and I not a word of French, but we found a common ground in my Spanglish with smatterings of Portuguese picked up from my years living in South America.

Daniel was attempting to break a world record for sailing the smallest yacht solo around the world, and planned to sail through the Torres Strait onwards to Africa to visit his adult children.

His tiny vessel had no room to move, he had to hand-pump sea water through a desalinating filter for an hour every day to produce enough drinking water, and there were no cooking facilities, so all he ate was dried packet food.

'I was exactly a hundred days at sea when I got into trouble. I have a heart arrhythmia that I monitor with a blood sample machine which tells me when to next take my medicine. But the batteries failed and for two days I could only guess my result,' Daniel said.

On top of this, 40-knot gale-force winds and 3-metre swells buffeted *Poisson d'Avril* so it bobbed like a wine cork. For two days Daniel didn't sleep, hoping to ride out the storm.

Fearing he was suffering a heart attack, he triggered his distress beacon. It was picked up by French authorities in the Pacific, who alerted the Australian Maritime Safety Authority (AMSA) in Canberra, which resulted in a daring rescue in which Daniel was airlifted by helicopter from his boat, which was left adrift at sea.

Daniel, like many adventurers who've suffered mishaps in the region, said he wasn't prepared for how rough conditions were in the Torres Strait, even with more than twenty years' sailing experience and having circumnavigated the globe 'three or four times, give or take, but in much bigger boats.'

Brushing his hands together, Daniel looked out to sea and smiled sheepishly. 'This crazy adventure is over for me – I am just so grateful to be alive.'

However, the adventure was far from over for *Poisson d'Avril*.

With conditions so rough, the little boat was thought lost at sea. But a couple of years later, when I'm belting up and down the coast of the Western Province with Ray on his DFAT junket, I stumble across a battered little hulk on the dark sands of the Treaty Village of Old Mawatta. There in plain sight is *Poisson d'Avril*, sitting on the beach.

Village Elder Jeffery Aber tells me the boat washed up on the beach the previous year.

'The children use it to play on now. We weren't sure where it came from,' he says.

Jeffery, a man whose whole life has been focused on survival – farming, hunting and fishing for his family and his village – looks at me blankly as I explain how Daniel planned to break the record of sailing the smallest yacht around the world.

Why would he want to comprehend Daniel's esoteric philosophical conundrum on the futility of existence and the desire in his remaining years to leave a mark on the world by conquering the elements?

Jeffery smiles. 'The old Frenchman is welcome to visit our village anytime and get his boat. We have borrowed some parts from inside it, but the boat is still in good shape.'

CHAPTER 10

GOING NATIVE

Some time at sea in 1849

KILL! – OR BE KILLED

Two men – such men. Repulsive in repose. Implacable. Blood-shot eyes simmering to blaze into animal fury – now veiled by a cold wariness pretending utter lack of interest in the other. Grim, deep-lined faces shadowing brutal mouths, beards matted with salt spray. Protruding bones made wretched the near-naked bodies seared with wounds from the cat-o-nine-tails, wounds festering under sunburn, wounds hellfire torture from salt spray.

One man would – must kill the other.

This extract is from the 1950 publication *The Wild White Man of Badu*, by the prolific Ion L Idriess, OBE.

Ion Llewellyn Idriess (20 September 1889–6 June 1979), or Jack, as he was known, was a prolific and influential Australian author. Releasing his first book at thirty-eight, he went on to publish fifty-three books in his lifetime. A soldier at Gallipoli, a prospector and a drover: he represented the quintessential Aussie bloke. He was largely shunned by Australia's literati; his hard-boiled style apparently left much to be desired.

Patrick White he was not. Despite the hints of Empire and language that is coarse by today's standards, referring to Indigenous people as 'blacks' and 'savages', it's obvious Idriess had an affection for the Strait. He spent time sailing around the islands and even lived in the Somerset homestead of the infamous Frank Jardine on the tip of Cape York, where he pored over Frank's journals. *Wild White Man of Badu* was cobbled together from tales whispered in the pubs of TI by old-time pioneer pearlers and notes from Jardine's journals.

It is the story of two convicts, Weasel and Wani, who in 1849 escape from Norfolk Island in an open dinghy with a sail. At the mercy of the winds, they cover some 1700 nautical miles to the Torres Strait. Wani kills and eats Weasel and sails into mythology.

Wani washes up on Badu Island during a thunderstorm and rather unbelievably slays the island chief and proclaims himself king, naming himself Wongai, which he mistakenly understands to mean 'warrior'. It's actually the name of a revered Indigenous bitter-tasting plum. Legend has it those who eat the wongai will always return to the Torres Strait. Wani inadvertently named himself after a piece of fruit. Idriess obviously had a sense of humour.

The people of Badu, the Badulgal, had a reputation for being fierce warriors and highly competent headhunters, the decapitated heads of warrior foes being the currency of the day.

Idriess's tale of Badu and its eternal feud with the neighbouring island of Moa, each making headhunting raiding parties on the other, sparked a boy's-own-adventure intrigue within me that belonged to my father's generation more than my own. Today, while severed heads are no longer legal tender, the people of Badu still flex their ferocity on the rugby field and in their traditional dance.

The basis of Wani's ability to dominate an entire population of fierce warriors is not just some fanciful creation of Idriess's, but also based on a belief of the Islanders in the *lamars*, the ghosts of the dead. White castaways were sometimes mistaken for *lamars* and supposedly accepted into Islander societies. On several occasions castaways or shipwreck survivors have been adopted into tribal life, thought to be the *lamars* of lost loved ones.

Wani's place in history is somewhat shrouded in mystery. He was probably called Weeni. His presence was noted by British naturalist John MacGillivray in October 1849, who was aboard the HMS *Rattlesnake* when they discovered seventeen-year-old Barbara Thompson, the sole survivor of a shipwreck near Horn Island in 1844, who had been living with the Kaurareg people. She had been adopted as a *lamar*, as the daughter returned from the dead of a chief named Pequi.

'Pequi was my chief friend, or father, as he called himself,' Thompson said. 'Others called themselves my fathers and mothers, but Pequi and his wives were considered my real relatives.'

Thompson told of how Wani was thought to have arrived on Badu in 1840, and when they met he had suggested she become his wife, which she apparently refused.

Once Thompson boarded the HMS *Rattlesnake*, she never returned to the Kaurareg people despite their heartfelt pleas that she was their family. She refused and sailed to Sydney, where she disappeared into history.

Thompson's account provides an insight into the Indigenous Australians' way of life and connection to Country a century and a half before Mabo's case in the High Court. She told of how land ownership worked, gender and family relations, hunting techniques, and ceremonial cannibalism and the ghosts of the deceased, the *lamar*. Historians John Maynard and Victoria Haskins in their book *Living with the Locals: Early Europeans' Experience of Indigenous Life*, suggest

Thompson thought the Kaurareg perceived white people as having a lack of compassion, and 'that made them something other than fully human in the eyes of the Kaurareg.'

Thompson said that after the death of an Elder she was told, 'Your people are like ghosts. They don't cry, they have no feeling. We are people, *garkigi*, we cry.'

Within two decades of Thompson's departure, the Kaurareg way of life had been destroyed.

In 1836, a decade before Thompson returned to Sydney, John Ireland, a cabin boy, seventeen, and William D'Oyley, five, the son of British Raj officer and gentry, were discovered on Mer, twenty-two months after their ship, the *Charles Eaton*, en route to India from Australia, struck the northern reaches of the Great Barrier Reef in wild seas and was torn apart.

One of the two lifeboats was lost at sea and the other was taken by some of the crew, marooning the passengers and the captain on the wreck. They made a raft, on which half the party, including the D'Oyley family, snuck off, leaving the rest, including John Ireland, to make a second raft and set adrift until they were discovered at sea four days later by an outrigger canoe of Islanders. Thinking they were being rescued, Ireland's party were taken to an uninhabited island where all but him and the other cabin boy, John Sexton, were bludgeoned to death with clubs and decapitated with bamboo knives. Sexton and Ireland were then taken to another island with a village, where they discovered the grizzly fate of the rest of the *Charles Eaton*'s passengers.

'Near the huts a pole was stuck in the ground, around which were hung the heads of our unfortunate companions. Among them I plainly recognised Mrs Doyley's, for they had left part of the hair on it,' Ireland later wrote.

The D'Oyleys' young boys, William and George, had been spared, having witnessed the murder of their parents. After some passing ships made the Islanders nervous, they went into hiding in the centre of the island for three months, before the tribe split into two parties and left in outriggers. The D'Oyley brothers were separated, John Ireland going with the younger William and John Sexton with the older George. The fate of John Sexton and George D'Oyley is not known, but presumably it was a grim one. John Ireland's party, after weeks at sea, eventually made it to the eastern island of Erub, where the two boys were bartered for two bunches of bananas with a Meriam man, Duppa, and his wife Panney.

By the time *The Isabella* approached Mer in 1836, ordered by the colonial governor to investigate the sighting of two white boys by a passing ship the year before, Ireland and D'Oyley were fluent in Meriam Mer language, having largely forgotten English. But Ireland was able to express that they had been treated with 'parental kindness', and when Duppa was coerced into trading the boys for linen, the captain said the young D'Oyley was 'crying and would not leave the black woman, who had charge of him'.

Three books were written of D'Oyley and Ireland's experience, one by Ireland himself, and historians Maynard and Haskins claim that 'the graphic details of the initial massacre of the shipwreck survivors cemented an enduring colonial fixation with shipwreck survivors being attacked and eaten by native cannibals,' with little attention given to the parental care the two boys received.

Professor Maynard, himself a Worimi Aboriginal man, told me how sensationalised accounts portrayed Indigenous Australians with 'aspects of cannibalism and warfare and all this sort of stuff ... The way you read these sorts of things, blackfellas are running around slaughtering people and putting them on the barbie.'

Maynard said that while the Indigenous history shouldn't be painted 'as utopian paradise, the reality is that Indigenous people on this continent have been here upwards of 50,000 years, come through ice ages, rising sea levels, which the Torres Strait is facing again now, droughts and fires, famines and floods, all of these things they were able to survive.'

However, Ireland's account certainly stirred the creative juices of Idriess in his 1933 book *Drums of Mer*, which opens with a gruesome 'dance of death', the staggering death throes of a body after decapitation. Again it is all about witch-doctors and swashbuckling adventures in which a white protagonist takes charge over the natives and becomes their leader. While there is no doubt of the brutality of the Islanders' headhunting culture, the years of rape, plunder and pillaging by passing European ships would have given Islanders a justifiable mistrust of these white ghost *lamars*, who lacked compassion and seemingly lived on these strange ships without a territory or home.

Although it may seem like mere titillation in a trashy novel, Maynard and Haskins argue that accounts like this 'fed into the fearful European imagination, providing justification for the slaughter of Indigenous people both on the mainland and in the Torres Strait.'

An interesting shift has occurred since these white castaways, victims of winds and the waves, washed up on unknown beaches and became members of societies unfathomable to colonial

Australia. While the castaways still arrived, the demographic shifted: these were misfits and madmen casting off mainstream society and going bush, getting off the grid.

Yankee Ned, a US Civil War veteran, deserted the United States navy in the 1860s and made his way to Australia on a whaling schooner. Edward Mosby left the ship in Australia after a fight with a crewman and made his way north to the Torres Strait and settled on Masig, where he married local girl Queenie. It took Ned a while to win over all the community, but he became their leader after helping fight off an incursion by a Mer raiding party; allegedly this defence was so brutally successful that nobody ever tried to attack Masig again. With his four sons he built up a successful bêche-der-mer and pearling business. He helped build roads and gardens and introduced cattle and horses. After losing a leg to coral poisoning he spent his twilight years sitting on his verandah scouring the Straits with a telescope, to guard a prized collection of pearls he had accrued over the years. One night, suspecting a Japanese pearl diver spying on him was going to rob him, Ned buried his treasure somewhere on the island, the location of which he took to his grave at the age of seventy-one in 1911. Ned's lost treasure passed into folklore, while his legacy lives on with the Mosby clan, a prominent Islander family.

An early reference to these wild white men of the Torres Strait appeared in the writing of English playwright and novelist William Somerset Maugham, who in 1926 penned a few South Pacific tales from the balcony of the Grand Hotel, which overlooked TI harbour, the same pub I and the family would go on Thursdays for ten dollar schnitzel night.

Maugham wrote of French Joe, a ninety-three-year-old he met who was waiting to die in Thursday Island Hospital. A former lieutenant in the Crimean War, Joe turned his back on the French empire and joined the communists, for which he was caught and sentenced to five years on New Caledonia.

With the help of a fellow Corsican, he slipped overboard en route.

Then came a long series of adventures. He cooked, taught French, swept streets, worked in the gold mines, tramped, starved, and at last found his way to New Guinea. Here he underwent the most astonishing of his experiences, for drifting into the savage interior, and they are cannibals there still, after a hundred desperate adventures and hair-breadth escapes he made himself king of some wild tribe.

'At all events you have had a fine life,' I said.

'Never. Never. I have had a frightful life. Misfortune has followed me wherever I turned my steps and look at me now: I am rotten, fit for nothing but the grave. I thank God that I had no children to inherit the curse that is upon me.'

Maugham also wrote of German Harry, a shipwreck survivor who refused rescue and lived as a hermit for thirty years. He is thought to be Henry Evolt, a Dane who, according to a 1951 *Sydney Morning Herald* article, lived on Deliverance Island until his death in 1928.

Maugham hitched a ride on a pearling lugger to Merauke and convinced the skipper to stop by the hermit's island.

He was a man of over seventy, very bald, hatchet-faced, with a grey beard, and he walked with a roll so that you could never have taken him for anything but a sea-faring man. His sunburn made his blue eyes look very pale and they were surrounded by wrinkles as though for long years he had spent interminable hours scanning the vacant sea.

I cannot say that he was pleased to see us. He accepted our gifts as a right, without thanks, and grumbled a little because something or other he needed had not been brought. He was silent and morose. He was not interested in the news we had to give him, for the outside world was no concern of his: the only thing he cared about was his island.

German Harry's story may have later inspired Gösta Brand, a Swedish hermit known as Ron, to live on tiny uninhabited Packe Island for forty years. Ron had a reputation for firing his shotgun at any boat that came too close to his one-room lean-to, so the island was consequently avoided by locals.

Ron died in 1981, the same year that twenty-five-year-old Lucy Irvine responded to an ad in *Time Out* magazine that said: 'WRITER SEEKS WIFE for a year on a tropical island.' Bored and restless with life in London, Irvine shacked up with Gerald Kingsland, an English writer twice her age, for a year on the uninhabited Torres Strait island of Tuin, near Badu. Kingsland wanted to live like Robinson Crusoe and all he needed was a young Girl Friday. The tumultuous experience gave Irvine the fodder to write her 1983 bestseller, *Castaway*, which was later made into a movie starring Oliver Reed.

Then there was Michael Fomenko, nicknamed 'Australia's Tarzan' by Islander kids when he paddled through Torres Strait from the Daintree to West Papua in a dugout canoe wearing nothing but a loincloth. Born to a Georgian princess in the Soviet Union in 1930, Fomenko's family fled Stalin's regime, travelling through China and then Japan before settling in Australia in 1941. Despite showing shining potential as a decathlete, Fomenko was troubled by language difficulties and feelings of alienation, and after reading Homer's *Odyssey* he spent most of sixty years living in the bush before ending up in an aged care facility in 2012. During that time he was periodically hunted down by mounted police and sent to psychiatric hospitals, where he received electric shock treatment.

Even on my watch there are still a few wild white men in the Torres Strait, like Leo the sun-withered Austrian, who lives in a shack at the back of the largely uninhabited Friday Island and has done for forty years. Over seventy, he has sired more kids than he can remember. A loner by choice, he told me when he came to the Torres Strait: 'I've bloody been all over the world and decided to just stop running, so I stayed.'

Leo bounds through my door one day, irate, dictating a letter to the editor in his thick Austrian accent, aimed at 'the bloody bastards who come over and shoot my goats with hunting bows'.

Crazy-eyed, he issues a warning to these weekend warriors. 'If they want to shoot at something, shoot at me, and I will shoot back!' He sighs. 'I just liked to look at the goats on the ridge tops. Can't bloody own anything up here, everything gets taken away.'

Then there's Helmut, another weather-grizzled hermit, a German man over seventy who lives at the back of Horn Island, away from the local village. He crawls around TI on a decrepit pushbike with old shopping bags full of power tools hanging off the handlebars. He often parks it in my driveway when he labours on boats dry-docked on the neighbour's slipway, scraping off barnacles, patching up holes and slapping noxious-smelling anti-fouling paint on the hulls.

With his Dali moustache and crazy white-blond hair and wild eyes, Helmut looks like the seventies BBC character Catweazle. Helmut, who at the time apparently looked like an Aryan Adonis, arrived in the sixties in a catamaran in which he'd sailed around the world with his equally beautiful girlfriend. Eventually the girlfriend left and the boat sank, but Helmut stayed.

The one time I spoke to him outside the bank, he talked breathlessly for an hour until I cut him short. A brilliant mind obviously ravaged by decades of isolation, Helmut told me of his meteorite collection, which was the envy of many a museum. He had written a tome on the subject but was too protective to ever show anyone. He changed conversational tack constantly, trying to cram as many stories as possible into our chance encounter.

'There were still little people here when I first arrived – I remember seeing one in the eighties when I was working as a labourer on the swimming pool. I saw children throwing rocks at something and when I went over I saw this little man, only three feet high. When I told people about it, they all laughed and said I was crazy, but the Kaurareg Elders tell they used to eat them, and that's why there are no more on Horn Island, the same reason there is no kangaroos. I believe there may still be some on the other islands, living in the crevices of the big boulders where we cannot reach them.'

In the Islands the little people are called *kidachi*.

As crazy as it sounds, there may be a basis in truth for the little people who inhabit the mythology of the region, a world Helmut has one foot firmly rooted in, the other on the fringes of the modern world. It has been postulated the *kidachi* refers to the pygmy people from PNG highlands.

On the tip of Cape York, I was taken into Country by rangers of Angkamuthi mob, who showed me the lay of the land as we bounced through scrubland in beaten-up Toyota troopies. Tapee Salee, a young bear of a man with a quiet voice, told me of the mischievous 'little people' or *bua buas* as we set up our swags to sleep on the banks of the Jardine River. As Tapee's wife cooked up fried damper scones and his young kids collected firewood, he told me they were terrified to pass through the patches of jungle where the forest canopy blocked out the light, as apparently that's where they lived, one foot in this world and the other in the Dreamtime. Tapee didn't scare easily – he was a member of the one of the fiercest local rugby teams, the Injinoo Crocs, who would train by swimming upstream in the Jardine River, which is full of large, mean salties, so when Tapee laughed nervously talking of the little people, I paid heed.

However of all the wild wild men I met in the Straits, it was Chris Burrell that made me realise they were all living relics of a bygone era. In his sixties, Chris is tall and wiry, with no teeth and a white moustache stained brown from chain-smoking. A taxi driver on TI, he blusters in through my front door with reams of old court records stinking of nicotine. He's angry – everything is 'fucking this' and 'fucking that' – and wants me to write his life story.

He came from a broken family, with a drunken dad who never got over the war and a mum who ran off looking for a better life, leaving behind Chris, his big brother and his little brother and sister. Chris also believes his generation was the last in the lineage of an Irish curse placed on his family by his maternal great-great-grandmother Ball.

'Her father went missing on the goldfields, and she put the curse on her own son – that was the Balls. My theory is maybe my great-grandfather killed my great-great-great-grandfather on the goldfields then disappeared to Kempsey. I don't know if that happened, but I often wondered how come he turned up with all this money and bought so much property, and why else would a mother place a curse on her own son?'

Sure enough, the next four generations squandered the family fortune in feuds and on the drink. One was gored to death by a bull, another fell off a horse, another was decapitated crashing into the back of a semitrailer.

'She said, "Your children will never find happiness, your grandchildren will never find happiness and there will be four generations that will never find happiness and will end up with nothing, the great-grandchildren will be drunks and criminals". I was the fourth generation, my daughter and grandkids are meant to be clear of the curse. The Irish curse came true.'

Chris's mum didn't want the responsibility of a young family, so she took the children from their home in rural New South Wales, 'she took us into Sydney to a picture theatre, got up and walked out and left us there.'

Thus began a long, troubled life. He and his siblings were separated and they bounced in and out of homes and foster families, abused sexually, physically and emotionally along the way.

Chris was a key witness in the Royal Commission into Institutional Responses to Child Sexual Abuse.

As a teenager he was released into the care of a wealthy alcoholic spinster aunt who had a love for the horseraces. This led Chris into the seedy underworld of the bookies and racecourses of Sydney, until he finally ended up a con man pulling scams up and down the east coast, and in and out of jail. A sharply dressed gangster, he had a brief relationship with a Torres Strait Islander girl and had a daughter, who he played no role in raising.

'Back then in the 1970s things were much more racist, and when a dark girl got with a white guy in society's eyes it brought them up in the world, it is a terrible thing to say but back then that was how it was seen.'

By the eighties he was a homeless alcoholic living on the streets.

Chris arrived on TI for a holiday about the same time I arrived to work. Chris came to visit his estranged daughter and never left, often sleeping rough when on the drink, until after a year he joined AA and has been sober ever since.

Chris describes his time in the homes as, '"criminal college", a lot of hardcore gangsters went through those homes.

'I've been in the system with the kids of the Stolen Generation. The difference between them and me is that they were stolen and I was abandoned, that was the only difference, so I know how they feel, being in those homes and being forced to do things against their will, I've been in that same position, so it goes past colour, and I am not prejudiced in that way.'

Chris is both tragic and enduring, an angry ex-con with a tenacious gentle heart despite everything he has been through. He wanted to set the record straight before his own passing, not for his benefit but for his family's. The Strait has softened the sharp edges of Chris's life.

'But I am the past – the present and the future belongs to me daughter and me grandchildren. It does not belong to me,' he tells me the last time he comes to my office.

While all these wild white men of the Torres Strait are outliers from mainstream society, and many of them undoubtedly in various degrees of madness and some may possibly even be murderers, they also all quintessentially have that essence of Australiana. They all shared the sentiment of the fuck-you aimed squarely at the establishment, and preferred to step off into shimmering haze of the Never Never than remain in the dark heart of our baseless, faithless and failing society. In a way it's what any decent free-thinking, self-respecting Australian should, but is too scared to do.

CHAPTER 11

THIRSTY ISLAND

Sometime in 1902

When Australia's poet laureate Banjo Paterson called Thursday Island 'Thirsty Island' in his 1902 short story of the same name, he did more than just describe the community as 'the outlying pub of Australia'.

There is a fort and garrison at Thirsty Island, but they are not needed. If an invading fleet comes this way it should be encouraged by every possible means to land at the island; the heat, the thirst, the horehound beer, and the Islanders may be trusted to do the rest.

A year after Australia's federation, Paterson was riding the wave of optimism in the lead-up to World War 1. The new nation was keen to carve out its identity, which was built on beer, bravado and brinkmanship, but the national psyche was still shadowed by Victorian imperialism. Paterson laid down the foundation of our Australiana, that bitter-sweet laconic larrikin outlook, with a rough-house rustic charm that makes us grin in the face of adversity. As endearing as it is to some, it also seems to me to be very white and perhaps founded on insecurity, hence its brashness and self-deprecation.

They were heady days for the country and for the Torres Strait, which was fast becoming the world's capital for pearl shell. At some £400 a tonne, the thousands of tonnes fished went a long way to building the state of Queensland. The industry grew, full of Islanders working alongside immigrants from Samoa, Niue, Rotuma, Lifou Island, Malaysia, the Philippines, Japan, China, Jamaica and Spain. Some stayed and made the region their home, influencing contemporary Islander culture and one of the first multicultural communities in the country, where today there can be found Fujiis, Nakatas, Laifoos, Seekees and Sabatinos. It's an era sentimentally referred to as 'Old TI', which went from 1890 until 1980, when the last of the pearling luggers vanished from the region as plastic buttons flooded the market, replacing those made from pearl shell.

The early days of Old TI saw the port town thriving. It was touted as the next Singapore, being a common pit-stop port for the many coal-fired steamers that traversed the region's shipping channels, now known as the Miner's Highway. Back then a garrison on a hill guarded the town with ten cannons, in case the Russians tried to take over the valuable port. (The guns were only ever fired once, at a vessel that turned out to be friendly.)

The first female mayor of Torres Shire, Vonda Malone, told me once that Old TI was 'A real gunslinger's town.' Old TI had opium dens, sly-grog shops and Japanese *Karayuki-san* brothels. The town was flush with money, not only from the pearling industry but also a reputed black market for PNG gold (the precious metal, not the cannabis). In a 1926 short story, William Somerset Maugham described how it was when French Joe arrived:

I went there since they told me in Sydney that it was the last place God ever made. They said there was nothing to see and warned me that I should probably get my throat cut.

Thursday Island-based historian John Singe described TI in his 1979 book: *The Torres Strait: People and History:*

The streets bustled with a motley crowd, wide-eyed Aborigines and Papuans seeing civilisation for the first time, trim Japanese skippers in neat white shirts and trousers, Chinese gardeners with baskets of tropical fruits, sleek Singalese shopkeepers – the craftsmen who shaved and polished the pearls – and resplendent in white suits and pith helmets, the European bankers, shippers, managers and administrators, striding through to lunch at the Grand

Hotel with its panoramic views across Muralug, Nurapai (Horn Island) and down to Cape York.

As well as mining the ocean floor for pearl shell, the pearlers plundered other resources. Islands were stripped of trees and food, and communities ransacked. Abduction of Islander women was widespread and rampant; this combined with the decimation brought by diseases meant that in a mere thirty years from 1900 the Islander population was halved.

By 1900 more than 3000 Japanese labourers were indentured to the pearling industry, forced to repay their upkeep and transportation to Australia. Thursday Island was often disparagingly referred to as being more a Japanese colony than a British one.

For those of brown skin, whether black-birded from the South Pacific, indentured from Japan, or just exploited locally, it would have been a grim time involving hard yakka. For them it was a culture of hard drinking and loose and wild times; if the sharks, crocodiles, sea snakes, stonefish or the bends didn't kill you, a dose of the clap could.

The white administration turned a blind eye to the brawling and the occasional brown body found dead on the beaches or in the back alleys of TI.

Today there are four pubs on Thursday Island for 3000 people; in 1900 there was seven for 2000 people. In Old TI racial tensions were always ready to boil over. While the Torres Hotel still gets a bit punchy on Friday and Saturday nights, like any north Queensland country town TI seems to have mellowed, as the tide of pearling industry receded and a layer of suburbia came in with the bureaucrats who have since inundated the community. But a few drinks in, the skin-deep tensions easily bust open – after a little Bundy Rum, a smile can become a snarl and a swinging fist at any time.

When I walk out to the edge of the sea-grass meadows at low tide, the receding water reveals shards of broken blue and white crockery, the remains of rice bowls discarded by the men who worked on the timber hulls decades before. Back in the Old TI heyday there was a Japan Club, a Chinatown and a Malay Town. Situated on the beach that the *Torres News* office now looks out on, the sailors from Malay Town used to slip their luggers at low tide. The remains of the bloodwood slipways, weathered by the salt water and the sun, still promise a good cut of timber. They are heavy to drag up the beach, even harder to cut as I slowly recycle the dense hardwood into park benches and picnic tables. Over my years in the job, my corner of the beach of old Malay Town has become my Zen garden, where I make mosaics from the shards of china, rake the sand and sit in the deep shade of a big beach almond tree. It's my quiet place to decompress after producing the week's paper, which years before must have been abuzz with activity, but has since become a hangout for kids.

I watch my daughter swim after school with the Islander kids, the genetic mix of those wilder times alive in their lithe builds and Asiatic features. They hoot and holler in creole, teasing each other about how tiger sharks will get them as they splash around in the high tide. At low tide they walk in packs across the exposed sea-grass meadows, spearing crabs with their three-pronged 'whap' spears. My daughter trudges behind them, spattered in mud, a doll in one hand and a found dugong rib bone in the other, until I yell, 'It's shark o'clock!' as the sun sets and the waters become dark and ominous.

Searching those waters for pearl shell were first the naked or free divers, usually Islanders working the shallows until the shell became scarce, and then in the deeper waters divers wearing heavy brass diving bell helmets. Many of the bell divers were Japanese, and it's estimated fifty percent of divers died on the job. The

Thursday Island cemetery has a whole section for the 600 Japanese divers buried there.

One of the free divers, an Aboriginal man from the Cape known as Treacle, or Treckle, had a very intimate encounter with a tiger shark (or in some accounts a hammerhead shark) in 1913 (or 1914). According to the *Medical Journal of Australia* of 31 July and 4 December 1920, Treacle dived into the sea from a ship and landed headfirst in the open jaws of a huge shark. The diver gouged out one of the shark's eyes and it released him. A one-eyed hammerhead shark was supposedly hooked a few days later while Treacle was recuperating in hospital.

'Sharks push, me push back,' Treacle was reported to have said. 'Bimeby me too strong – sharka he let go ... That sharka nearly eat me, but he no make me lose my job, too ... No plurry fear!'

If you believe the account Ion Idriess gave two decades later, the reason Treacle got into trouble was because of a curse put on him by an Aboriginal witch-doctor while on 'walkabout in the wilds of Cape York'. The witch-doctor said that when he next sailed, he would 'put his head into the belly of the Devil'. Idriess told of how Treacle was saved by the magic of the 'white man doctor' and reported that he later made money showing his scars to passengers on the passing steamers.

The lacerations on his head, neck and left shoulder were sewn up, and a few weeks later he was back on the job – or so the grandson of the surgeon who stitched Treacle up, a Dr Wassal, told me on the one hundredth anniversary of Dr Wassal's death from stepping on a stonefish. The grandson, himself old and frail, had flown up to hold a ceremony for his late grandfather and was keen for his ancestor to be remembered in a place that seems to want to forget much of its colonial past. Nobody but me and some last-minute ring-ins turned up for the event.

Often old folks come back after lifetimes away, wanting to feel the salty sea breeze of their halcyon days, old diggers and doctors, people who spent their childhoods on TI, now in their dotage. An old man who spent a couple of years in the force back in the seventies insisted on taking me for a beer, wanting to share his stories of being a copper.

'It was a beautiful and wild place back then. I remember the last time a black flag was ever raised on a lugger, meaning a diver lost his life at sea. Back then the worst insult you could say to a sailor was to call him a dugong fucker – apparently the females have genitalia that resembles a human's, and apparently it was sometimes just too tempting for a sailor too long out at sea,' he chuckled, his sun-mottled hand quivering under the weight of the six-ounce beer he brought to his pallid lips.

'There were only a few cars on TI back then and it was very quiet. When the hunters took a mother dugong, the night was filled with the sound of a baby dugong crying for its mother out at sea, it was very eerie.'

He then passes me a faded photograph of himself in the day, smiling in footy shorts and holding a skull.

'The police station used to have a bar out the back, and there was this skull, it was apparently the skull of a fierce Torres Strait Islander warrior, and to be a member of the club you had to drink out of it.' Seeing my raised eyebrow as I examined the skull in the photo, he stammered, 'But was a different time back then – it had an innocence.'

I later discover the police social club, called the 278 Bar, still has the old warrior's skull stashed away somewhere. The name 278 refers to the price the police got paid for providing prisoners in the watch house a meal, $2.78.

The bar's insignia is a skull wearing a sombrero, which appears on the beer mat on the bar. Above the beer fridge is a fake skull, the real no doubt kept discreetly out of sight, perhaps saved for special occasions.

Octogenarian Uncle Seaman Dan tells me one day, sitting on a beach in 2014, how he navigated the days in Old TI. I doubt he drank at the 278 Bar.

Uncle Dan is stooped, withered and slight of frame, but is a giant in his community, a living legend with five albums and two ARIA awards under his belt. He didn't record his first album until he was in his seventies, although as a young bloke he was always knocking about with a guitar under his arm, which he started playing at the age of eight. The Torres Strait crooner's fusion style blends Polynesian, Melanesian, Nat King Cole and a dash of Sinatra with TI Hula tunes.

'We used to drink at the Mangrove Hotel,' he says smiling a near toothless grin.

'The Mangrove Hotel, I never heard of that one.'

'When we were working on the pearling boats, we were under-age, so we would get someone to buy rum and wine from the pub, then we would sneak into the mangrove swamp to have a party. They were simple, happy days. But now the doc says no more hard stuff,' Uncle Dan tells me while squeezing my knee and chuckling again.

Uncle Dan always chuckles.

We're sitting in the shade of a beach almond tree, as a BBC crew get ready to interview him for the series *The Coast*.

I don't mind the show, but the Scottish presenter, Neil Oliver, seems to be clinging to a lost youth. He really could use a haircut. He insists on holding his canvas manbag in every shot. I sneak a peek when he puts it on the bench next to me and Uncle Dan so he can preen his hair. Inside there is hand cream, sanitising gel and a spare cravat.

The crew fuss and groom a spot on the beach to make it look more 'authentic' for them to shoot a scene, snapping off low-hanging branches, kicking rubbish out of frame or covering it with sand.

Uncle Dan's grandfather was a Jamaican skipper on one of the boats that brought the missionaries to the region, and his great-grandmother was a chief's daughter from New Caledonia.

Uncle Dan was born on TI in 1929. He tells me he remembers how the outdoor cinema on Thursday Island was segregated so the whites and blacks did not sit together. By eleven Uncle Dan was mustering cattle on horseback in Far North Queensland, then as a young man he came back to the Torres Strait and worked on the pearl luggers as both a diver and a captain.

I asked if he ever met Mr Crocodile while diving for pearl shell.

'Ooh, sometimes working around the mouth of the Jardine River, it was very cloudy, the water so dirty you couldn't see your hand in front of your face. I never saw a crocodile, but it was pretty scary. But if you didn't come up with a bagful of pearl the skipper would just send you down again,' he says, chuckling.

Uncle Dan, who just finished recording another album, is recovering from a heart issue. For a petite man, he has the heart of a lion, and he's still smiling after living as a second-class citizen for the better part of a century on his own Country.

Looking out at sea he squeezes my knee again, winks and says, 'Ah, it's a beautiful day to be alive, whoopee.'

CHAPTER 12

A DOG ACT

15 December 1897

'WHEREAS it is desirable to make provision for the better protection and care of the aboriginal and half-caste inhabitants of the Colony...'

These are the opening words of the Queensland Government's 1897 *Aboriginals Protection and Restriction of the Sale of Opium Act*. It was the first of many Acts that removed many basic freedoms of First Nations people, and similar Acts were introduced by state governments around the country.

They became known as 'The Act' or the 'Dog Acts', as they treated First Nations people no better than animals.

To get permission to work or travel, an 'Exception Certificate' had to be granted by the government, which became known as 'dog licenses'.

At the turn of the twentieth century, along with Federation in 1901 and the rise of a new nation, came the Commonwealth Constitution and it's Section 127 which stated '...in reckoning the number of people.... "Aboriginal natives" shall not be counted.' It was a means of both ignoring their rights and controlling their affair. Section 127 was not removed from the constitution until the 1967 referendum.

Torres Strait Islanders, who had already been subjugated by twenty years of the London Missionary Society, were then, like all First Nations peoples, stripped of what little autonomy they had left. They were underpaid for work and overcharged for goods purchased at the government store, which ensured that at the end of each pearling season they would be slightly in debt, binding them to further indentured labour. They could not freely choose who they would marry, and their movements between islands were restricted and required consent from the so-called Government Protector, a white overlord whose position was established under the guise that the 'natives' were not capable of looking after their own affairs. In actuality it served to reinforce the white society's pecking order.

By the 1920s, at the height of the pearling industry, these Dog Acts also served to create an abundant supply of cheap labour to help fund the state's economy.

The Act was enforced by the 'Protector', the regional head of the Queensland government's Department of Native Affairs, known as the

DNA, which represented the government's fervour for white paternalistic control and systemic and institutional racism. Part of that control was based on the foundations laid by the missionaries and the schools they had built in each community. A white teacher became the proxy for the DNA in each community, and not only instilled the DNA's draconian ethos but also delivered a substandard education, effectively preventing Islanders from developing academically past the Grade Four level, known as the Mark. Each government-appointed teacher acted as a superintendent-magistrate, supervised Islanders' movements, and made decisions about the items and credit they could receive from the government stores.

Gela tells me the DNA also used food rations to pressure Islanders to give up their culture. 'Mum was not allowed to speak in lingo – if you spoke your language at that time, then it would have an impact on your food rations, under their rationing system, so we grew up not being able to speak fluently our mother's tongue.' He says it means for his generation part of their culture has been eroded, 'a result of colonialism, as a result of past policies that were in place, policies of segregation and assimilation.'

Under the guise of the Act, the Gela's parents' and grandparents' generations were denied access to their wages, which were instead spent on public infrastructure projects hundreds, sometimes thousands of kilometres away from where they lived in poorly built public housing with rundown schools and hospitals. In many cases the money was simply stolen by corrupt officials and employers. Governments not only withheld wages but also child endowments and benefits, savings, inheritances, soldiers' pay, maternity payments, trust funds, deceased estates, unemployment benefits, lump-sum compensation payments, aged or disability pensions, and workers' compensation.

Of the estimated $500 million in stolen wages siphoned off by the Queensland government using wage control legislation under the Act between 1939 and 1972, less than ten percent has been repaid over three repayment schemes, in 2002, 2006 and 2016. This meant the small proportion of people who received a compensation payout only got a fraction of what was owed, and yet they had to sign a discharge notice preventing them from pursuing the rest of their money.

Many others got nothing because they couldn't provide enough evidence, for the simple reason that they never received adequate paperwork from the government of the day. In fact, the Stolen Wages Commission stated that this lack of documentation was not due to poor bookkeeping, also because the records were deliberately destroyed to cover the fraudulent use of this money.

The contribution Aboriginal and Torres Strait Islander people made to Australia's economy with their largely unfairly paid or unpaid work is a history seldom told.

As Dennis Eggington, chief executive of the Aboriginal Legal Service of Western Australia, told Australia's national Indigenous newspaper, the *Koori Mail* in 2010: 'Aboriginal people are often denigrated as being a drain on the nation's economy, but if you look at the facts it's actually the other way around, with Aboriginal labour being used to build the economy without due payment or even recognition ... It's a terrible injustice that has been perpetrated over many decades, with the truth hidden from the official version of Australian history.'

Western Australian Greens Senator Rachael Sievert told the *Koori Mail* in 2007: 'There is no doubt in my mind that this country's strong economy was born on the backs of Aboriginal labour.'

Gary Highland, the national director of Australians for Native Title and Reconciliation told the *Koori Mail* in 2017, 'When I was in school, I was told that Australia developed on the sheep's back. I now know that it developed on the backs of thousands of Aboriginal men, women and children.'

'This is just more boiled lollies, thrown to the ground,' spat Bishop Saibo Mabo at a community meeting on TI discussing the stolen wages.

Bishop Mabo is referring to the era of the Department of Native Affairs, which had a total of three protectors, or 'emperors for life', during the twentieth century, the last being Pat Killoran, appointed in 1948, who for the next four decades presided over the forced evacuation of families from their land, the detention and separation of children from parents, and the commandeering of Indigenous wages, savings and child endowment payments in what was described as an 'evil regime'. I heard rumours that the guy was a lech as well, often recruiting the prettiest Island girls to work in his office until he grew tired of them, and he would fire them when he'd found a fresh muse.

Killoran, who was behind the failed relocation of Milton Savage's grandfather Elikiam Tom and the other Kaurareg living on Horn Island in 1950, was also responsible for the forced relocation of the Cape York Aboriginal community of Mapoon in 1963, where residents were forced at gunpoint out of their homes, which were then burnt down, so mining giant Comalco could establish a bauxite mine. The event is said to be the inspiration for Midnight Oil's hit song 'Beds are Burning'.

Bishop Mabo said of the Queensland Government's 2016 Stolen Wages offer: 'When Killoran come round to our community he would throw boiled sweets onto the ground for us kids, that is what this offer from the government is now, boiled lollies on the ground.'

'Boiled lollies' has become an expression among many of the older Islanders to describe the racism and disempowerment they have suffered and the intergenerational hardship it has caused for them and their families – and, as one political adviser suggested over a quiet beer, trapped them in a mindset that effectively keeps them under the colonial thumb.

Torres Strait film producer, Aaron Fa'Aoso, told me over coffee one day on TI's esplanade, '*Bala,* the contribution our people have made to the Queensland economy in the early days basically built the state, and that's never been recognised. The pearling industry created hundreds of millions of dollars, and that was all from our sea country.'

However, despite the Act and the wages it stole from Torres Strait Islanders, there were a couple of times they challenged this injustice. In

January 1936 the Islander divers had had enough of being ripped off, so using the protector's cargo ship, spread the word through the Torres Straits to have a strike. The message spread quietly in language, and even in messages left underwater for divers to read. Some 400 pearl and trochus divers refused to work, protesting not only about poor working conditions but also the Islanders' right to control their wages and manage their own affairs. It brought the industry to a grinding halt for nine months.

While the government didn't relinquish all its hold over the Islanders' lives or their earnings, it was a partial victory – curfews and travel bans were removed, and some control was taken from the teachers and given to elected island councils. The momentum was again manifest on 23 August 1937 on Masig, where thirty-four elected Island Councillors from fourteen communities formally gathered for the first time to make a series of demands from the Queensland government. Two years later the state government passed the *Torres Strait Islander Act 1939*, which incorporated many of the recommendations discussed at the conference.

The Islanders yearned for more in the way of autonomy, but then World War II broke out. Just after midday on 14 March 1942, Japanese Zeros bombed Horn Island. For the next seventeen months the islands and airfields of the region were subject to sporadic attacks. In total nine people were killed, and at least twenty-two were injured. TI itself was never bombed, only Horn Island. There was a rumour that a Japanese princess was buried in TI cemetery but that has never been verified; the fact that so many Japanese pearl divers were buried there may have been a factor.

The Strait was ready for the air invasion, having dug in and erected bunkers and anti-aircraft guns, and formed Australia's first all-Indigenous battalion, the Torres Strait Light Infantry Battalion. It had 880 men – impressive considering the region's population at the time was only around 4000 people, and it represented all but ten of the men of age. Not surprisingly, the Torres Strait community had the highest rate of enlistment per population in the country.

While all of these troops were enlisted, not conscripted, recruitment tactics included drill sergeants firing pistols in the street to scare young men into joining. When they did, they were often transported immediately to the base on TI without the chance to even tell their families they were going. Yet despite these coercive tactics, many of the men hoped serving in the army would improve their aspirations for self-autonomy after the war.

The Australian Government did not initially approve of the battalion as the men were not of 'European origin': they were only paid half as much as their white counterparts, could not ascend higher than the rank of corporal and did not receive any family allowance. They weren't even allowed to wear the digger's signature slouch hat. In December 1943 a similar protest to the 1936 maritime strike was held, and despite the threat of them being shot for disobedience, it resulted in their pay being raised to two-thirds that of the white soldiers.

It took over forty years for the Australian Government to pay these old diggers the discrepancy in their wages compared to the whitefellas, and it was not until 2001 that the few remaining were recognised for their unique efforts with the awarding of their service medal, the Torres Strait Star.

In 2014 the Chief of the Australian Army, Lieutenant General David Morrison AO, came to Thursday Island on the ninety-ninth anniversary of ANZAC Day and gave a formal public acknowledgement and recognition of the contribution of Indigenous servicemen and – women. He was the highest-ranking officer to ever come to the region.

He said: 'Sadly, for too long, many Australians were blind to the reality of our history. The celebrations of our victories in war were blind to the mixed emotions that they may have engendered in those who called this land home long before it was called Australia. On this day that we pay tribute to the soldiers who stormed ashore on a foreign beach, we must also consider that some Australians remembered men from across the world coming here to take their land.

'Today I think all have a greater understanding of the significance of this land to Aboriginal and Torres Strait Islanders.

'Today I wish to pay tribute to the many Indigenous men and women who have served in our armed forces in every war since the formation of the Commonwealth in 1901.

'Those first soldiers who fought in World War I, of which a third were killed or wounded. They fought for a nation that did not even fully recognise their rights and status as human beings, let alone citizens.

'Yet their love of land and Country preceded any flag or crown, so they went to war as proud warriors – that made their unselfishness and sacrifice even more remarkable...

'It seems to me that ANZAC is a sort of Dreaming for Australians. Of course it is a war story. But its moral tale is about the qualities that no single race of people may lay exclusive claim to – love for country, love for friends and family and the willingness to bear terrible suffering to protect what we love.'

After the formal pomp and ceremony of dismounting the catafalque party in ANZAC Park, I shared a beer with Morrison at the barracks of the 51st Battalion, Far North Queensland Regiment, Charlie Coy – also known as 'the Sarpeyes', creole for 'sharp eyes'. The country's most northerly regiment is known as 'the eyes and ears of the north' and is still predominantly made up of Indigenous soldiers.

Morrison said, 'We have always recognised the service of Indigenous Australians, but we haven't been as public in our recognition than has been warranted.'

Morrison formally recognised the contribution of the Sarpeyes with an unveiling of a plaque renaming the barracks after them, and the ANZAC Day lunch and beers at the barracks bar went well into the night. The regiment did their Sarpeye dance – an adaptation of a traditional warrior dance, but in army fatigues rather than headdresses. Instead of bows and arrows, machine guns fired off rounds of blanks in perfect unison, in time with beating of the *warup*.

While punters played two-up and Crown and Anchor, many Islander Elders, including

Bishop Mabo who did the dawn service, performed island dancing and singing as the rum and beer flowed freely. Must be one of the rare occasions rum, guns and gambling made a good mix for a party.

Of course, as brazen as Morrison's speech was, the alt-right haters were quick to spit the dummy. In a burst of online vitriol, anti-Islamic, anti-gay, conservative Brisbane blogger Bernard Gaynor said Morrison's speech was used 'to promote the lie of "Invasion Day"'.

Gaynor, an Iraq War veteran, was kicked out of the Australian Army in 2013 for making sexist and homophobic comments.

In 2018, on the seventy-fifth anniversary of the formation of the Torres Strait Light Infantry Battalion, Mayor Fred Gela, whose father was the first to enlist, said: 'When our men enlisted, our community, our mothers, took up the responsibility to not only care for children and elderly, but the sick too as well that was in our communities. I want to pay tribute to my mum. I want to share a story through her eyes. On Erub, a Japanese submarine came out at Kemus, Elders still share that story today. They came on shore, the same place as the Coming of the Light in 1871 (the arrival of the missionaries). The women carried the woven baskets they used to carry food, and carried children, firewood and food into the bush to hide, they were defenceless. The men were away protecting everything else, but inside our communities the only person protecting our families was God.'

At the same event Member for Leichhardt Warren Entsch said a little discussed impact of the war was that the Islander troops 'were fed army rations, so they became used to a lot of Western food'.

'For the first time these young men had experienced that, and afterwards, continuing to focus on that Western food, a lot of the issues we talk about in diabetes started to emerge within the communities.'

While most talk of stolen wages is about something that happened in the past, this form of systemic racism has once again permeated the political landscape with the Work for the Dole scheme introduced by Prime Minister Abbott in 2014. In the bush it is called the Community Development Program (CDP), which targets remote communities and forces participants, eighty-three percent of whom are Indigenous, to work up to three times as many hours as people on similar programs in the cities, and for around half the minimum wage. This 'jobs program' is an endless form of indentured labour, in which participants earn meaningless certificates in pushing wheelbarrows or shovelling concrete, in places where there are few or no work prospects, often while non-Indigenous FIFO case managers and consultants on fat salaries with all the perks work next to them. It is essentially modern slavery, a form of credit bondage that perpetuates cycles of poverty.

I was never able to interview anyone on these programs, they were all too scared it would result in being cut off completely from welfare. An out of work fisherman, in his 50s, once told me, 'It's like we're on a chain gang, it's bullshit, we do all the dirty work for councils and government, but we get no sick pay or super, we have no choice in this – they should be giving us jobs to mow their nature strips or work on their building sites.'

On some of the outer island communities where there are little to nil work opportunities, participants are often corralled into public events or health workshops to bolster the numbers, to allow department organisers to tick and flick it as community engagement.

A lady in one of these more isolated communities told me, 'It's adult day-care, they make as do stupid arts and crafts, but we have no choice.'

Yet Islander community leader Kenny Bedford, who works with the Torres Strait's

CDP provider My Pathway, says it is not as clear cut as that.

'The community don't want sit-down money, people feel ashamed sitting at home doing nothing, at least CDP gets them out doing things for their community. It's all fine and good talking about paying people properly and giving them jobs, but the reality is the money and opportunity are just not there.'

Even so, the whole thing reeks like a rort to me.

On the eightieth anniversary of the 1937 Island councillors meeting, their contemporaries in the Torres Strait Island Regional Council held a re-enactment and read out the minutes of that historic meeting. It described the aspirations of Islanders to have better working conditions and greater autonomy over their affairs, to establish property rights and to resolve issues within the community.

It was uncanny to sit there and hear these aspirations of eighty years ago, as it sounded like much of what I hear from our present-day leaders.

Despite this, the ever-positive Councillor for Masig, Frazier Nai – the dreadlocked joker I befriended in my first week on the job when he told me that taking his photo would steal his soul – said: 'The minutes of the 1937 meeting revealed a system of authority was in place, of consequences and order. The type of thinking they had back then was about responsibility about our nation. It is important to realise that change is not a single event but rather an ongoing process. I hear people say there is no silver bullet solution, but there is. The silver bullet is *youmi* (you and me), it lays inside all of us. It's not about having more resources, but being more resourceful. It's not what lays before us or what lays behind us, it is what lays inside us.'

Despite all that his people have endured, Frazier is always looking at the glass half full, an enthusiasm I suspect he shares on the various the boards he sits, from regional health to the PM's advisory committee. As I fly out of Masig later that afternoon, I look down at the coral cay shaped like a tear and remember the first time I came to the island, to cover a Fisheries meeting. On that trip, Frazier stole me away for a tour of the island. Around behind the runway in the last remaining stand of jungle, he told me of his thirst for his people's prosperity, his aspiration of the Torres Strait pulling itself up its bootstraps and finding its own way economically, free of the meddling hand of the Queensland and Australian government.

Sitting in the cab of his ute in the shade, listening to the rise and fall of cicadas, he said: 'Have you heard of the Masig monkeys?'

'That sounds like bullshit, Frazier.'

'No, really – we think they may have been introduced by the Malay pearl divers back in the day. Look up in the treetops there – there's one there, I think. There's not many left but they're around.'

I turn to where he is pointing, straining to see through the canopy, thinking that maybe I can see something, until I feel eyes staring at the back of my head.

I turn to look at a grinning Frazier.

'Ah, fuck, Frazier!'

Frazier breaks out into a laugh, the sort of schoolboy giggle all Islanders do: a laugh in the face of adversity, the bitter-sweet laconic laugh of a larrikin, but one that runs much deeper than Banjo Paterson's century-old Australiana.

CHAPTER 13

FLOWERS FOR A WATERY GRAVE

'Mine will be a watery grave, I feel it in my bones. Men will me in canvass sew, and weigh me down with stones'
Bernard Shaw

14 October 2005

Torres Strait Islander immigration officer Wilfred Baira pleaded with his white boss, Garry Chaston. 'Is it possible that I could spend another night on Saibai so that the wind goes down before I can go back to Badu?'

Baira had real concerns over the seaworthiness of the new Immigration Department vessel *Malu Sara*, already having experienced the hull leaking when under anchor. The weather on Saibai, just a couple of clicks south of Western Province, was going from bad to worse.

'Garry's response to Wilfred was that the department could not afford to pay for another night on Saibai,' says an emotional Patricia Mooka, a colleague of Baira's, at a coronial inquest two years later.

That fateful day in October 2005, just after noon, Baira reluctantly obeyed his boss and set off from the island of Saibai, bound for the island of Badu, 55 nautical miles south, in an unseaworthy vessel in rough and windy seas. Meanwhile, Garry Chaston flew home to Thursday Island in a helicopter to be in time for dinner with his wife at the local bowls club.

Chaston, who had a reputation for being 'heavy handed', the inquest later found, left a junior officer, Jerry Stephen, in charge of ensuring the vessel returned to Badu. The officer ended up working a twenty-four-hour shift while Chaston took the night off.

The *Malu Sara* had neither a GPS nor a marine CB radio, as Chaston had previously described the Islanders operating the vessel as 'two generations behind', who 'would not be able to handle that equipment,' a witness told the coroner.

Baira was given a satellite phone, which he had not been trained how to use, nor had he been trained how to operate the new vessel – a vessel that both leaked and had engine issues.

Baira, thirty-eight, fellow immigration officer Ted Cyril Harry, fifty-four, an experienced seaman, and their passengers, Valerie Saub, thirty-four, Flora Enosa, thirty-four, and her daughter, Ethena Enosa, five, all drowned at sea some time after their vessel sank early the following morning – despite multiple calls on Wilfred's satellite phone explaining their plight.

The Thursday Island police officer Sergeant Warren Flegg, who was in charge of the search for the missing *Malu Sara*, admitted during the coronial inquest that he did not believe Baira's distress calls were real, a judgement that fatally delayed the order of a rescue attempt by three hours, by which time it was too late.

Senior and Corey reported on the tragedy from the day it happened until the coronial inquest two years later, which they attended at Thursday Island Magistrate's Court, and covered it all in the *Torres News*.

Under cross-examination Flegg admitted he should have done more.

Just after 8p.m. on 14 October, Jerry Stephen informed Flegg the boat was lost. It was dark and the weather was deteriorating, and they had been at sea for over seven hours. Baira had activated his Emergency Position Indicating Radio Beacon (EPIRB) some time earlier. Flegg wrongly told a Canberra-based officer from AusSAR, the Australian Search and Rescue organisation, that the vessel was equipped with the usual navigation equipment: 'they've got a compass and everything on board.'

The vessel in fact had a compass and nothing else.

Stephen continued to try and maintain phone contact with Baira, but it kept cutting out due to the worsening weather. At 9.28p.m. Baira managed to call Stephen and inform him they were still lost in open and rough seas, and the boat was taking on water. It is thought the motor cut out some time after 10p.m.

'They're apparently sinking now,' Flegg told Cairns police headquarters at 2.32a.m., minutes after Stephen had his last conversation with the vessel. It was only then Flegg first made requests to send out a helicopter and a search vessel. Baira's satellite phone disappeared off the network between 3.28a.m. and 3.57a.m., which is the time the vessel most likely sank and the passengers, all wearing yellow life jackets, were plunged into the water. It is thought five-year-old Ethena Enosa did not have a child-size life jacket.

At 3.38a.m. Flegg told AusSAR: 'they've just told us that they've started taking a little bit a water, so that's why we really haven't gone out to pick them up because they weren't ... in that, that much trouble. They've also run out of oil and they've started taking a little bit of water, so I'd say that the other reason is that they're sick of being out there and want to get home.'

'They will keep me up all night with these bloody alerts,' a Canberra-based AusSAR officer said at 6.01a.m.

Flegg replied, 'I've been on this thing for bloody – we were notified at 19:30 local ... and it just started out, you know, that they were lost, and now it's gone and turned into, "Oh we're sinking. Can you come and get us?"'

The AusSTAR officer replied: 'Funny how these things develop.'

At 6.45a.m. a Thursday Island Volunteer Marine Rescue boat laboured out in rough seas to the last reported location of the EPRIB. There were 30-knot winds, poor visibility and 1.5-metre waves, which later increased to 3 metres as the futile search progressed. Only then did Flegg request again for a helicopter to do an aerial search, which was approved at 9.30a.m. It located the EPIRB adrift at 10.30a.m. with no sign of the vessel. AusSAR initialised a full aerial search at midday.

The following day at 2.30p.m. three witnesses in the same plane claimed to have sighted someone in the water, wearing a yellow life jacket and waving, but the helicopter that arrived at that location twenty minutes later found nothing.

The search grew over the following week with nineteen aircraft as well as Customs, police and navy vessels, and people from the community of Saibai; the search area grew to include the Western Province coast of PNG. By 21 October the search was suspended.

On 23 October an Indonesian fisherman found a body near Deelder Reef, about 50 nautical miles west of the last known position of the *Malu Sara*. It was subsequently identified as Flora Enosa. This was the only body ever recovered.

At the coronial inquest the former head of Queensland Police Search and Rescue Robert Graham said the activation of EPIRBs in the Torres Strait did not always signify an emergency. He said: 'Up here EPIRB are known as "Empty Petrol I Require Boat" – they know a big white man helicopter would come across the horizon and drop fuel to them.'

Stephen, who was left on a twenty-four shift while his boss went for dinner, testified that he had received calls from the *Malu Sara* concerning their situation and at each call had informed Chaston.

Stephen said when he first informed him the *Malu Sara* was having trouble pumping out the water, Chaston said: '"Well, they better (expletive) bail faster, hadn't they?", or words to that effect.'

Stephen said he had thought the authorities were handling the search and rescue once he passed the information on to Chaston and the police. 'I thought they were handling it and my role was to receive information and pass it on. I didn't think it was my job to be telling authorities how they should respond,' Stephen told the inquest. 'Looking back, I'm kicking myself that I wasn't more forceful. I thought the authorities were in contact with Wilfred and my understanding was that was all I was to do.'

The coroner, Michael Barnes, concluded the five deaths were a 'totally avoidable' disaster that would not have happened 'if any one of a number of those involved in purchasing, building, operating or searching for the vessel had faithfully and diligently discharged his duties.' Barnes said none of those on board were at fault and they were the victims of shocking and incompetent mistakes made by police, boat builders and the Department of Immigration.

The shonkily built *Malu Sara* was never designed for the open waters it sank in, and despite reports of it leaking, it was kept in commission by Chaston, who also refused to have the vessel fitted with GPS and marine radios. As the coronial inquest delved into the case, many of the department's records were reported to have mysteriously gone missing.

It was another two years before the head of the Immigration Department, Andrew Metcalfe, finally apologised, but only after my boss Senior pressured him to do so when Metcalfe attended a memorial service to mark the fourth anniversary of the tragedy.

In a radio interview on the ABC's *The World Today* in October 2009, Senior said: 'Indeed, I suggested to Mr Metcalfe last week that that term had never been used, while the department had apologised many times, but the term "sorry" had never been used. 'Cause I pointed out to him how important it was to the families and the community that the word "sorry" be used.'

Senior said the apology was only a fraction of what the families of those who died were fighting for.

'The first is that there needs to be some legal charges laid. There needs to be some people charged over it. There has never been any charges made and the people with whom the coroner apportioned blame still remain free and going about their lives. The second thing is they wanted sorry to be said. Well, that has now been done and the third is the compensation issue.'

While the victims' families were paid compensation the following year, there were never any legal repercussions for Flegg or Chaston.

In March 2014, eight years after the tragedy, Flegg was cleared of all wrongdoing by the High Court and reinstated with all privileges. He continues to work as a police officer in the Cape. Chaston resigned with full entitlements before any internal action could be taken by the Department of Immigration and Citizenship.

In remembrance of Wilfred Baira and Ted Harry, DFAT named two conference rooms in Canberra after them.

The families of the victims were left devastated. George Nona, from Badu, told me after the High Court decision: 'The fact that Flegg has been reinstated and that Gary has retired to a life of luxury while the families of the victims have been left with this mess is just wrong. In our culture once upon a time, when there was a war between islands and a neighbour island attacked another and took the bones of an enemy back, it was seen as the greatest insult. That is how the families feel about two conference rooms in DFAT's Canberra office being named after Wilfred and Ted Harry. The families want these names removed as they see it as a huge insult. They tried to blame Wilfred, which is so wrong, saying he was too tired, that is shocking. He was a very good seaman, I went fishing with him many times. So much evidence was not used in this case, it is so wrong. It makes us feel so small, the system has let us down.'

Some months after Flegg was cleared of any wrongdoing, and nearly nine years after the *Malu Sara* was last at sea, I'm standing on a beach on Mer, near the community hall where a politically charged meeting is underway between the local fishers and the Australian Fisheries Management Authority (AFMA) – the same hall in which Justice Martin Moynihan held a session of the Queensland Supreme Court for the Mabo case in 1989.

Half submerged in sand at the high-tide mark is the hull of a boat, the outboard still attached but the cowling cover long gone and the motor corroded beyond repair. The bloke from AFMA, who is white and from down south, has given me a lift out to Mer so I can cover the meeting. He raises his hands in exasperation. 'This boat was given to them here to help develop their local fishing industry, but it's never been used from when it was delivered, just sat here on the beach – the cowling cover is in someone's garden being used as a flowerpot. They said the boat had bad *puri puri*.'

The boat was from the same builder as the *Malu Sara*. It was built at the same time and was the same design. On a low-hanging branch of a majestic beach almond tree, someone has carved deep into the timber: *MABO*.

As is clear from the *Malu Sara* tragedy, being let down is something Islanders – like most Indigenous Australians, and indeed Indigenous peoples the world over – continue to experience. It's always patriarchal, top-down decision-making that fails to engage those who are directly affected.

After the AFMA bloke is called back to the fisheries meeting, I wander around the community. Not far from the abandoned boat on the beach, I find the upturned cowling cover. It's overflowing with beautiful purple flowers, perhaps a quiet memorial for those lost at sea and a middle finger salute to the white patriarchal 'we know what's best for you' that gave them unseaworthy boats.

I smile at the bittersweet irony of these flowers for the Malu Sara's watery grave.

CHAPTER 14

SOUTH OF THE BORDER

July, 2013

'Eat all the seafood you want, *bala*, just don't touch the coconut chicken or the beef curry,' a burly Islander fisherman mutters under his breath. There are three trestle tables set out with plates of lobster tails, huge prawns, iced oysters and mussels, sweet and sour fish and *namus* – Spanish mackerel pickled in vinegar, sugar and chillies. At the end of the tables is one pot of coconut chicken and one of beef curry.

Only two weeks into the job I'm covering the annual Protected Zone Joint Authority (PZJA) stakeholder meeting, which saw the PZJA board fronting up to an angry mob of Islander fishers, who vented their frustrations at the bureaucratic process that managed their traditional fishing territory. Islanders have been fighting for their ambition of a hundred percent ownership, and their claim that commercial fishers were overfishing the stock and depleting their traditional fishing territory. With acronyms I didn't yet understand, names I couldn't spell and state and federal government ministers I didn't know, it was tough story to write correctly and fairly.

At the lunchbreak, no doubt sick of the sight and smell of their product, the fishermen wolfed down the chicken and beef, leaving the seafood for the bureaucrats and the other FIFOs. There were actually lobster tails left over. I later discover the heads and legs are popular bait for fishing. A cartoon strip we periodically run in the *Torres News* captures this ambivalence: a child of a hard-up Islander family seated at the dinner table says, 'Ah, Mum — not *kayar* (lobster) for dinner again.'

Many call *kayar* their bread and butter, but it's something they'd rather sell than eat.

The PZJA was formed as a result of the Torres Strait Treaty that was signed on Daru in November 1978, but not ratified until 1985 after a more than decade of intense negotiations.

Three years before PNG's independence from Australia, in 1972 Prime Minister Gough Whitlam suggested our fledgling sovereign neighbour's border be the 10-degree south mark, being the halfway point between the two countries. The border went all the way to PNG's Western Province coastline, as part of Queensland's territory grab in 1879 to gain control of the international shipping channel between the Pacific and Indian Oceans as well as the pearl shell, trochus and bêche-de-mer fisheries. The ten degree south line would have resulted in the Torres Strait Islands of Saibai, Duaun and Boigu falling under PNG territory, and the idea sparked the resistance of a near decade-long grass-roots movement by Torres Strait Islanders, with its war-cry of *Border No Change*.

Queensland Premier Joh Bjelke-Petersen, who revelled in the opportunity to firstly attack Whitlam's Labor Party and later rattle Prime Minister Malcolm Fraser, seized the opportunity to grandstand the issue. A staunch opponent to native title and land rights, Premier Joh became an unlikely ally for the Islanders, championing their rights to remain part of Queensland.

In 1976 ten years before his wild drunken night in the notoriously seedy Admiral Benbow Hotel in Memphis, where Fraser was robbed of his Rolex and wallet, and found drugged staggering with no trousers around a foyer frequented by hookers and dope peddlers, Fraser willingly took off his pants in the name of diplomacy in the Torres Strait. He graciously put on a traditional *lava lava* (sarong) to break the ice and mucked in with the mob, but to avail. It took another two years of negotiation until a treaty was signed in 1978, keeping the existing border. Many years later, staunch advocate for Torres Strait land and sea rights, seen in the archipelago as the grandfather of Torres Strait independence, George Mye said: 'Torres Strait is the only part of Australia that is interfacing with a foreign country, and that's something we've got up our sleeves and we're proud of it.'

Rather than a linear border, the final result was a box on the sea. This awkward, permeable, shared territory allows residents of only thirteen of the 120 PNG villages in the Western Province and residents of the northern cluster of islands of the Torres Strait to pass freely back and forth without visa or passport to fish, maintain family connections in both countries, and continue traditional activities. It has also placed an indefinite moratorium on mining in the region. The treaty was a world first, because there is no fixed boundary line, and it recognises that traditional inhabitants have precedence over two sovereign territories.

It is at times a difficult marriage, which is often exploited by illegal fishing, dubious border activity and friction from communities on both sides. Occasionally PNG leaders call for abolishing it all together, leaving Islanders in fear of an unimpeded flood of desperate and impoverished Papuans. Annual treaty awareness visits are conducted in order for the situation to be monitored on the ground and remind everyone of the rules of play. It was on one of these visits in 2014 that I joined Ray from DFAT, on the thirty-year anniversary of the treaty.

Australians consider themselves an island nation cut off from the rest of the world by an expanse of ocean. But the Torres Strait Treaty resulted in Australia's proximity to our nearest neighbour being much closer than a banana boat ride to Daru, and for the Torres Strait island communities of Saibai, Dauan and Boigu, there are many worries.

Only a couple of kilometres from the PNG mainland, a steady stream of banana boats crosses to buy supplies, sell mud crabs and artefacts, or cadge a day's work for a couple of Australian dollars. At low tide even deer have been known to swim across to Saibai and Boigu.

With up to 50,000 crossings made by villagers each year, the treaty also makes Queensland Health medical centres in these communities the front line to deal with tuberculosis and other communicable diseases, which are increasingly ignored by Port Moresby but occasionally make an inroad into Australia. A couple of outbreaks have killed Torres Strait Islanders. The region has had some of the world's worst infection rates of multi-drug-resistant tuberculosis, and many of the

Western Province villagers seeking medical attention at Queensland Health outposts are infected with it.

The treaty is not without its challenges, especially considering much of its impact is dealt with by local government. The Indigenous Torres Strait Island Regional Council is unique in Australia, in that it is the only local government that has to negotiate international relations on a near daily basis. It has to deal with the asylum seekers occasionally reaching Saibai, the steady influx of the infirm, and the PNG raskol smugglers doing contraband runs over the uncharted shallow waters. Rumours of child trafficking have slipped from loosened Border Force lips at the Torres Hotel, telling of underage girls from PNG villages held in Torres Strait households as 'house girls'. There are also Chinese, Indonesian and Vietnamese fishers poaching the remote waters. It's a far cry from the rubbish, rates and roads that local councils elsewhere in Australia have to deal with.

In August 2015 *Blissful Reefer* was intercepted and impounded by PNG authorities at Daru, having most likely passed through the Torres Strait and possibly fishing illegally in the region.

While the name sounds like a peaced-out Bob Marley song, the reality was anything but. *Blissful Reefer* was a Thai fishing 'slave ship': on board there were eight victims of human trafficking from Cambodia and Myanmar, who had been forced to catch fish, which often ends up in American supermarkets.

Blissful Reefer was thought to be part of a fleet of thirty or more similar vessels working a patch of water known as the Dog's Leg, on the western edge of the Torres Strait territory mapped out in the treaty. These trawlers belonged to a huge human trafficking operation involving hundreds of people, believed to be part of a far bigger syndicate operating further east in Indonesian waters north of the Northern Territory. They edge closer to Australian waters each year as their own local fish stocks become more and more depleted.

In international waters the laws of nearby sovereign states do not have jurisdiction; rather, it belongs to the nation of the flag raised on the vessel. The vessels frequently change their national flags and paint over registration numbers to outwit authorities, effectively creating a lawless place where little or no crime gets reported.

Calling from Sigabadaru, a PNG Treaty Village near Saibai, community leader Kebei Salee tells me that slave ships and illegal fishers passing through the region are nothing new. 'The route through the Dog's Leg area is the one they always follow. Sometimes they shelter in the islands around there when the weather is too bad, then they continue on their way. These vessels are often crossing our waters.'

Most people have no idea all this occurs within our sovereign territory – territory that the Border No Change movement had to fight hard to keep.

Getano Lui senior, a leading Island Elder spokesman at the time, captured the sentiment of the Border No Change movement when he said, 'If you take our water and the seabed then you take our lives.' He also captured the spirit of the treaty: 'We are happy to share what we have in the Torres Strait, but we will not give – not a teaspoon of water, not a grain of sand.'

The Border No Change resistance fortified Islanders' resolve to stand up for their rights and seeded the dream of making the Torres Strait an autonomous territory. To counter this growing unrest, the Queensland government in 1984 established the Island Coordinating Council (ICC) with elected chairs from each island community and the tip of Cape York, giving Islanders for the first time a democratic local government structure. Border No Change activist George Mye was made its first chair. Four years later, on Australia's Bicentenary, he declared at a 400-strong meeting on Thursday Island that his people wanted nothing less than 'sovereign independence from the state of Queensland and the Commonwealth of Australia'. The aspiration, which would remain unfulfilled, was to go to the UN and claim independence, similar to that of Norfolk Island.

In the same year, the Hawke government, keen to repair relations with Indigenous people, created the Aboriginal and Torres Strait Islander Commission (ATSIC), with elected Indigenous representatives from sixty regional councils; the Torres Strait was to have the Torres Strait Regional Council (TSRC). It was a decision that was met with disdain as Islander leaders were concerned with yet another political structure when there were already some thirty-five government departments managing the lives of 8000 people. The Commonwealth's compromise was to appoint the ICC councillors as the TSRC's representatives. A subsequent review of ATSIC and pressure for greater autonomy in the Torres Strait saw the TSRC get upgraded into an independent statutory body, the Torres Strait Regional Authority (TSRA) in 1994.

George Mye's cousin Getano Lui junior became the TSRA's first chair. Lui junior saw the increased powers of the newly formed TSRA as a new beginning and a 'significant milestone' to autonomy. He aspired to have that independence occur in the year 2001. Lui junior also saw the

TSRA as a 'transitional arrangement' until the realisation of autonomy in the new century made it redundant. They were heady political days in the Torres Strait, eight years after the Treaty had been ratified and two years after the High Court decision on the Mabo case.

Another important thing to emerge from the formation of the treaty was yet another acronym, the PZJA – the Protected Zone Joint Authority. The PZJA, controlled by state and federal governments, manages the large sea territory shared between PNG and the Torres Strait, and the fisheries within it. In the decades to follow, it would become a bone of contention, as would the fisheries across the region, because Torres Strait Islanders' desire for autonomy extends to the fishing industry, as it is the only viable economic driver for the region.

By the time I arrive in 2013, I realise I am one of the only sources of local news trying to understand and navigate a bitter ten-year stand-off between the non-Indigenous commercial fishers and the traditional inhabitant fishers, who want 100 per cent ownership of the most profitable fishery, the tropical rock lobster. They have long claimed that the tropical rock lobster has been overfished, and that their tribal fishing territory has been encroached on by non-Indigenous commercial operators.

After our lunch of lobster, and curry for the fishermen, Maluwap Nona, an Islander fishing representative, stood up at the meeting and quoted Article 3 of the *United Nations Declaration on the Rights of Indigenous People*: 'Indigenous peoples have the right to self-determination. By virtue of that right they freely determine their political status and freely pursue their economic, social and cultural development.'

Nona added, 'Any management process that is decided upon has to give respect to Torres Strait Islander fishers, it's the only way there will ever be a paradigm shift. The bureaucracy has been a failure; they haven't listened to the people managing and working with the resources. It's not about black or white; it's about self-determination and ultimately about us controlling the export market and controlling our own freedom.'

Nona had long been politically outspoken on the fishery. Back in 1998 he and another fisher, George Gesa, were in a dinghy off Mer when they sighted three other dinghies from which commercial fishermen were working. Nona and Gesa approached and told them to 'get out of our area' while brandishing a crayfish spear. They confiscated their catch and sold it to their community on Mer, but were later charged with stealing the fish with violence.

The jury acquitted them after they pleaded they had an honest claim to the fish under the Torres Strait treaty, which establishes a zone whose purpose is to acknowledge and protect the traditional livelihood and way of life of the traditional inhabitants. Nona changed his name after the victory from Ben to Maluwap, which means 'ocean fish'.

He said at the time: 'To stand against the might of government in this country and the might of the commercial fishers, you are fighting a losing battle. But my ancestors are with me to do something about what has happened over the past 100 years. Our things, our rightful things have been taken away, which is why I had to take this stand.'

In 2001 Nona was appointed as an organiser of a working committee to develop a native title sea claim to the whole Torres Strait. The TSRA's claim would cover some 44,000 square kilometres.

In 2010, after a nine-year legal battle, the TSRA made a successful native title claim to the area of sea between Cape York Peninsula and Papua New Guinea. This was the largest native title claim in Australia's history. The Federal Court judge determined that the applicants enjoyed non-exclusive native title rights to access, remain in and use their maritime areas and to access and take resources for any purposes, which included commercial purposes. However, this was later overturned on appeal by the Queensland and Commonwealth governments in the Federal Court, as there was a precedent for commercial fishing activity extinguishing native title.

It was another three years until the High Court overturned the Federal Court decision, just a couple months after I started in the job. The *Akiba vs Commonwealth High Case* was a subtle victory, as for the first time it established a precedent that native title rights extended to not only traditional activity but also commercial activity.

However, the result has been claimed as a hollow victory. Mayor Fred Gela noted that all commercial fishing activity by traditional hunters still required a state or Commonwealth fishing licence. 'This is a disappointing outcome as it merely documents what is presently, and has been for some time, the situation in the Torres Straits and provides nothing new,' Gela said. 'Torres Strait Islanders are one with their lands and seas, but I wish to see in my lifetime the laws of the Commonwealth of Australia and state of Queensland recognise and protect this spiritual partnership, in turn realising the vast, golden economic opportunities contained within for the betterment of all Torres Strait Islanders,' he said. 'My father has always said to me, if you are going to do something, do it properly or not at all.'

CHAPTER 15

HANDSHAKES AND POISONOUS SNAKES

1 February 2014

Some 165 years after Wongai butchered his fellow seaman and washed up on a beach on Badu, I too am cast onto its shores. I cadge a lift in a chopper with then LNP Assistant Minister of Aboriginal Affairs David Kempton, the Member for Cook. This is the first of many visits I will make with politicians, state and federal, to outer island communities, visits that largely seem like a waste of time and taxpayers' money – serving as no more than opportunities for some happy snaps to prove they were 'on Country', and to shoot off some rhetoric of closing the gap before maybe buying a souvenir and retreating to the capital.

The experience would always leave me feeling a little dirty, like I had whored myself to fill some column space. Media, like politics, can be a dirty business.

Late-fifties lean, tall with a slight stoop, an ex-lawyer and the son of a NSW pastoralist,

David Kempton is in his first and only term in a traditional Labor stronghold. Kempton has a wet-fish handshake and a gaze that often drifts mid-sentence to a soft, mumbling, middle-distance stare. Dressed suitably 'country' in a tieless shirt with the sleeves rolled up to look ready for hard work, Kempton looks awkward in his fine Italian leather shoes.

He declines a photo in front of the chopper. '*The Courier Mail* crucifies me in the press for government exorbitance with other photos of me getting around in choppers.'

On finding out our bird only has a solitary engine, he laments dryly: 'I'm not allowed to fly in a single-engine chopper. I'm sure my number must be coming up soon – spent so much time flying around the electorate in one of these things.'

Despite this he still darts for the front seat like an anxious schoolboy. 'You can have the front on the way back.'

The first time I met Kempton was 29 November the year before, when he opened a new wing of the TI hospital. Designed to cater to the diabetes and renal disease that are rampant in the region, it was originally rather coarsely named the Chronic Disease Centre, which then became the *Adgir Gubau Giz* Community Wellness Centre when Kempton came to officially open it. But Kempton's ribbon-cutting good-news story soon turned sour when he was greeted by angry protesters from the Kaurareg community.

Harry Seriat, son of a Kaurareg Elder, told me: 'Kaurareg Elders were not invited to participate in the original groundbreaking ceremony before construction and again at a ceremony to pay respects to ancestral spirits before demolition of the old morgue ... we were not invited to take part in the naming process. Not only were we not consulted about the choosing of the name, but a Meriam name was chosen by an Elder from Mer. This is Kaurareg Country and therefore it should have been selected consulting a Kaurareg Elder. How would Elders of Mer like it if we were to name buildings on their land?'

Kempton was on the back foot, and despite the brushed aluminium lettering mounted on the front of the building, dropped the *Adgir Gubau Giz* (Meriam for 'Our People's Journey Healing Centre'), and the centre was christened the Community Wellness Centre.

Hand on the breast of his 'floral Friday' yellow shirt, Kempton told the crowd: 'I fully recognise the concerns of the Kaurareg people and I promise we will be having a strategic meeting with them to do what wasn't done before. What we need to establish, once and for all, is a political protocol to avoid these issues in the future,' Kempton offered, but this is something neither he nor any other politician has since sought to do.

In 2016, with a notable absence of ceremony and fanfare, the centre was discreetly renamed *Dhoeynidhan Padh,* which is Kaurareg for 'Healing Place'.

To add more salt to Kempton's wounds, the new morgue in the medical centre also caused insult to Islander and Aboriginal residents alike. The morgue sat on the ground floor beneath consultation rooms, and it was deemed culturally inappropriate for people to be 'walking on top of the dead'. It took three more years and a new state government to build a new morgue, while the dead were kept in a refrigerated shipping container, which was beautified with a bit of wood veneer and potted plants when community complained it was a bit shabby and lacking in appropriate respect.

No doubt Kempton is hungry for some good press in the region. He straps in to the single-engine chopper to dart out through a hole in the monsoon clouds to Badu, and I sense there's a sleight of hand I can't quite identify.

Up until this day the people of Badu, the Badulgal, have lived on their land under a Deed of Grant in Trust (DOGIT), determined by the *Community Services (Torres Strait) Act* and the *Community Services (Aborigines) Act* of 1984, which were drawn up by the Bjelke-Petersen state government, in which a young Bob Katter was the Aboriginal and Islander Affairs minister. At the time Katter touted it as 'a refreshingly precise and forthright method of transferring control into the hands of the local people,' but subsequent Acts governing DOGITs ignored the Torres Strait Islander process of customary tenure and nullified any sovereign rights after Queensland annexed the region in 1899. They also lacked the same benefits available to citizens on ordinary freehold land, who can individually own their homes or own land for a commercial business, or draw a loan against its equity. Fifteen of the Torres Strait Island communities – excluding Mer, which was drawing battlelines for the Mabo case – and nineteen mainland Aboriginal communities came under DOGITs by 1985.

Mayor Fred Gela compared DOGIT, to the 'Dog Acts,' as a continuum of the White Australia Policy and the patchwork of patriarchal policy laid down by Sir Joh and his cronies.

Kempton waxes lyrical at the Badu handover, which occurs in the lead-up to the passing of Queensland's *Aboriginal and Torres Strait Islander*

Land (Providing Freehold) and Other Legislation Amendment Act 2014. The government is touting it as the most radical reform to Indigenous freehold in decades. Kempton calls it a move in the right direction for Indigenous people's autonomy, and says that the government 'respects your rights and self-governance'.

While the new *Freehold Act* theoretically allows for land ownership, the steps required are time-consuming and expensive. The state has not agreed to fund this or to pay for the establishment of essential services, such as sealed roads, the cost of which now falls to the Traditional Owners. There is also the potential for the Act to extinguish native title on tracts of land, opening up communities to non-Indigenous investors.

Similar freehold Acts in the United States and New Zealand have had disastrous results for their Indigenous peoples. It is part of the 'normalisation' process successive governments believe is required to improve the lot of Indigenous people, but has been criticised as being assimilationist, undermining Indigenous culture, and breaching articles Eight and Ten of the *Declaration on the Rights of Indigenous Peoples*.

The (white) anthropologist Patrick Sullivan, who has studied the engagement of Aboriginal people with the Australian Public Sector in a paper about normalisation, thinks this policy era in Indigenous affairs, which began in the 1990s, has 'turned its back on the vision of a semiautonomous, de-colonised and modernised discrete realm for Aboriginal and Torres Strait Islander people ... Normalisation is a positive goal if this means that Aboriginal people can expect a standard of living at the national norm. It is a challenge if it means that Aboriginal people are required to reflect socially, culturally and individually an idealised profile of the normal citizen established by the remote processes of bureaucratic public policy making.'

Sullivan suggests normalisation policy stems from the widespread political belief that semi-self-autonomous Indigenous communities were essentially 'failed states' due to unsuccessful government policy, abandoned infrastructure, the removal of the heavy hand of colonialist and 'maladapted Aboriginal culture, naively inadequate and ideologically ill-prepared non-Aboriginal assistance.'

Sullivan also suggests much of the failure of the 'closing the gap' policy is driven by this same normalisation ethos.

Although Kempton's 2014 Badu handover has a warm fuzzy feeling, it also reeks of normalisation policy and the one-termwonder Campbell Newman state government's slash-and-burn economic rationalist approach, in seeking to cut financial ties.

During the traditional Island dancing, as a chorus of Creole fills the community hall, Kempton leans into my ear and says, 'Aren't they beautiful?' It is beautiful – it's genuinely uplifting every time I'm graced to witness it – but Kempton's words sound detached, almost cheap and nasty.

Kempton later tells me he believes the Freehold Bill is the first step to greater autonomy. 'The magic of this is the community decides and is in control of their own land, and this represents the death of paternity, it doesn't happen in mainstream communities, so it shouldn't happen here either. There is some concern the land will sold off, but it is a free market economy and it will sort itself out. Next we need to shift the economy over, there are a lot of services and infrastructure that we provide that the community could do for itself. This is the first step to allowing these communities to becoming more normalised like the rest of society.'

Mayor Gela, whose constituents in the outer island communities of the Torres Strait were the most affected by DOGITs, is more pragmatic in his support of the *Freehold Act*, saying, 'at least that choice is going to be there for any individual who wants to enter the realm of achieving the great Australian dream of owning their own home and establish their own businesses.'

Despite the introduction of the *Freehold Act*, Kempton continued to struggle in the public arena. Two months after his Badu junket, *The Courier Mail* declares him to be the MP who has spoken the least number of times in Parliament in 2014 – a paltry nineteen occasions.

With an election on the horizon, ally Warren Entsch sent Kempton up on 1 July to participate in the Coming of the Light re-enactment that Enstch had been in year before. Kempton's portrayal of missionary MacFarlane, however, lacked Entsch's high drama. Kempton appeared distracted, often gazing off into the middle distance, and fidgeted with his fine Italian leather shoes during Bishop Mabo's fire-and-brimstone sermon.

The Torres Strait was not kind to Kempton, particularly during the Coming of the Light. A Customs zodiac was called in to help push his longboat to shore as the currents and winds threatened to whip him past his beach landing and into the churning washing machine kicked up the angry Kaurareg god Waubin.

Perhaps it was an omen of Campbell Newman's shock loss of government in February 2015, in which Kempton's seat was part of the collateral damage. He lost his seat to Indigenous ALP candidate Billy Gordon.

I even had Bob Katter bound into my office in his ten-gallon Stetson, all white hair and toothy grin, in the lead-up to that state election, looking for a foothold in one of the country's largest electorates. A larger-than-life Katter dragged in a meek Lee Marriott, a young Cape York farmer with 'Vote 1' Katter Party posters under his arm. Marriot, not yet thirty, wore a Stetson too, although his was still dripping after the wind blew it from his head into the sea, where it was rescued by a couple of fishermen.

'Would you be able to put these posters up for me?' Marriott stammered.

'That probably wouldn't be appropriate, mate – might be seen as the press taking sides,' I said diplomatically.

'Sit down, boy,' Katter boomed to Marriott, while giving me a bone-crushing handshake and the charismatic smile of a sociopath.

'I've got an economic plan for the Torres Strait,' Katter croaked, spreading his arms wide in a Jesus Christ pose. 'Coconuts. All the young people, it's all they want – coconut oil, coconut this, coconut that. The Torres Strait could become the coconut capital of the world! There's even an island called Coconut Island, let's put a plantation there.'

Katter's insalubrious yet infectious grin stretches across his face. I look at Marriott, who's looking at Katter's every move. Marriott figures he should smile too.

'But Coconut Island is tiny and it's disappearing into the sea – there's less of it each year,' I said.

Without so much as a flinch Katter segues into a delicious diatribe about how much the bush had been neglected by those city folk and how gays and greenies were collectively wrecking the country, along with all the refugees. I tell him my wife and I are both green and immigrants, to which Katter winks at me as if I'm being ironic. With another bone-crushing handshake he nods towards me and booms at Marriott, 'I like this man's style. If you ever need a job, give me a call.'

But Marriott, like Kempton, was swept away in the changing political tide at the polls a month later.

Incensed by his loss, Kempton lashed out at the media and the unions. He posted vitriol on Facebook titled 'not sour grapes' and accused Gordon's union mates 'such as nurses, teachers and Ergon workers all paid government employees who for weeks have had a concerted campaign of despicable lies to scare Indigenous voters. Things like "LNP will take your welfare benefit off you, cut your power, close the hospital, sell the school, take your job and cut your pay". All intentional lies and against the electoral laws.'

Kempton's successor, the new Member for Cook Billy Gordon, as well as the new Minister for Housing and Public Works, Leeanne Enoch, were the first Indigenous members of the ALP to be elected in Queensland. Shortly after Premier Annastacia Palaszczuk took office with her minority Labor government, a smear campaign began against Billy Gordon, which Gordon suggested had been instigated by Kempton and Entsch. The petty criminal past of his youth was exposed, as well as some outstanding tax returns and unpaid child endowment payments to an ex-wife. He was also accused of domestic violence, so in all it was sufficient for Premier Palaszczuk to drop him like a hot potato. He subsequently resigned from the Labor Party and remained in the seat as an independent.

However, Gordon's ousting from government transformed him from a backbencher to holding the balance of power, along with the two Australian Katter Party members who also won seats at the state election. But instead of exploiting this position, Gordon went to ground, especially after allegations that he was sexting women photos of his 'private member' – a claim he did not deny to me, only saying on the record that he acknowledged: 'This is not becoming of a public figure; it is very unsavoury.'

Gordon eventually emerged and I found myself again an island-hopping media whore, watching as he dry-shaved with a razor in the seat in front of me, using his phone's selfie mode as a mirror.

Sipping a couple of beers and swatting sandflies during an overnight outer island visit to Iama Island, I had a chance to yarn with Gordon beyond the politicking.

Iama, in the Central Island cluster, was the territory of the fierce warrior Kebisu, who was said to have ruled the seas in the late eighteenth century with a fleet of outrigger canoes. Iama was also the home of the island's first London Missionary Society teacher, whose great-grandson was Getano Lui senior, one of the leaders behind the Border No Change movement and the formation of the Torres Strait Treaty. His son, Getano Lui junior, is a political stalwart who continues his father's legacy of pushing for regional autonomy.

'White guilt champions black mediocrity,' Gordon tells me, in discussing how the cycle of government normalisation policy grooms Indigenous bureaucrats for positions of power, where they end up doing no more than perpetuating the problem on fat pay cheques. Despite a shaky start, Gordon seems earnest in his desire to better the lot of First Nations people. But he doesn't contest his seat at the 2017 election, when Cynthia Lui, Getano Lui junior's daughter, stands as the ALP candidate for Cook. She becomes the first Torres Strait Islander to gain a seat in Parliament.

As a revolving door of politicians comes through the region, as I join them on their junkets, the head-nodding, the furrowed brow of concern, the chequered shirtsleeves rolled up 'ready for hard yakka', regardless of the colour of their political stripes, it just feels like nothing more than an opportunity to be seen by the constituents while being a voyeur of the exotic, a footnote in a future memoir reflecting back on adventures on the frontier.

Riding on their coattails and thumbing lifts in their charter planes in return for some favourable press, I am also a voyeur, gazing over the wide expanse of the gap that each successive government fails to close, noted here in my own memoir. But the longer I live in the Strait, the more embedded I become and the more I want to make this not my memoir but the Torres Strait's, as a way to offer a mirror to the nation.

Another FIFO junket really drives this home, when newly appointed Federal Assistant Minister for Agriculture and Water Resources Anne Ruston visits some of the islands. Her portfolio includes the region's politically charged fishing industry.

While Ruston doesn't have the chequered shirt or the Stetson hat, she has donned the RM Williams boots, standard for farmers and workers of the land – and politicians going bush. I realise on the runway at Horn Island on our way to Mer that she is just another political tourist.

'Pretty cool to be getting to go to Mer, home of native title and where Eddie Mabo is buried,' I say.

Ruston pushes her aviator Ray Bans down her nose and looks over the top. 'Really, is Eddie Mabo buried there? Are we able to go and have a look?'

'Well, you have to be invited by Elders...'

I'm not sure if Ruston hears me as the whir of the engines grows louder as the plane starts to taxi down the runway; I'm not sure if her reply, as she pushed back up her aviators, was meant for me, or if it is just her thinking out loud. 'We give these people so much.'

When we arrive on Mer, Ruston is surprised that there is no welcoming committee on the runway.

A dilapidated ute, more rust than metal, squeaks to a halt. Under her breath, the Senator says to us, 'Imagine if that was our car.'

A dreadlocked Islander leans out the window. 'Wanna lift?'

With no other option but to walk, we climb in, me riding with a bunch of old coconuts in the back tray, which is punctured with rust holes that blur with the blacktop beneath.

At a community meeting of fishers Ruston furrows her brow and nods as they express their concerns and frustrations.

'I haven't come out here to talk, but to listen,' she says earnestly, while her two assistants thumb their phones, huffing at the poor reception, without a notebook between them to jot down the constituents' points.

Bob Kaigey, a young Mer fisherman and up-and-coming political leader, says that while he appreciates the minister taking the trouble to visit, 'Every time the government comes through here we ask the same things and we are told there is no magic wand. Governments go in and go out and nothing changes, we are not getting anywhere. When will there be change? There should be documents of what we have said before, but we say the same things. We have been fighting for this for decades, we are losing our Elders and still nothing is happening.'

Ruston nods sympathetically while her two assistants continue to fondle their phones.

After the meeting Ruston is shown around the community, where she meets Celuia Mabo.

'Hi, who are you?' Ruston says, reaching out for a handshake.

'Celuia Mabo, daughter of Eddie Mabo.'

Ruston looks blank.

'Eddie Mabo, the pioneer of native title,' Celuia says curtly.

I step away, cringing as Ruston squirms some response about the great contribution her father made to the country.

A fisherman leans towards my ear. 'These politicians come out here with their handshakes, which turn into poisonous snakes.'

Ruston is then taken to a backyard fishing operation, where one of the fishermen opens a lid to show how they salt the bêche-de-mer before it's sent off to Chinese buyers, but he opens the wrong bin, revealing instead a catch of even more lucrative yet illegal endangered sandfish.

There's a nervous chuckle from everyone bar the minister as the fisherman closes the lid and opens the right one, like a street tout's three-cup shuffle. Ruston appears blissfully unaware of either the error or the subterfuge.

En route from Mer back to TI, we arch around Warrior Reef, the fishing territory shared with PNG, coming in low for a look at what may be bêche-de-mer poachers, whose banana boats retreat back to the PNG coastline on our second flyover. An ex-pilot herself, Ruston is given the tiller for a bit of a joyride, titillating for her – a white-knuckle ten minutes for the rest of us.

It was one of many white knuckle flights I experienced throughout my tenure as *Torres News* editor, from landing in a little single engine Cessna in 67km cross winds, or mid-monsoon skidding to a stop on the wet blacktop of Mer's runway, one of the nation's shortest, or as on my very last day on the job in December 2019 returning from Erub with Entsch. He invited me along for the tombstone unveiling of the 'grandfather of Torres Strait independence' George Mye. Entsch, his wife Yolanda and I were all dozing in the afternoon sun after a long day of ceremony and feasting, when for one sickening second, the engines cut out, the continual drone abruptly stopped to a deathly silence as we felt our stomachs rise to our throats. After the longest second of my life the engines spluttered back to life, I looked back Entsch who was clutching the seat in front. We shared a gaze only those who have cheated death know, 'fucking geezus,' Entsch growled with a grin.

It reminded me of that first flight with a politician back in 2014 with Kempton, after the official ceremony of his government's *Freehold Act* on Badu. The monsoon had started to close in again around Badu, so after a flurry of handshakes, and wolfing down a couple of cray tails, Kempton and I, the mild white men on Badu, dashed back to the chopper as black clouds swallow up the horizon and our window of opportunity to return to TI started to close.

He graciously let me sit in the front for our return trip, the end of my maiden political FIFO junket.

Looking at the dark horizon he said: 'As long as the number of take-offs matches the number of landings I'm okay with flying, I guess.'

Maybe aware the political tide was already turning against him, he lamented to me about something Bongo told him at the medical centre opening a couple of months earlier. Bongo, a mountain of an Islander man who often comes to my office booming his anger at the injustices faced by his people, originally supported Kempton, throwing his weight behind his campaign in the Strait. However, he told Kempton in November in 2013 during the protests at the medical centre's opening that he'd 'rather speak to the horse's mouth than the horse's arse'.

Kempton sighed as the pilot strapped us in and closed the perspex door. 'When I look in the mirror at night I ask myself, am I really all those things they said I am?'

Kempton needed to get to back to Cairns for the opening celebrations of the Chinese Year of the Horse. I wondered if there he would be regarded as the mouth this time and not the posterior.

CHAPTER 16

MIND THE GAP

A dark and stormy night, 26 March 2014.

Lightning strikes around the small dinghy buffeted by gale force winds and three-metre waves, lost at sea in the middle of the night. Phoebe Pilot clutches her three children, aged seven to twelve, as she recites the prayer of last rites.

The dinghy struggles, punching through wind against tide as the sea becomes rougher and the currents stronger. Unable to activate their emergency EPIRB beacon and way out of mobile phone range, they are at the mercy of the elements.

Phoebe's husband worries the dinghy will flip and drown his young family. There are no life jackets on board.

When the family left their home on the Top Eastern island of Erub that morning, sea conditions were calm, but as they pass the coral cay island of Poruma, the half waypoint of their 200 kilometre journey, things deteriorate – the dinghy's outboard labours throughout the night, drying up nearly all their fuel reserves.

A rosy-fingered dawn stretches up from the horizon, and with what little fuel they have left, Pheobe's family just make it to the island of Nagie before their outboard splutters to a halt. It's some 50 kilometres short, north-east of their destination of Thursday Island.

With a mobile phone with a dying battery and a weak, intermittent signal, Phoebe calls for help and they are rescued later that afternoon.

As horrific as this is, it's the second time in six weeks Phoebe's family has nearly been lost at sea. The first time the battery on their GPS failed en route, leaving them to guess their direction. They ended up at Mount Adolphus Island, 50 kilometres east of Thursday Island when they realised they were lost and activated their EPRIB after a night sleeping in their dinghy.

Why did Phoebe's family make this life-or-death dash across what's considered by some as the most treacherous waters in the world?

To visit the dentist, Thursday Island having the only practice in the whole region.

A few days after her near-death voyage I chat with Phoebe on the beach just down from my office, near her dinghy tethered to the foreshore rocks.

She is stout and looks bookish in her half-rimmed turtle-shell glasses. For a mother of nine children she looks no older than mid 30s and speaks, like many Islanders, so softly it's almost inaudible. My first impression is that she is stoic.

'In the ten years I have lived on Erub, I have never seen a dentist come out and when I speak to Queensland Health they tell me I have to go to Thursday Island.'

With airfares charging around $550 one way, per person, transporting a family for basic medical needs, such as dental work, becomes prohibitively expensive. Even taking the treacherous dinghy option still costs Phoebe's family nearly $500 in fuel alone.

'Both me and my husband work casually, so when we take time out to do this, neither of us are getting paid, so it adds further strain upon us. Many people with dental issues on Erub cut their gums with glass to release the blood and reduce swelling, they even try to pull loose teeth themselves, as they simply can't afford to make the trip to TI to visit the dentist.

'But I was not brought up like that. I want my children to be able to gain access to the dentist like any other kid in Australia.

'When you are a parent and your children need medical help you do whatever it takes, but then when we have to risk our lives to do it and they look to you for protection when we're in trouble on the water, it's a terrible feeling.

'It's not good enough.

'Queensland Health told me that they are "working on" the dental shortage on Erub, but I wonder how long that will take,' she said.

Publishing this story causes Queensland Health to scramble into damage control, realising it's not a good look to have a family twice nearly die at sea just to visit the dentist. Acting Chief Executive Officer at Torres Strait and Northern Peninsula Hospital and Health Service Philip Davies admitted it's a 'less-than-ideal situation.'

'Unfortunately there is a long standing distinction between one's mouth and the rest of one's body, so the rule is only in a medical emergency can a person be evacuated by air,' he said. 'So only if a problem that started out in your mouth became an acute medical issue can a medical evacuation occur,' he said.

That's bureaucrat-speak for they won't fly patients into TI for dental work unless it becomes a life threatening infection, but realising how unpalatable that sounds, Davis also promises to bring in an expert to review and maybe resurrect the 'dental drover?' A $780,000 white elephant, the dental drover is a mobile dental clinic on a back of a truck designed specifically to be driven onto a barge and service the outer islands – it's never been used and sits in a vacant lot since its unceremonious arrival nearly two years earlier. Apparently a flat battery rendered it unmovable for the first six months, needing a specialist to repair it, only to then discover the undercarriage clearance was too low for it to drive up the ramp to the barge. An embarrassing oversight indicative of the bureaucratic blundering that often occurs in the region, and a delicious source of ribbing for the *Torres News*, where I christen it 'Queensland Health's expensive garden gnome?'

Shortly after, during a visit by Minister of Indigenous Affairs Senator Nigel Scullion, I collar him for a response on the issue.

An ex-fisherman that lived in the Torres Straits in the 1990s, Scullion has the swagger of a cowboy, all cock-sure and confident as he shoots down Queensland Health with: 'It is completely unacceptable that people in the Torres Strait don't get access to dental care.'

The screws further tighten when the review finds that preexisting, but never used, dental clinics on the five outer islands of Erub, Iama, Warraber, Moa and Mabuiag could be made operational, and not just used as storerooms where expensive equipment gathers dust and rust under boxes of discarded paperwork.

Dental reviewer Dr Ralph Neller tells me if Queensland Health was serious about resolving this, they need a short-termto-interim solution 'to start getting things going', and then a more permanent solution put in place.

Nurses in the outer island health clinics told Neller they 'desperately need dentists to come out here.'

The stop-gap results in dental patients being flown in to the clinic on TI from all the outer island communities, at Queensland Health's expense, to remove the embarrassing backlog of glass-chewing, abscess-ridden patients. Then after a couple of years pushing pens and counting beans, a new mobile Dental Chair starts rotating throughout the outer island communities, finally providing access to a level of dental service similar to the rest of the country.

This dental debacle not only highlights our failure as a nation to resolve our relationship with our Indigenous people, but also reveals a more subtle and insidious impact, that of institutional racism. The Anti-Discrimination Commission Queensland (ADCQ) defines institutional racism as: 'a form of racism which is structured into political and social institutions. It occurs when organisations, institutions or governments discriminate, either deliberately or indirectly, against certain groups of people to limit their rights.'

It's a layering of prejudiced government policy over the years that is incremental and, like leaving a frog in water brought slowly to the boil, is almost unnoticeable. It wasn't until a plain brown envelope was slipped under my door three years later that I gain an understanding of an issue most white mainstream society has no idea even exists – it's a photocopy of a single page of the ADCQ report on the issue, which was meant only for Queensland Health's upper echelons and certainly not for the media. The single page was a report card showing all sixteen of Queensland's hospital and health services were identified as having high levels of institutional racism, of which ten were rated as 'extreme'.

Bongo, long since pissed off at what he saw was an acute failing by government on many levels, had with some others in the community formed the Social Justice and Human Rights Advocacy Group. I ask him his thoughts on the report.

'The report shows the failing of the whole mainstream thinking behind public health systems,' Bongo booms. 'It is a merry-go-round where we audit public health systems to determine whether or not the systems are doing what they are supposed to do, and if the systems are treating us with the same equity as all other Australian citizens. We are beyond being sick and tired of the times we have had to knock on the Queensland Premier's and the Health Minister's door, only to be turned away with trivial and meaningless excuses while our people are dying from lack of appropriate health care.'

This subtle form of racism only adds to the mistrust many Indigenous people have of government, where in health it may mean a reluctance to even visit a doctor. But institutional racism infiltrates not only health but all layers of government bureaucracy. ADCQ Commissioner Kevin Cocks AM later tells me: 'People need to understand what institutional racism is, it's about the practices and policies that are part of the institution.

'It doesn't necessarily mean people who work there are racist, it might be unconscious bias. It's about dismantling those institutional policies or practices, and the best way to do that is through your governance and your structures, by bringing highly skilled Indigenous people into the workforce to resolve the problem. It's very important to have the voice of lived experience of Aboriginal and Torres Strait Islanders in collaboration in the reform of what was identified within the audit, and it's going to take a number of reiterations, especially when you think of how long Queensland has been a state. It's going to take a long time to undo the institutional racism that exists.'

After being leaked the page of the ADCQ report, I was given the whole transcript, which stated that:

...there appears to be no dearth of good health policies to improve the health and life expectancy of Indigenous Australians ... the problem appears to be more a case of the slow up-take and implementation of those policies by public hospitals and health services at a local level, and a lack of accountability mechanisms, reinforced by legislation and regulation, to make them do so.

The findings of this report are unacceptable for contemporary health service provision in Australia.

The lesson to be learned from this report is that if Aboriginal and Torres Strait Islander health policies are not reinforced in the relevant legislation, then those primarily charged with implementing them, namely the HHS boards and their executive management teams, as this audit demonstrates, will invariably ignore them.

The report also highlighted the lack of accountability of Closing the Gap funding, so while there may be grand ideas, nobody was checking if the money was being spent where it should be.

Cocks told me: 'As far as Closing the Gap, it needs to be an important objective of all governments and it will take courage by all parties to work collaboratively together. From a human rights perspective I think everyone in Australia understands that health issues for Aboriginal and Torres Strait Islander people are needed to be addressed to close the gap, it's a huge gap and it needs to be closed.'

Apart from the coverage in the *Torres News* of the leaked report, and an article I wrote for SBS online, no other news outlet covered the story after I broke it, showing either how unpalatable the subject is or, more likely, there was a care factor of zero.

About the same time as Bongo leaked me the ADCQ report, a report by Victoria Tauli-Corpuz – the UN's Human Rights Council Special Rapporteur – came out after her visit to Australia, which included Thursday Island, where she met with Bongo and his advocacy group. She appeared a meek and mouse-like, middle-aged Philippine woman, who viewed me with a guarded disdain, despite my warm introduction by Bongo. Can't blame her really, I must have personified everything that was wrong with Australia – a white male being a prominent voice for the region's mostly Indigenous population. It couldn't have helped when I said, while taking a photo of Bongo and his advocacy group standing in the shade of a mango tree, 'It's no good, you're all too black.'

Looking up from my camera I realise my faux pas, 'I mean the shadow, can you step forward? Of course you can never be too black.'

After a pregnant pause that lingered for eternity, Bongo chuckled.

Tauli-Corpuz however, is anything but meek. A champion of Indigenous people worldwide, on a Philippine Government's 'terrorist' hit list, she had no qualms ripping into the Australian Government in her report of her visit when she said:

...deeply disturbing the numerous reports on the prevalence of racism against Aboriginal and Torres Strait Islander Peoples. Racism manifests itself in different ways, ranging from public stereotyped portrayals as violent criminals, welfare profiteers and poor parents, to discrimination in the administration of justice.

Aboriginal doctors and patients informed the Special Rapporteur about their experiences of racism within the medical sector and their reluctance to seek services from mainstream medical providers...

...There are also more subtle elements of racism stemming from the failure to recognize the legacy of two centuries of systemic marginalization. The mainstream education system contains inadequate

components on Aboriginal and Torres Strait Islander history and the impact of colonization. The non-recognition of the socioeconomic exclusion and the impact of intergenerational trauma on indigenous peoples continue to undermine reconciliation efforts. In order to truly recognize the situation of Aboriginal and Torres Strait Islanders today, there needs to be much greater public awareness of their perspectives on history and the consequences of past policies and legislation, including the long-term damage and rupture of social bonds caused by the forced removal and institutionalization of their children.

While Australia has adopted numerous policies aiming to address the socioeconomic disadvantage of Aboriginal and Torres Strait Islander peoples, the failure to respect their rights to self-determination and to full and effective participation is alarming. The compounded effect of those policies has contributed to the failure to deliver on the targets in the areas of health, education and employment in the 'Closing the Gap' strategy and has contributed to aggravating the escalating incarceration and child removal rates of Aboriginal and Torres Strait Islanders.

Aboriginal and Torres Strait Islanders also told the Special Rapporteur about their feelings of powerlessness, loss of culture and lack of control over their lives.

An endless string of top down, patriarchal politics has disempowered a demographic that, over the short span of less than a dozen generations, has had to adjust to the seismic shift that colonial encroachment has had to a way of life unchanged for millennia. Even three generations ago, faded sepia photographs of Islander men in the pearling heyday show a population lean and muscle-ripped, whose vitality often led to long lifespans.

Diets were low in fats and refined carbohydrates and high in fish protein, while the high energy outputs of gardening, hunting with 'whap' spears and fishing from outrigger canoes provided plenty of exercise. But healthy habits started to change when the whitefellas introduced the devil's drink and tobacco; then with the onset of WWII came the widespread availability of flour, sugar and tins of bully beef. The outboards and dinghies replaced outriggers, cars replaced walking, and the supermarket replaced gardening. And like the rest of Australia since World War II, obesity levels rose.

The world-wide correlation between poverty and obesity is starkly apparent in the Torres Strait and other Indigenous communities, where calorie rich, nutritionally poor processed foods are cheaper than lean meats and fresh fruit and vegetables, partly due to increased freight costs.

In addition, Islanders typically earn twenty-five percent less than the average Australian.

Today Indigenous Australians are three times more likely to get diabetes than their urban counterparts, and those in remote communities twice as likely. Like many Indigenous populations around the world, diabetes, obesity, heart and kidney disease are rampant. I often see Islander kids with a pack of potato chips and a litre of soft drink for lunch, parents who routinely give toddlers chocolate and lollies wherever they ask, and Elders with ankles bandaged from diabetic sores loading up plates of pan-fried scones and damper at community functions. It's also common to see people piling buffet food onto plates at community events to take home – it's part of the celebration process for Islanders, ensuring the rest of the family at home also gets a feed.

The emotional impact of food insecurity on generations struggling to put food on the table has triggered the feast or famine response, where people become conditioned to get a feed wherever they can, no matter the quality of the food. The irony being that Islanders know how to have fun. They belly-laugh, eat, sing and dance, despite many living at or below the poverty line, while white Australia gets richer, meaner and more unhappy.

When then Health Minister Tony Abbott came to Thursday Island in the noughties, he said that Islanders should do some exercise and eat healthier.

'How the hell can they do that when a cabbage costs ten bucks, when they can feed the family with hot chips for the same money?' Senior blustered over the phone as he told me the story. 'I told the bastard as much when he said that – the idiot's got no idea.'

This disconnect, this gap between two worlds, this failure to fully appreciate cultural ways and cultural appropriateness is ever-constantly present, from the mispronunciation of a tribal group during an 'acknowledgement to Country', to the design and naming of the new medical facility, the Community Wellness Centre on TI.

Not only has the cost of living added to the burden of Islanders, but so has the cost of dying. A taboo subject, Sorry Business has become big business for those servicing Indigenous communities, from unscrupulous funeral funds hard selling expensive policies to grandiose tombstones families feel obliged to buy. Transporting the dead to the only functioning mortuary on TI is also an expense that falls on families from the outer islands.

This all gave me plenty more cannon fodder to fire at Queensland Health, also fuelled by the concerns of Barry Williams the region's only funeral director. Close to retiring, Barry worried about what will happen when he shuffles on and leaves a vacuum that can only be filled by more expensive funeral parlours from Cairns. Always with a suntanned smile, and always in a sun-bleached, threadbare singlet and board shorts, Barry doesn't have two brass razoos to rub together. He drives a clapped-out early model Toyota Camry and his 1970s hearse is on its last legs. Barry does too many jobs on the cheap and a few for free, especially after families have to pay for plane charters – the compassion has made him world weary.

Up until 2005, Queensland Health footed the bill of transporting the deceased to where they are prepared for burial and necessary paper work is signed off. Since then, families struggle to pay charter flights on top of funeral costs. It's a cost that, if Barry doesn't absorb it, the local Indigenous council often does.

Mayor Fred Gela told me: 'We have had situations where patients have been transported by Queensland Health down to Cairns to see a specialist, where during that process they pass away, and the family have had to foot the bill to get them back home, because they didn't die in the hospital. It's ridiculous.

'We had another situation where an Elder became ill on an outer island and went to the Queensland Health medical centre, where a medivac was ordered, but the patient died before the helicopter arrived. The helicopter then refused to transport the body back to Thursday Island Morgue for bureaucratic reasons, even though it flew straight back empty. That cost the family thousands of dollars for no reason.'

Again, with Barry's insider information and a year's worth of defaming stories, I was able to help pressure and shame Queensland Health into discussions to address the cost of dying problem. While they still don't foot the bill of transporting the dead to Thursday Island, they did finally agree to establish morgues in the outer island communities. However, that then failed to move any further as Fred Gela's council stalled, much to Barry's frustration.

'It's such a taboo subject, nobody wanted to talk about it, but thanks to you at least we're doing that now,' Barry said one afternoon as he stopped by my office with a steaming hot banana damper, his wife's speciality. Their way of saying 'thanks.'

When the new morgue finally opened three years later, giving me the delicious headline, 'New morgue, better later than never', Cr Frazier Nai was standing next me as Barry gave a speech ripping into everyone from Queensland Health to council for stalling with outer island morgues.

Avoiding the elephant in the room, I whisper into Frazier's ear.

'So is it business as usual now at TSIRC, you guys have been sworn in again, haven't you?'

'Yeah, but we do it a little differently to other councils, we have a smoking ceremony where all the Elders stand in a row, and we have to walk past them as they swear at us for all the mistakes we're going to do over the next term – it's pretty full on.'

'Wow.'

Then Frazier gives me his signature shit-eating grin, and I know I have fallen for another of his wind ups.

While there's always going to be speed bumps with mob taking care for their own, all indications are that grassroots autonomy is still the better way to go. The government's impotent Closing the Gap strategy to reduce disadvantage among Aboriginal and Torres Strait Islander people with respect to life expectancy, child mortality, access to early childhood education, educational achievement, and employment outcomes in twenty-five years has failed on nearly all fronts since inception in 2008.

'Growing our own' has been the grassroots outcry from many Indigenous leaders as the only way forward, and although still statistically under-represented in universities, there is a slow growing pool of well-educated, experienced Indigenous professionals.

Dr Jackie Huggins AM, Indigenous author, activist and Co-Chair of National Congress of Australia's First Peoples, has called for the need of indigenous medicos in Indigenous community medical centres to help bridge the cultural divide and bring about real shifts in lifestyle – and she's not the only one to see the intrinsic value in this common-sense approach.

'I think it's imperative ... our people, who are health practitioners in their own fields and communities, be able to transcend the barriers and do the most culturally appropriate work,' Huggins told ABC's *The World Today* in 2017.

'To give an example, when [my uncle] went into a health service he was so happy that there was an Indigenous doctor there. He said, "my spirit is healing already from just entering that health service and seeing an Indigenous doctor there.

'...the situation is still the same. It's getting worse, really, and that's a sad reflection on Australia as a very rich nation in terms of Aboriginal people – we are the sickest and the poorest, and the least housed, job-wise. Every social statistic in our country is with Aboriginal people at the lowest ebb.'

In her speech at the Redfern Statement Breakfast at Parliament House, Canberra, on 14 February, 2017, after the handing down of the ninth Close the Gap report that revealed failures on six out of seven fronts, Huggins said: '...we have come to a time where we cannot continue with the cycles of failure.'

Not for the first time, she called for 'A new relationship where we have a seat at the table when policies are developed ... and for Aboriginal and Torres Strait Islander people to be equal partners in decisions made about us.'

Huggins later lamented how the government has failed to listen to them and how there is a 'stop start' effect from the constant revolving door of bureaucrats, where the incoming have to be brought back up to speed, so nothing really happens, or happens really slowly.

'...we have the car but we don't have the wheels. And I think that's the case for a lot of our organisations that are attempting to get into those issues.'

My sledging and shaming campaign of the Torres Strait dental debacle not only helped turn the tide on dental health, but also garnered me a couple of awards, one from the community and from my peers, where I bumped off the ABC and *The Australian* for the best Indigenous Issues Reporting mantle at the 2014 Queensland Clarion Awards. A small victory for a people that only wanted what the rest of us take for granted, my dental scoop profiteered me kudos, commending my 'crusading journalism on a local scale.'

It was all drenched in *gratis* red wine and whisky at a black-tie affair in Brisbane's Southbank, where few hundred newshounds whinged about the collapse of the Fourth Estate and the rise of social media banality until the carpet was sticky and the bar closed. I joined the stragglers who continued to howl into the abyss until the witching hour at a string of closing nightclubs, until I was alone at the casino, the only place still serving a stiff drink.

Walking it off over the bridge back to Southbank, to pick up my carry-on to do my dash for the early redeye run back north, dawn's rosy fingers pushed shards of morning light into my eggshell mind until my temples throbbed. I fumbled into the breast pocket of the now creased in all the wrong places and dank-smelling suit I've worn for the first time since becoming *Torres News*' editor, and found the 'spear' my PNG smuggler friend had given me at the Torres Hotel a few months before. The cigarette of

PNG bush tobacco was hand-rolled in newspaper, whose text seemed to be *Tok Pisin* or PNG creole. Not a smoker, I promised myself a victory puff if I won, so I cadged a light off the coffee cart at the end of the bridge, sat on the kerb sipping my fortifying double-shot latte while acrid bitter smoke tightened my chest and infused my blood with a dizzying double shot of nicotine, in my own private smoking ceremony.

As the spoils of my dental *coup d'état* subsided in the unforgiving light of day, I was left with the nagging feeling of how it was all bullshit, how everything was completely and utterly meaningless, self-congratulatory crap. I was no better than the other vultures and hyenas picking at the kill of lions. My career may be gaining a belt notch, but the gap between the Indigenous and non-Indigenous Australians was still failing to close, and I was just another 'white cunt'.

CHAPTER 17

THE ZOO

A sunny August afternoon, 2015

Buffeting across a squally sea in a water taxi, Pedro Stephen, mayor of most of the inner islands of *Kaiwalagai* clustered around Thursday Island known as Torres Shire, smiles at me.

The fully enclosed ten metre, yellow twin-hull runabout, called *Sea Cat*, has rows of plastic chairs welded to the deck, which we bounce about in as we return from Horn Island Airport to TI. It is the end of a long day flying out and back to some of the outer island communities.

The small twin engine Islander had buzzed noisily over endless ribbons of shimmering reefs, where the occasional massive cargo ship, one of 4,000 or so that pass through the Straits annually, is dwarfed, not by the 1,000 feet of sky between us but more by the great expanse of brilliant blue the extends to the gentle convex of the horizon. Inching along the miners' highways (the routes of mainly commodity vessels) of the Great North East and Adolphus Channels, the white wakes of these slow-moving vessels resemble snail trails.

There is a profound sense of the region's remoteness and vastness to be gained from bouncing around the outer islands: *Gudamaluilgal,* the hunting islands or Top Western group of Boigu and Saibai, swampy mudflats that eyeball the Western Province coast of PNG just a couple of kilometres to the north, where banana boats dart back and forth; and Dauan Island, the small granite pyramid that represents the most northernmost outpost of the Great Dividing Range: *Meriam,* the Eastern Islands or gardening islands, a ring of extinct volcanoes of Mer, Erub and Ugar with rich red soils sitting on the edge of the continental shelf in the Coral Sea; *Kulkalgal,* the fishing islands or Central Islands of low lying sandy coral cays of Poruma, Warraber, Masig and the basaltic outcrop of Iama; lastly: *Malvilgal,* the Inner Western Islands of Badu, Moa and Mabuiag, the midway point of the Straits, high granite hills that represent the remnant of the land bridge to PNG swallowed up 7,000 years ago. Each island cluster also has its own variations of cultural practice and language.

It's still uncomfortably warm as sea spray and the late afternoon light streams in through the open door at the bow of the water taxi as it banks left and right, weaving between sandbars and reefs invisible beneath the churning water.

'That's one of the meanings of the *Dhari*, it represents the whitecaps,' Pedro pipes over the whine of the two 225 Mercury outboards. He's pointing out at the white sea foam on the crest of the waves, whipped up by the wind.

Dhari is the Meriam Mir word from the Eastern Islands meaning 'headdress' (in the central and western islands where Kala Lagaw Ya is spoken, the headdress is called *Dhoeri*).

The *Dhari* has become the icon of the Torres Strait, appearing in the centre of their green and blue flag. It appears on everything from clothing and tattoos to business logos, including in the masthead of the *Torres News*.

Customarily *Dharis* are only worn and made by males for ceremonial purposes, and the designs vary from island to island. Traditionally they are made from frigate bird and Torres Strait pigeon feathers but may now be made from heavy cardboard, plywood, chicken feathers and cane.

'You can imagine how dramatic it would've looked with the warriors dancing at night with their *Dharis* glowing white in the light of the camp fire. Reckon it have been bloody scary,' Pedro chuckles.

Short and stout, and in his early 60s, Pedro is immaculately dressed in a silk floral shirt and a round polished pearl shell hanging around his neck, symbolising his status as a community Elder.

Pedro is the longest-serving living mayor in Queensland and one of the first Indigenous ones. With two decades in the job, Pedro and mayor are synonymous for many in the region. Also a very pious man, Pedro was a preacher before he became a politician and consequently he was also a great orator to quote for copy. There was always a hint of fire and brimstone in his speeches, regardless of whether he was addressing heads of State in front of the whole community, or just a pedestrian opening of a newly constructed zebra crossing to half a dozen onlookers.

And he never swore, so the utterance of the word 'bloody' to me is more than just a casual aside, but represents a watershed. I feel like I am being imbued with sacred knowledge, while letting me have one foot into the fold.

With over a couple of years on the job, it's a feeling that's been on the brew for a while, I suspect, as my editorial reveals I'm trying to give a fair representation of the Islander's side of issues. I first noticed it when Pedro started asking, like a doting uncle, if I had eaten, making sure I had grabbed a feed at the various functions as I race around with my notebook and camera.

It seems to be happening by osmosis throughout the community as well, where I am increasingly called *Bala* (brother), even '*Bala* Aaron,' rather than a curt, 'hey *Torres News*.' But I have never been told overtly that Islanders are starting to warm to me. As one Islander said, 'Whites talk too much but does too little, we don't need to talk so much, it's annoying.'

Being a 'white' man, editing the only newspaper of a 'black' community puts me in a unique and at times awkward position. While everyone treats the Island journo with a cautious, atarms-length friendliness, I have felt till now as if I was too white for the blacks and too 'black' for the whites.

TI, the region's hub where every State and Federal government agency has its offices, has become essentially an apartheid society. The glut of bureaucrats, fly-ins from the southern metropolises, usually stick to its own and rarely fraternises with the 'natives.' They even refer to themselves as 'expats', while Islanders call them 'two year tourists.' They often have an air about them as if they are doing a tour of duty or are on safari. Many of them often bemoan the Island's slow pace, and what they considered double standards where the Islanders got it all too easy. Some of the dinner party set, so unaware of their white privilege, would say they suffered reverse racism, when overlooked in a promotion to what they feel a less qualified Indigenous colleague. One bored (white) housewife of a public servant described the ex-pat vibe as 'living in a caravan park.'

Many promise to write me a scathing letter to the editor of *Torres News* when they leave, to expose what they perceive as hypocrisy. But they never do. Perhaps nostalgia envelops their disgruntlements with time and distance.

These 'expats' are nearly always white, middle class and with brutal suburban outlooks. They often seem almost Aryanist in their dinner party cliques or tearing around on the weekends in expensive over-powered boats. Islanders are left in their wake, not just in their little tinnies in which they traverse the width and breadth of the Straits for subsistence and survival, but in their inability to snag the expats' lucrative salaries in employment, or even get a decent roof over their heads. Old Helmut the Horn Island hermit describes it as a 'bureaucratic dictatorship.'

The constant turnover of public servants has driven up the real estate market to prices similar to Sydney's. This has pushed Islanders out and into often over-crowded government housing where it's not unusual to have three generations cram into a three-bedroom-asbestos-fibro house, where each room houses each sibling's own family.

One Islander lady tells me of her joy after their decade-long wait for a new home under government housing, 'But the kids didn't know what to do with themselves, they kept wanting to sleep in our room, they had never had their own bedroom,' she laughed. Islanders know how to laugh in the face of adversity, where maybe only one or two breadwinners would cook for twenty people every night, no one ever turned away. These old-fashion family values and strong sense of community are something our selfish suburban, nuclear-family mainstream culture has long-since lost.

The housing issue provided me another indication that I was slowly becoming embedded in Islander consciousness, at a rally organised by angry residents of government housing in February 2015. With myself the sole spectator I soon realised the whole thing had been organised for my benefit. Various residents stood up to speak their piece on the concrete stage at ANZAC Park, where all the many marches and gatherings culminate in the community.

The rally had been triggered by a letter sent to all residents from the Department of Queensland Housing, informing them they would be evicted if their household income exceeded

$80,000 dollars a year. With sometimes up to twenty people living in the one house, if ten of them were on welfare, that alone would push them over the cut-off. Understandably, this agitated a demographic, people who already felt like refugees in their own land, and who earn on average $25,000 less a year than the median national income, coupled with often intergenerational unemployment and one of the highest cost of living of any postcode in the country.

The Department of Housing formally apologised for this 'automated letter sent in error', acknowledging the prohibitively expensive rental prices even for high income earners, where the reality is that if a house is not chucked into an employment contract, it is effectively untenable. But this letter, not the first time such an 'automated' correspondence had been sent out, opened a wound. Banners were painted, agitators rallied – and I asked to attend.

The main organiser, Frank David, late twenties, who is a direct descendent of Kebisu, has a wild intensity in his eye that transcends his slight wiry frame and hardship-battered demeanour.

'The $80,000 household income threshold keeps us at the bottom, discourages us from getting more qualified to get better paid jobs,' he bellowed down a microphone on the podium. 'If we climb the ladder, we will lose our housing, so we don't climb. I have been getting eviction notices for ten years, but I don't care.

'Generation after generation of our leaders do nothing, we want the Minister to come up here and make a new policy with us, no more marching with no outcomes.

'We struggle to feed our families while the whites come and take our jobs and take our houses.' Frank paused for moment and glanced at me sitting alone in the front row. Smiling nervously he covered the microphone with his hand, 'But not you, *Bala*.'

Turning back to the group he thundered back down the mic, 'So we will get *Torres News* to put this out there to make them listen.'

Which it seems they did.

A week or so after going to print, where I reported on one resident who had been waiting five years for the Department to replace a toilet floor full of rot and a ceiling about to cave in, tradesmen miraculously arrived and did the repairs.

'Back to the Rock,' Pedro sighs as our water taxi edges closer to Thursday Island.

I shrug, not understanding.

'That's what people call TI, the Rock.' There is both a hint of irony and indignation in his voice.

Taken aback by the almost grim connotation, I wonder if it's a slight, comparing TI to the infamous U.S. island prison Alcatraz – a tropical hell for public servants whose modernity and mediocrity is constantly maligned by *Ailan* life and the tyranny of distance that is completely incongruent to the Government's paper shufflers and bean counters.

The Rock also conjures up an allegory for the whole planet, the third rock from the sun, and on it is captured a tiny cross section of humanity with all their failings, aspirations and struggles.

Interestingly, the Rock's demographics are reversed to that of the rest of the country, as there is a predominately Indigenous population and a minority of white 'expats' (or immigrants, to call a spade a spade). However, what's not reversed is the fact the white minority make up most of the over-privileged bureaucrats and business owners, while majority of the population are the Indigenous have-nots. This demographic flip still provides us 'whites' plenty of navel gazing – a sense of 'being different' or on the outside of the community's culture, and where English is a second or third language.

Each year it gets easier for me to spot the new expats who arrive on the Rock. Apart from getting to know, or at least recognise, every face on the island, the newbies all have the same stunned mullet expression I had on first arriving. It's an expression that shows the uncertainty of living in a remote Indigenous community, the jarring realisation that you are for the first time a minority on the outside of a close-knit society.

It's a similar expression day trippers have who venture up from their road trip pilgrimage to the tip of Cape York. It's either grey nomads shuffling around in the unforgiving midday sun, enfeebled by the humidity, or bow-legged Akubra cowboys – old men in new hats or young bucks with sunburnt Southern Cross tattoos. Their wide rabbit-fur brims are stained with sweat and pig's blood from their bush-bash up the Old Telegraph track in their V8 SUVs – giant Ned Kelly helmets that ejaculate diesel smoke, Bundy Rum cans and shotgun shells into the pristine wilderness as they rumble north to the end of the road.

A fluoro-coloured sticker on their chest with their first name allows them to be easily mustered up at the day's end by their tour guides and shipped off back south on the afternoon ferry.

But it's often the bleeding heart liberals that suffer the most. Middle-aged women with short hair and fat bead necklaces, or young metrosexuals who find themselves suddenly transplanted into a room full of burly Islanders of few words. They build a career up around noble ideals of helping the disenfranchised, but are surprised at how confronting it is to finally be in a room full of them.

They would wither with fear at a good old fashion Queensland country-town bar fight or recoil in horror at a dugong hunting trip – and when they get on ground they suddenly realise it.

The Islanders realise fraternising with these people will open doors and get the funding and help that they need. But it makes for some stilted conversation at coffee break. Apart from many Indigenous communities voting left of centre in most State and Federal elections, Islanders, like many Indigenous Australians, tend to be religious, conservative in their political outlook.

I wonder if Islanders and other Indigenous Australians sometimes prefer the overt rum-loving racist redneck, the typical pig-shooting fisherman, which while loving the great outdoors is happy to work down a mine or clear-felling forests. Rarely mincing their words they wear their racism on the sleeve, calling a spade a spade. Much easier for mob to reciprocate and call them a white cunt, and then maybe share a drink and a fishing yarn. It's the micro racial aggressions that the well-meaning liberal-minded let inadvertently slip under the radar that often assails their dignity.

'It's like a zoo,' Pedro says, smiling again. 'A zoo full of bureaucrats. They come here for a couple of years and try and re-invent the wheel, throwing out the last person's plans because they have got some great idea they thought up in Canberra or Brisbane or learned at university, then they go and the next one comes up and does the same thing – nothing actually changes. They have no idea of our culture, they think it's just *Ailan* dancing and *Dharis*. Like our clan groups and totems, they're real, it's not just some story we say – you see it when someone is dying.'

Pedro's role as both preacher and politician are often transcended by his role as an Elder people turn to in their hour of need. My boss Senior, a long-time friend of his, tells me Pedro is often called out at all times of the night to the hospitals or people's bedside.

'Those of the Crane Clan will bend one leg up like the bird just before they die, while those of the lizard or snake stick out the tip of the tongue and the ones of the turtle make a popping sound with their lips,' Pedro says as he mimics the action with his mouth. 'But all these people that come up here talk about is our mythology, it's not myth. It's just how it actually is, but they will never get it.'

Pedro shakes his head.

'There are three kinds of people that come to the Torres Strait, the mercenaries who come for the free housing, free relocation and extra remote living allowance, then there's the ones that can't get a job anywhere else, and then there's the ones that actually care,' he says, grinning again. 'But there seems to be a lot more mercenaries these days.'

I chuckle and smile back but daren't ask him which one he thinks I am.

I like to think I am a well-meaning madman misfit, but in my heart I know I am a combination of all three.

CHAPTER 18

WHITEWASHING AND BLACK CLADDING

February 2018

Squeezing my hand, bringing me in for a shoulder to shoulder tap and slap on the back, Shane Duffy, a Mount Isa boiler maker, former Broncos fullback and Kalkadoon man, greets me like an old mate.

It is the first time we've met.

He's both affable and rough and ready, and seems like a knockabout bloke. He is also, for the past fourteen years, the CEO of the Aboriginal and Torres Strait Islander Legal Service (ATSILS), Australia's largest Indigenous legal service. He frequently locks horns with prime ministers and heavyweight bureaucrats.

'Hey, bruzz – good to finally meet ya,' he says with a cheeky grin as his eyes sparkle. Twenty years off the footy field and he's still in pretty good shape.

Beneath the personable touch, faded jeans, T-shirt and thongs, Shane is an astute shaker and mover of Queensland's social justice for Indigenous people.

Since the late 1980s Shane has worked his way up the justice food-chain, starting out as a court support officer for Aboriginal kids in trouble and ending up in more strategic policy making and reviewing roles in government.

'I've got no quals per say other than my trade, but that's how you learn things, by creeping up,' he says, lounging at a forty-five degree angle draped in the chair across from my desk.

Even though he's streamlined ATSILS's operation on limited funds, knocking out nearly 50,000 legal advice matters a year, he says funding is always a battle and they are constantly having to justify their existence.

'We can't control funding and legislation, then there's always the argy bargy between the State and the Feds. We have to meet an ever-growing demand, having minimal funds while being blocked by government.'

But Shane isn't afraid to kick the Government's gift horse in the nuts over how it's failing to 'Close the Gap'.

'There's more money being invested into black affairs now than in the entire history since colonisation, but everything is going the wrong way — the data's going south. If you stood for a private corporation, for your shareholders, and said you've fucked up, you're gone, but the bureaucracy gets rewarded for its inability to get outcomes on taxpayers' dollars.' Shane laughs at this, as do I, even though neither of us thinks it's funny.

'It's the system that's broken, they've got no black content in government any more, they are reducing government departments, we are getting less and less and less, there's no historical content. It's the same story over and over again, next mob comes through, same story over and over again, it's because they don't even have the bureaucrats underneath them that can give them proper briefing, it may be a briefing from back six or twelve months ago, but nothing historical. If you keep funding someone money and keep getting the same result and it's not a great result, why would you keep funding them?

'What we find in government is that they have these very high-level bureaucrats who make the decisions off government direction, and then they get voluntary retirements. Then they come back as consultants, or go to the large NGOs and they get more government funding because they've got a relationship with their former peers. While they might involve Aboriginal and Torres Strait Islanders, where are they in the upper echelons of the organisation, for the development of strategy? We are not there.'

Shane has good reason to be pissed off. While money keeps flowing to government bureaucrats and consultants, little seems to reach indigenous communities in areas where it would do the most good. For example, from the first quarter of 2017 until the first half of 2020, over 40,000 Indigenous Australians have been imprisoned. This is sixty-four percent more than ten years ago and, during that time, the number of Indigenous women in prison has risen by seventy-seven percent. Indigenous people comprise nearly one third of the nation's prison population, while only representing two percent of the overall population

Over the past decade the Indigenous prisoner rate has increased exponentially compared to the overall Australian prisoner rate.

'I really challenge the Prime Minister in a respectful way to redefine what justice means. From their perspective justice just means incarceration, but we need a blueprint for change, looking upstream or at the drivers of why people are coming into the justice system, and dealing with the root causes and underlying issues.

'Not many people we serve earn much above the poverty line, so it's an essential service that we look at from the human rights perspective.

'It costs $180,000 a year to keep someone in prison. If we put that taxpayer's investment into health, housing, disability, employment and training, if you ensure through measures they actually work across their own bloody agencies, building more KPIs on how they engage with Aboriginal and Torres Strait Islander people on the ground, they will more often than not come up with cost neutral, cost effective solutions.

'As I said to the Prime Minister, we've got to be closer to getting it right by involving those it impacts upon, rather than looking at it as a problem rather than the solution. 'Come to us, sit down with us and get performance indicators that show they are not consulting after documents have been printed but that they actually listened to people on the ground who know it and live it and breathe it every day.

'But it's because locking people up is popular.

'And now it's all about privatisation, corporatisation of social services, all based off profit and a return of dividends to shareholders.

'Serco in the UK are running the prisons, and we've got a couple private prisons here now too, it's in their best interests for people to be fucked up because they make money.'

Shane was also critical of how the Church is also getting their cut.

'With incarnation and homelessness, contracts are being awarded to Churches of Christ, Life Without Barriers and the Salvation Army.

'With our funding state governments are really good at giving *gamen* way (Creole for being fake or insincere). Say they give you a $100,000, and there's an unexpended amount say $3,000 – they'll take that off you next year giving you $97,000, so your funding in real terms decreases, plus there's no CPI built in.

'But the church groups are different, they give nothing back, because anything unexpended gets collapsed in the broad structure of the church. The church groups are at the front and centre, bruzz, they don't pay tax and they use their line of their "poor broke" status to actually stick their finger up our arse.

'We can't compete, us black fellas can't compete with corporations that go in joint ventures with church groups, they are a tax deductible – it's big money.'

Shane questions even the so-called successes the government claims with the seven Closing the Gap goals.

'The one indicator achieved was the Year 12 attainment, which is based on quantitative data – but the qualitative was full of shit. The qualitative was these kids were finishing Year 12, but they were coming out with Year 7, 8, 9 education standards.

'All the money going out is getting invested into business, public servants and houses for public servants.

'Like with remote Indigenous housing, it's bullshit, we're losing jobs, which has a flow-on effect in these remote communities, which can pressure someone to hit the charge, then there's domestic violence – so the flow-on effect and the unintended consequences are their inability to actually engage and understand the intense good of sustainable change. I was talking of transformational learning with Government, which no one had done before, and which makes way for new learnings, but they don't brother.'

'I challenge the level of skill at a critical decision making level, there should be a skills-based board with expertise in specific areas in line with government appropriation, but I've been around long enough to know we're not going to get it and of course whether at a national or a state level. Government workers, whether they are blackfellas or not, they want to protect their interests.

'When it's remote everyone flies in flies out, drives in drives out, so it's all remote, the service delivery and the infrastructure.

'We need to look at self-determined community control, but Government is trying to have it all boxed up with black cladding. We are worse off today than under the Act, we're getting more kids removed than under the Act, highest prison rates, but I s'pose we're not getting shot and poisoned but it's the same thing but with different ways, bruzz.'

Black cladding is where non-Indigenous businesses try to make a grab at the lucrative cash cow known as the Indigenous Procurement Policy (IPP), a Federal government initiative launched in July 2015, aimed at stimulating Indigenous economic development by leveraging Commonwealth spending.

When Indigenous businesses are not able to meet the demand, it's then that unscrupulous non-indigenous businesses may attempt to grab a share of the lucrative contracts by pretending to be Indigenous, a practice dubbed 'black cladding'.

Lawyer Terri Janke, from a hundred-percent-owned Indigenous law and consultancy firm that specialises in this field, told me at a forum on the subject that, while describing the IPP as the 'most successful government policy ever', she said: 'Remote Indigenous communities are the most at risk of black cladding ... we often get called by people saying how they are not even getting a look in, in the business they have gone into partnership with, or they don't really even know what the deal is.'

Ms Janke said some of the examples of black cladding involved the use of 'front companies' which falsify payrolls, give kickbacks, use absentee management and 'pass through' invoicing to create the appearance of indigenous engagement.

And it is a feeding frenzy.

Researcher Sarah Hudson's 2016 report, *Mapping the Indigenous Program and Funding Maze*, for the Centre for Independent Studies, exposed almost six billion dollars a year have been spent on more than 1,000 Indigenous-specific programs across the country – over ninety percent of which haven't been audited for effectiveness.

A month after publishing her report, she told NITV: 'Lots of money has been spent, but the problem is that we don't know where it went and how much money was actually spent overall. We do know where some has been spent, but there is a lack of evidence in terms of the amount spent on Indigenous programs.'

Ms Hudson believes a large amount of money is wasted.

'Lots of money has been spent on 'Closing the Gap', but we are not seeing a big change in the gap.

'A lot of the programs that are being created are not meeting the needs of Indigenous people. In many instances, the programs are not undertaking any consultation with the people they are targeting. Often decisions (regarding programs) are coming from centralised government and told to the communities.

'What needs to happen is that communities (need to) have more say where money is needed and where the programs should go. Evidence says that successful programs come from Indigenous people and suggestions from community.

'I think there needs to be more transparency. I often call it 'the funding maze', because it's hard to track the funding.'

My mate Rahm Adamedes eloquences it a little more blunt: 'It's chequebook diplomacy, so they can say, "see we give you six billion bucks and you blackfellas still fuck it up," it's like the government is setting them up for failure so they can turn around and take away their ownership and self-determination.'

Anthropologist Jeremy Beckett, who has worked with Indigenous Australians since the 1970s, was an expert witness on the Mabo Case and the 2013 Sea Claim Case, called this process 'welfare colonialism'.

In his 1987 book: *Torres Strait Islanders: Custom and Colonialism,* he said:

Welfare colonialism, then, is the state's attempt to manage the political problems posed by the presence of a depressed and disenfranchised indigenous population in an affluent, liberal democratic society. At the practical level it meets the problem by economic expenditure well in excess of what the minority produces. At the ideological level the 'native', who once stood in opposition to the 'settler' and outside the pale of society, undergoes an apotheosis to emerge as its original citizen.

Beckett says this form of colonialism is 'solicitous rather than exploitative, and liberal rather than repressive.'

The National Partnership Agreement for Remote Indigenous Housing (NPARIH) scheme, a ten-year plan that commenced in 2008 to tackle the housing crisis in remote Indigenous communities, was a good example of this. It often led to million-dollar houses being built by all-white contractors that fly in, fly out, leaving houses that Community had no say in how they were designed, and have no sense of ownership of.

In fact many of the government-funding construction projects in remote Indigenous communities are rolled out like that, not even with black cladding, other than a couple of token blackfellas pushing wheel-barrows to fulfil Indigenous employment requirements often set for contractors awarded the big ticket jobs. Sometimes even that is side-stepped with a red-tape dodge and weave, like the multimillion dollar rebuild of the aged care facility on Thursday Island.

When Warren Entsch turned the sod with Traditional Owners and the Mayor on that project, there were rousing speeches of how it would create local employment, but like most of these gigs it never did.

The chequebook diplomacy approach of chucking money at things without community consultation, time and time again, creates white elephants, such as the federally funded upgrade to the desalination water treatment plant on the outer island community of Boigu, where residents faced water shortages in 2015.

The new water inlet pipe that draws in seawater became exposed at low tide leaving the impressive looking new plant high and dry, and its large adjacent reservoir permanently empty.

The community had to ration a couple of small tanks for the whole community till the next high tide, which effectively meant no running water for the hottest part of the day.

The brand-new holding dam remains permanently dry.

TSRIC Mayor Fred Gela showed me around the impressive yet defunct facility in 2015: 'It's not rocket science, these engineers come up from down south with their degrees, but lack common sense. The old system they replaced provided this community with fresh water 24/7.'

'I thought an upgrade was meant to make things better, but now there are water restrictions when previously Boigu had twenty-four hour access to fresh water,' Gela said. 'We had the same problem on Mer, they installed a new de-sal plant, but the inlet pipe stopped just metres short of the continental shelf, so it ran out of water at low tide. We had to install the last few metres to ensure better water access.'

The project, like nearly all major federally funded ones in the Torres Strait, is managed by the Torres Strait Regional Authority (TSRA), the region's federal representative body for Indigenous people. Since the political heady days of inception, the TSRA has increasingly become a behemoth, and instead of serving the Indigenous people it was designed to represent, it ends up often working against them.

An Islander once told me: 'The only way you can close the gap in the Torres Strait is to get a job with the TSRA.'

A Kafkaesque example of the TSRA's bureaucratic boondogglery with this chequebook diplomacy is a nineteen-home subdivision they built, for mainly white TSRA executive staff on Thursday Island – it is thought to have cost around nineteen million dollars. The site, which became known as the Clarke Street Development, was originally pegged for an affordable housing project to help alleviate the overcrowding issue.

With a chronic shortage of community housing on the island, the TSRA used unconsolidated funds that could have been used to invest into projects to help the region's Indigenous people, to build instead nineteen-million-dollar-homes on a hill with some of best views of the island, overlooking the overcrowded community housing underlings. The builders were from down south, and snared the contract with the agreement of employing a few blackfella wheelbarrow pushers.

When Islander Derek Brank from neighbouring Muralag Island knocked on my door, he was a bit skittish about sharing his example of being a 'token black' on the job. Derek, thirty-seven, lean and sun-weathered with a salt and peppered goatee and mullet, told me how he'd been working in the region as a sub-contractor 'on and off for twelve years' but his excavator and truck have been sitting idle in a shed at his Muralag Island residence for the last two years.

While Derek has been getting casual work as an excavator operator on the project, one of the building contractors hired by the TSRA to do the development declined his request to use his equipment, and instead shipped up units from down south.

Both the project contractor and the TSRA were tight-lipped about Derek's situation and refused to comment.

'People from down south have been coming up and cutting my grass,' Derek said. 'On this job there are four mini excavators and I said to the boss that I have my own machine but he won't use it. My boss is charging me out at like a $100 an hour, so he's making a mark off me, and then the foreman excavator is getting a cut out me operating his machine. But what about my machine? It's sitting on Prince of Wales [Muralag] doing nothing for the last few years, which is just wrong.

'I thought these projects are meant to help people in the Torres Strait, but I got knocked back. I want to know why, these are the questions I want answered.'

Derek said he bought his own machine six years ago to try and build a small business and also to employ some locals, but due to inconsistent opportunities and limited access to big projects like this one, he said: 'It just doesn't work. If I was given the contract I would have bought three other excavators and employed locals, but instead I am just working for two other companies as an operator.'

Derek said he had three operators working for him previously but without continued work, he had to let them go.

'I am the only blackfella operating up here. I feel like just another black face so they can say they are helping us, which is rubbish.'

The job was cursed from the first day the bulldozers pushed into the area in 2014 and straight through a Kaurareg Traditional Owner sacred site. Despite TSRA's assurances it had commissioned, 'a qualified cultural heritage consultant to produce a Cultural Heritage Assessment Report,' a check of the Aboriginal cultural heritage database revealed they had only checked if there were any listed significant sites of cultural importance on the land on November 14 – after the Kaurareg raised issue with the works that commenced, and I had asked the TSRA for an explanation on November 11.

Traditional Owner Harry Seriat told me that the site was a traditional meeting place, a place of ritual, initiation and black magic as well as a natural water spring and several garden plots of banana and cassava.

It seemed that the TSRA had breached the Queensland Government's *Aboriginal Cultural Heritage Act 2003*, which states in its preamble that the Act *binds all persons, including the State, and is intended to provide effective recognition, protection and conservation of Aboriginal cultural heritage.*

Seriat said what happened was similar to a process a couple of years ago when the TSRA planned to develop the Affordable Housing Project on the same site, but the project stalled when they allegedly voiced concern about their cultural heritage.

'Back then TSRA put up a sign of a planning permit to build a housing development, and one of our people brought it to our attention. That's when Traditional Owners objected and put a stop to it. They didn't have a cultural heritage plan or even consult with us,' he said. 'Now they have done it again, but this time going straight in and starting to cut the hill up without ever talking to us.'

A neighbour abutting the development site also told me that the start of works did more than disturb them at 6:30am with the surprise sound of bulldozers. Caroline Cloudy said that on the night after the bulldozers started, she and her family experienced spiritual disturbances.

'It started Tuesday night and is still going on a week later. We can feel the presence of something in the house, we have been hearing stuff being thrown around underneath the floor. Inside the house there has been a rotten stench, like rotten meat while there is nothing actually there. My husband said it smelled like the smell coming out of a morgue. Even my eldest son also felt something in the night pulling his sheets and trying to pull him off the bed.'

It's not often as a journo you get to put a story of ancestral spiritual disturbances on the front page of a newspaper.

The ongoing PR disaster of the project, from its spiritually cursed inception to the below-the-radar completion that was without its customary blessing and opening ceremony, carried on long after the white mercenary contractors flew out and white executives quietly moved into their houses on the hill.

TSRIC Mayor Fred Gela called for a thorough review of the TSRIC Act, as he saw the democratically-elected board function as no more than a token role to rubber stamp decisions by Canberra's FIFO'ed executive staff, where the CEO can trump anything the board decides.

'They need to look into the Act of the TSRA itself, and I have been saying this for quite some time now,' Gela said. Within the Act of the TSRA, it provides the CEO with a role of delegated authority and power, where the CEO can a make a decision that goes against the wishes of the board, if the CEO perceives it's not in the best interest of the organisation. Under those types of instruments and clauses of the Act, why the hell do you need a board? It's a token gesture.

'The proof's in the pudding, look at the Clarke Street Housing development on TI. Millions and millions of dollars has been invested into this development, first I was told it was nine million, now I'm told it's nineteen million – but I've yet to see a board resolution on it. So if there is no board resolution on that, we need to ask, who made that decision? What people in the region need to realise is that nineteen million, if it is in fact nineteen million, that investment was not an external grant.'

Gela said the Clarke Street money came from budget surplus that was put into a consolidated account.

'Really that money should have been spent in all the communities, into the various programs. But instead that investment was used to build the TSRA's empire.'

Gela said while the TSRA builds its executives new homes, residents on the outer islands of Poruma and Boigu were in a crisis situation with a dire need of a seawall.

'That money could have gone into preserving communities, or alternatively used to fund economic development projects in the region.'

My continued airing of the TSRA's dirty laundry, with the project and the failings of the TSRA Act, resulted in Federal Minister Nigel Scullion defending the TSRA's reputation as being the 'high water mark' of Indigenous Rep bodies, and denying the Board was a toothless tiger.

'Now there's always allegations of the tail wagging the dog,' Scullion told me in an interview about the TSRA, 'but I can't but help but think this is just Canberra covering its arse. If it were possible – and it's not, as in all boards – for the public to see exactly how that operates, they'd know it is also a nonsense.'

As we are walking out of the TSRA office after the on-therecord chat, Scullion gives me a good punch in the arm and grins.

'How's things mate, I see you've been busy then.'

A couple of years later, native title activist, and former TSRA Board Member Maluwap Nona complained to me outside a Federal Court hearing, 'It's like the TSRA has become the DNA'

– the former authoritarian Department of Native Affairs.

Nona was a respondent on what should have been a straight forward native title case management hearing for the remaining sea country, where the historic 2013 High Court ruling recognised that fishing commercially in the waters of the Torres Strait did not extinguish native title rights.

However, that time Nona and other Traditional Owners were battling the TSRA, the very body that was meant to be supporting them.

Another of the native title claimants on the case, Ned David, another direct descendent to the warrior Kebisu, described the TSRA's actions as 'a great plot for a John Grisham novel.'

It became a saga where the TSRA hired over a dozen lawyers to do everything in its power to, as the presiding judge said, 'derail' the legal process, a move that left everyone scratching their heads as to the TSRA's motive.

The judge described the TSRA's role as 'increasingly disturbing on a number of fronts.'

Warren Entsch, when hearing of the TSRA's court case said it: 'beggars belief ... this raises a lot of questions about the TSRA ... I have serious concerns of the level of nepotism in the organisation.'

Long term dissatisfaction with the TSRA and the top-down, over-governance of the region has prompted local leaders to push for an agenda of regional control, the most recent being in 2014, called the 'One Boat' policy, and the idea has been bandied about ever since.

Gela said: 'One Boat would absorb the roles, responsibilities and powers of all of the local governments – TSIRC, Torres Shire Council and Northern Peninsula Area Regional Council and the TSRA, our Commonwealth Statutory Body.'

Gela expressed to me many times his frustration with the seas of red tape and duplication of services at both State and Federal levels, as well as endless consultants and viability reports soaking up all the funding, so there is nothing left to actually hit the ground with and really help those intended. Gela thinks, and with good reason looking at the government's track record, they could do it better themselves.

'It's not a new model, but rather it builds on the work already done in the 1997 New Deal, and the 2011 Bamaga Accord. This agreement is not forgetting our aspirations to form a territory.'

Professor Martin Nakata from the University of New South Wales (UNSW), who is the first Torres Strait Islander to receive a PhD in

Australia and Chair of Australian Indigenous Education, agrees with Gela.

'Twenty years ago when the 1997 House of Representative Standing Committee on Aboriginal and Torres Strait Islander Affairs first recommended the establishment of a Regional Assembly as a joint Commonwealth-State Government Statutory Authority, and as a launching platform for regional governance, Islander leadership struggled to manage the ensuing consultations with the community,' he said. 'The negotiations became less about *what* the Assembly was to determine in the region and more about *who* was to determine it.'

Nakata told me that establishing a Regional Assembly could well set the Torres Strait on a path towards self-government under Territory status, but the process continually stalls for what seems like personality politics.

On face value Nigel Scullion told me he supported the idea, but said: 'If you want One Boat, you've got to start sinking some. I think the One Boat model is a good model, but the transitional arrangement will require life jackets. It's all pretty heroic until you get to the point where they have to say, "two-thirds of us will lose our jobs."'

And therein lies the problem – who will sacrifice a cushy government pay cheque for the benefit of all?

That's the heart of the problem with chequebook diplomacy, welfare colonialism, or a funding maze – it gets comfortable to have one's snout in the trough.

Billy Gordon's line – 'White guilt breeds black mediocrity' – seems apt when considering this killing them softly approach.

Ned David is not convinced the government bodies from local, state and federal levels will succeed with the One Boat idea, but said: 'We need a new agreement that outlines some clear thinking around what we as a region, as a group, are able to make some decisions around where public investment is made and how it is made, rather than somebody in Brisbane or Canberra saying here's some dollars and this is how you're going to spend it. We know what the problems are and I think we know what the answers are, all locally based decisions and solutions. We own it and if mistakes are made, we own the mistakes as well.'

One time when I was travelling with Gela to Boigu Island to look at some NPARIH housing, which his council had commandeered control of the construction process, a wiley old Islander builder, lean and leathery with a neat close cropped white goatee, quietly had a chat to me.

Samat Ketchell mentors the young Islander apprentices working for the council, making sure they stay on the straight and narrow. He explained what it was like working as a carpenter forty-five years ago in the region when he first started in the industry, back when authoritarianism was not sugar-coated and colonialism was just the good 'ole fashioned oppressive version'.

'I started in 1967, working for the Department of Native Affairs (DNA). These boys today have power tools and all the mod cons, but in my day, they just threw the materials off the barge and we had to swim with it and pick it up off the beach,' he said quietly.

'We had no cement mixers, no wheelbarrows, we had to take sand from the beach and smash rocks in the hills to make aggregate for concrete. We had to haul water in buckets and drill bloodwood with hand drills. What tools we had we treated like gold. We used to push the wire nails into a block of soap to make them slide into wood easier.

'We got paid twelve dollars a fortnight, then when you wanted to go to the shops to spend your money there was still apartheid. If there was a white person inside, we had to wait until they came out before we could go inside.

'These boys today don't know how lucky they got it.'

CHAPTER 19

LORE OF THE LAND

9 August 2017

'See, that's the body of the dugong, facing back towards the Torres Strait from where he came,' NBA star and Australia's second highest paid sportsman Patty Mills tells me over the wail of the small Islander's engines. Part Torres Strait Islander and part Aboriginal Kokatha from South Australia, Patty is all Indigenous, something he wears as a badge of honour both on and off the court, and he considers himself an ambassador for his people.

In the Torres Strait, where he spent part of his childhood, he's considered nothing short of a hero. Patty recently re-signed with the San Antonio Spurs for a cool $65 million making him the most successful Indigenous Australian sportsperson ever. But he doesn't forget his roots, making sure he comes back to Country every year or so – this is the third time I've met him. It's just two days before his 29th birthday.

In 2014, after the San Antonio Spurs won the NBA Finals, Patty brought the Larry O'Brien

Championship Trophy, which he nicknamed '*Bala* Lazza,' to the Torres Strait.

The name itself represents a blend of cultures. The Language word, *Bala* means brother, and the Lazza, 'Stralian vernacular for Larry.

Patty and his team-mate, fellow Queenslander Aron Baynes, carried the $40,000 solid sterling silver, gold-plated trophy through the streets of Thursday Island community.

And nearly everyone got the chance to hold it and get a photo with it and Patty.

Later after a function dinner *Bala* Lazza was put on the lawn as Patty, his father Benny and the Elders danced around the trophy late into the night.

That sense of shared achievement is something Patty brought all the way from Texas to the Torres Strait.

Approaching Mer, Patty's grinning like an excited school boy as the small plane banks preparing to land on the second shortest runway in the country, the shortest being the runway on the Torres Strait island of Mabuiag. Patty's nose is pressed against the window looking down at of his father's home island. I too feel a surge of coming home. A complete outsider, a whitefella, I have been to Mer more than any other island in the Torres Strait and it's one where the community has made me feel at home, always embraced as a brother from a different mother.

Mer, and its neighbouring two islands Dauar and the crescent shaped Waier, are the remnants of an ancient volcanic eruption, with what's left of the volcano rim constituting the archipelago. But the Traditional Owners, the Meriam Mer people, believe Mer was formed by a boy named Gelam.

According to the legend, Gelam and his mother Usar were left alone on Moa Island in the central islands of Torres Strait, where they were terrorised by an evil, baby-eating monster called Dhogai. All the kids of the Torres Strait are scared of this bogeywoman, even my daughter can retell Dhogai stories in full creole.

So fearing Dhogai, Gelam decides to leave Moa and his mother by building a dugong from a wattle tree and travels east to Mer Island, where the dugong becomes a large hill in the shape of the animal.

Looking out from the plane window on the approach toward Mer, Patty points out the ridge line of the island, the dugong's backbone, and the rocky west-facing escapement, the dugong's head that looks back at the Torres Strait. A Mer Elder told me one visit that when the new school was being constructed just below the ridge, they struck bands of white clay every few metres when laying footings.

'That's the rib bones of Gelam,' he told me.

Mer, also known as Murray Island, is a tiny dot of land, less than five square kilometres, with around three hundred people living on it, and is the furthermost Eastern Island in the Torres Strait, sitting on the edge of the continental shelf and at the beginning of the Great Barrier Reef.

An hour's flight east from Horn Island, we passed the low-lying sandy coral cays of Warraber, Poruma and Masig, whose short runways completely transect the small islands, and whose sandy fringes are constantly encroached and nibbled away by a slowly rising-sea.

Low lying clouds swallow the plane for the last leg of the flight until Mer, Dauar and Waier, silhouetted in the morning light, are suddenly revealed as we drop altitude on approach to land. Falling hard and fast to a very short tarmac, my stomach rises to meet my tonsils as I white-knuckle deep into the upholstery. We bounce and skid like a stone skimmed across a pond, the aircraft stopping on the last few metres of runway, past a rocky drop off to the sea below — I never get used to this landing.

Stepping out on the blacktop, Patty is greeted by community leaders.

We pass through a gate exiting the runway under a metal archway fashioned like the jaws of Beizam, the tiger shark, an important totem animal.

Mer is not open to everyone; permission to visit the island must be granted by the Traditional Owners of this all-Indigenous Islander community.

Traditional Owner Doug Passi grabs Patty Mills in a bear hug, then moves his way to a more formal handshake with rest of his party, eyes twinkling, his wide grins revealing a patchwork of remaining teeth as he booms: 'The tarmac is under the law, L.A.W. – Australian law, but as soon as you step through the shark's mouth and on to Meriam Mir land, you are under the lore, L.O.R.E. – Meriam Mir lore.'

I've heard Doug say this to many people entering Miriam Mer Country through the jaws of Beziam.

After Patty's entourage has passed, Doug winks at me. '*Wis wei bala?* (which way – meaning how are you?) – why aren't you wearing a *lava lava?* Next time you come if you're not wearing one we'll make you walk down the hill naked,' he chuckles as he drapes his arm over my shoulder.

Patty told me while flying that Mer always sets his hair on end, and it's easy to see why. That sense of cultural lore is palpable on a landscape draped in mystery and tropical rainforest.

On other visits, Elders tell me of some of the powerful entities that inhabit Mer, such as a bogeyman that only lives in the shadows, whose long conical shaped head is similar to *Weris*, their traditional woven basket sardine scoops.

'When we were young and we only had the hurricane lamp, we'd see him all the time in the shadows, it made us pump that light all night,' laughed an Elder on another trip when I overnighted on Mer. 'We don't see him as much now we have electric lights and streetlights, but you still see him in the shadows sometimes – it's why after all these years I'm still scared of the dark.'

Then there was *beisosok*, a mythical black dog the size of pony that lurked in the shadows as well.

Another Elder tells me of an entity that lives in the creek bed that runs from the beach up the hill to the site of the school.

'We would never go into the jungle after dark as it didn't want us there then. One time me and my wife were looking for fruits in the jungle and we forgot the time. When the sun started to set we heard this noise like a bulldozer coming up the creek through the bamboo, crashing and making a terrible noise.

We wanted to run but I signalled for my wife not to move as it came right up to us, but there was nothing there – not a single piece of bamboo even moved. It wants to lure you into the jungle, but if you go you will never come out.

'When they built the road to the school which crossed the creek, it disrupted its path and sometimes at night, when driving over the creek, we feel like we are being pulled out of our bodies, like we for a moment get lost and don't know where we are, it's trying to draw us into the jungle.'

This sends the hairs on the back of my neck on end. Earlier that night, I had borrowed a car and driven along the road and over the creek bed. A strange mist clouded my windscreen, one which neither the wipers could clear on the outside nor my hand on the inside. As I crossed the creek I felt the strangest sensation of not knowing where I was, like I had become lost in twenty metres of road as I drove through the grove of ten metre tall bamboo. In a timeless moment I had become strangely disorientated as the night jungle hissed and creaked, inviting me in.

Patty's visit to Mer is in his role as an Ambassador for the 2018 Commonwealth Games, and he has chosen Mer for two reasons – to raise awareness of the Games, and to show the world the importance of Mer's unique culture and its significance to the rest of the country. But there is also a third reason – he is overdue to reconnect with his Meriam culture.

All scheduled engagements are cancelled soon after arrival as his uncles steal Patty away for dance training. He has no choice in the matter. This much to the dismay of Events and Tourism Queensland, for whom I'm moonlighting as a photographer, and who got me to Mer with Patty, GOLDOC representatives, a Channel 7 crew, and the Associate Editor of *GQ Magazine* Richard Clune, who's scheduled to do a feature on Patty.

With the run sheet out the window we all sit listless on the beach, with no choice but to slip into *Ailan* time, now also servants to the lore of the land.

Mer, considered the birthplace of native title and final resting place of Eddie Mabo, sees more than its fair share of government leaders all wanting to be seen paying their respects. Just on my watch, I've accompanied members of both State and Federal Government, including a premier, a prime minister and a couple of governor generals. But life is languid on Mer, where kids catch tuna off the beach as tiger sharks loll at the water's edge, gorged on the schools of sardines that literally jump onto the white sand. The sharks actually chase them on to the beach before flopping back into the sea like gigantic mud skippers.

With Patty out of sight I decide to shoot off some B roll stuff, so I wade out into the sea to a young boy no more than ten and his younger sister, both up to their waist fishing with hand lines. A two-metre Shovelnose shark casually swims between us.

'Don't worry about them ones, you're all good here, but don't go in the water over there,' the boy nods up the beach a hundred metres, where three dorsal fins circle.

'Tigers?' I ask. The boy just grins. With sharks being one of Mer's totems, I guess we must be okay, here, I hope.

Cultural lore runs as a strong undercurrent through all aspects of Islander life, from the fear of *puri puri* – *Ailan* voodoo – to the coming of age ritual of Shaving, where a young boy coming to manhood is taken off by all his uncles and has his head shaved, before marching to the beat of *warups* to a gathering of the women of the family, who all lie on the ground as he walks over their bodies.

Lore is also used to deal out justice, in one grim case a friend told me how a teenage boy broke into her house while she and her young children slept, waking and terrifying them.

When she approached the parents, the father of the youth said he would take care of it, 'I will take him away in dinghy fishing and hunting and talk to him.'

The next time she saw the youth was when he came around to her house to apologise, missing the end of his ring finger, which his father had chopped off as punishment.

Cultural lore, like all culture, is also something in flux, not static – I've seen traditional dance retelling stories of the pearling luggers, of the World War II Japanese Zero air raids, and the impacts of sea level rise.

Some cultural practices, such as *puri puri*, were marginalised with the influx of European law and religion, and pushed into the shadows, while others have been accepted but not formally recognised, such as traditional adoption, or *Ailan* adoption, an ancient custom still widely practised in Torres Strait Islander communities and is in fact widespread throughout most Pacific Island cultures.

The custom is where there is a permanent transfer of a child from one extended family member to another and where children are likely to be returned to their original parents. In Torres Strait Islander culture, people are considered greedy if they have too many children and do not share them with others. The underlying principle of Torres Strait Islander adoption is that giving birth to a child is not necessarily a reason for raising the child.

Ailan adoption is used to maintain the family bloodline by adopting (usually) a male child from a relative – this is linked to the inheritance of traditional land in the islands, to keep the family name going by adopting a male child from a relative or close friend into the family, to give a family who cannot have a child due to infertility the joy of raising a child. A married couple may give a child to either a single person or another couple, and relinquishment is not restricted to single parents. *Ailan* adoption is also used to strengthen alliances and bonds between the two families concerned, to distribute boys and girls more evenly between families who may have children of only one sex, to replace a child who had been adopted out to another family – this may occur within the extended families, to replace a child into the family once a woman has left home so that the grandparents still have someone to care for, and to provide company and care for an older relative, usually an older child in this case.

Ironically under the colonialist patriarchal rule of the DNA and Sir Joh Bjelke-Peterson, *Ailan* adoption was largely ignored and tolerated as black fella business, but with the decline of his regime and the dismantling of the DNA, the new Community Services departments did not recognise the practice, nor did successive governments since the 1990s, and so began an intergenerational problem of an age-old custom becaming illegitimate in the eyes of the law.

The lack of recognition of this cultural practice creates acute hardship for many families where children, unable to get birth certificates, miss out on schooling, healthcare and employment opportunities. Often children are unable to get high school certificates, driver's licenses or passports, or even open bank accounts.

It has also created problems in settling estates.

The issue came to prominence in the early nineties when the Queensland Government was lobbied by the Kupai Omasker Working Party for Legal Recognition of Traditional Adoption, including making submissions to parliamentary committees in 2008.

Chair of Kupai Omasker, Ivy Trevallion has been lobbying for *Ailan* adoption recognition for over three decades. Her eyes always water when she talked about this with me. Softly spoken with a demure, gentle presence, Ivy's tenacity in a struggle that's cuts close to her bone is admirable.

'This has been practised since time immemorial. It's the giving of children to strengthen family ties, to give families support who haven't got or can't have children, or if a woman marries off, so she can replace herself in the family,' she told me once at the fruit and veg stand at the supermarket. 'The sad thing is that in the Queensland constitution, it says in the preamble that they honour the Aboriginal peoples and Torres Strait Islander peoples, the First Australians, whose lands, winds and waters we all now share, and pay tribute to their unique values, and their ancient and enduring cultures, which deepen and enrich the life of our community.

'But this is not happening. They talk about closing the gap, it's very disheartening because we have people waiting for something to happen, generations of people waiting for an outcome with this.'

She believed the Queensland Government is in breach of Article 11 of the *United Nations Declaration on the Rights of Indigenous People*, which states: 'Indigenous peoples have the right to practise and revitalise their cultural traditions and customs.'

'So why can't they recognise our practice? Legally recognising this is needed for our children.'

Ivy was nothing but stonewalled when she took this to Premier Palaszczuk in Brisbane in early 2017, despite support from within her cabinet. It started a campaign with Ivy, *Torres News*, and Independent Member for Cook Billy Gordon to put pressure on the government to change this impasse.

Ironically, the practice reached legal status in the Court of Appeal for Indigenous people in British Colombia in the 1990s, and they used the Mabo case as a precedent. Eddie Mabo himself was *Ailan* adopted.

It was finally tabled as an election promise for the Palaszczuk Government at the end of 2017, along with the nomination of the first Torres Strait Islander candidate, Cynthia Lui, for Gordon's seat of Cook. The intention was two-fold, win the votes of the Torres Strait and get rid of Billy, who had been kicked out of Palaszczuk's government at the start of term.

While winning the election by a slim margin and gaining the seat of Cook, the move was seen for what it was by community leaders. TSIRC Mayor Fred Gela said: 'This is certainly a way of winning votes. Sadly, I hate to say this, this could have been resolved well and truly before the election. Sadly it has come to this. If this is what it will take then that's something that we have to wear, which is sad.

'This matter has been on Anastasia's lap for sign off for quite some time, Government better be fair-dinkum about it. We are well and truly way past the consultative phase, that's been well and truly exhausted. It's time to act.'

The *Meriba Omasker Kaziw Kazipa (Torres Strait Islander Traditional Child Rearing Practice) Bill 2020,* was introduced to Queensland Parliament on 16 July 2020, by Member for Cook Cynthia Lui. It finally will start the path to legalising this cultural child rearing practice.

Other elements of cultural lore, such as Tombstone Unveilings, were subsumed by the incoming belief paradigm of Christianity.

In earlier times when an Islander died, the family would place the body on a platform and allow the elements to reduce the remains to bones. When the skull naturally disconnected from the body it was considered the sign when the family was to collect the remains and place them in a sacred place. The skull was given to the spouse or next of kin of the deceased.

But after July 1, 1871 when the London Missionary Society landed on Erub Island and 'gave them the light,' with the subsequent spread of the Christianity, Islanders began to bury their dead.

However, in true Islander style, they managed to merge elements of their older culture. Just after a person died the inlaws of the deceased organised the funeral, as the family was busy in mourning.

Traditionally, five years later, when the coffin collapsed in the grave, the grave stone would be erected and the family would have a ceremonial unveiling of the tombstone and throw a big party. Tombstone Unveilings, or 'Stones', as they are known, signify the end of grieving and are a celebration of the person's life, with feasting, dancing and singing, with the whole community is invited.

Much preparation goes into these events and family are expected to travel from all over the country to attend.

The year before Patty Mills brought the Larry O'Brien Championship Trophy home, he'd returned to Thursday Island for the Tombstone Unveiling of his Grandfather. An upbeat affair, I was invited to attend by Patty's father, Benny. There too Patty donned the traditional red *lava lava* (sarong) and danced with family late into the night.

Patty Mills' grandfather's Stone was one of many I came to attend. Within weeks of starting my job in 2013 I found myself at my first Stone, that of a respected Elder on neighbouring Hammond Island.

The old man's gravesite was cordoned off with palm fronds and a ribbon, to be cut by the priest after his blessings.

The grave was covered with brightly coloured cloth with prints of frangipanis, and gifts which were later divvied up between the in-laws – it's the family's formal presentation of gratitude for their help while they were mourning. Some of the gifts included dugong and turtle harpoons, clothes and toys. An Elder told me, in earlier days money was also pinned to the cloth and the hall where the subsequent feast was held was decorated with more gifts for everyone who attended.

Senior, my boss, said that nobody does death better than Torres Strait Islanders.

It was a quite a heart-warming spectacle to watch, with all the old man's sons and grandsons dancing and singing around his grave, everyone smiling, whistling and whooping.

However, there is a downside. These Stones can cost families anywhere in the tens of thousands, creating real financial hardship – the granite headstone, feeding three hundred people, transport costs from all around the country – it must be a serious financial burden. I have heard of it creating tensions in some families for this reason.

One Islander told me, 'In these modern times some people just want their cultural obligations to be over with quicker, it's like everyone is in more of a hurry these days.'

It's seems the 'hurry disease' that affects so much of the world is also permeating *Ailan Time.*

Walking back from the Tombstone Unveiling ceremony, I inadvertently passed the preparation of not one but five *kupmurris,* the Strait's version of a hāngī or ground oven.

I watched as the men, who traditionally prepare the meats and tend to the fires, carve up deer, wild pig, dugong and turtle. There was a hypnotic sound of knives chopping in unison, as a group of young men diced a mountain of garlic and ginger, and the air was rich and sweet with its bouquet.

A large turtle lay on its back waving its flippers helplessly as an older man slit its throat. Every part of the turtle was used, the flesh, the organs, the blood.

One of the delicacies is the freshly butchered liver slapped straight on the BBQ, which the men ate for lunch to sustain them during their preparations, which in this case had taken four days.

I watched the young kids play with the turtle eggs, rubbery ping-pong-ball-like things.

The meats were marinated with the garlic and ginger, malt vinegar and soy sauce. The latter I'm guessing is the influence of the Malay and Japanese ancestors who came to the region as part of the pearling trade.

Three of the *kupmurries* were dedicated to cooking meat, while the other two were for damper and *Sop Sop,* which is yams, pumpkin and red and orange sweet potatoes doused in coconut milk and wrapped in banana leaves and foil. These dishes were prepared by the women.

The science of the *kupmurrie* is simple but elegant. Dig a shallow hole in the ground, layer it with kindling and stones, set fire to it and let it burn down. The hot rocks are then spread out, a layer of split banana tree trunk is laid on the rocks and the food placed on top. The food is then covered with leaves which both help trap the heat and provide a source of steam.

This is all covered with a blanket, then plastic sheeting and lastly buried in sand. It is then left for an hour or two to cook.

Bush foods such as turtle and dugong have been hot beds of contention, as both animals are endangered and many environmental groups are outraged at this traditional hunting practice.

And with the onset of social media, where young hunters have posted photos and videos of their kills, it has led to shock and dismay amongst the so-called latte-sipping-metrosexualmiddle-classes.

Tensions are high on the islands too. As I watched the meat being prepared, a stocky middle-aged Islander in a singlet, and wielding a bloodied machete, told me in no uncertain terms, 'Don't you be taking any photos of this. All eyes are on you – you will be run out of town if this ends up in the media.'

The lines can be blurry. A legal Indigenous hunting right of endangered dugong and turtle is considered above board when the meat is used during traditional cultural practice such as a Stone, a Shaving, or other significant cultural events. However, rumours of eskies of this meat being flown down for families on the mainland for general consumption is something that riles people, including Member for Leichhardt Warren Entsch, who tells me he's heard of it sold in pubs in Cairns and Townsville. A political backlash to Indigenous traditional hunting started brewing with strange bedfellows of environmentalists and conservative MPs.

The way dugong was traditionally hunted was only achieved by the craft of a master huntsman. At low tide, sea-grass – the dugong's only food source – was scoured to see where it had been grazed, and as the dugong is a creature of habit, often returning to the same patch, the hunter would build a platform near the grazing site, climb on top and wait patiently for many hours for it to return.

This is a far cry from modern hunting practice which involves dinghies with outboard motors and rifles. This is enough to make some choke on their food, including me when I swallowed my guilt as I later politely gnawed on dugong spare ribs and a turtle steak, given to me by family members of the Stone celebration. I'm not a fan of either turtle or dugong. Turtle, if overcooked, can be like chewing on a wetsuit, and while the huge dugong ribs are like a tasty pork belly – the guilt of gnawing bones of an endangered animal always makes me queasy.

Catching turtles is still done in the traditional way, the turtle rodeo, diving off a dinghy and grabbing a turtle – this usually happens in breeding season when two turtles are preoccupied in coitus.

But is it fair to criticise traditional hunting for the demise of these creatures?

Gulf of Carpentaria Gangalidda Traditional Owner and political activist Murrandoo Yanner captured it eloquently, shooting down the ex-TV and radio shock-jock-turned-Senator Derryn Hinch on an Indigenous radio show in 2017, when Hinch criticised the use of outboard instead of traditional canoes with talk of passing laws against traditional hunting.

Yanner shot a rapid-fire stream of consciousness with the gravel of smoker's voice: 'The whole thing with big outboard motors and dinghies is that they're still a proper hunter under native title. They are going out for the same purpose, the same amount of dugong, then you come back, the outboard motor simply makes it quicker and faster. There's a thing called cultural technological adaptation, you guys would still be on the bows and arrows, you wouldn't have the guns and you wouldn't have an air force or army if it wasn't for Marco Polo, a European bloke stealing gun powder from the Chinese. We're the ones that look after the dugong population across northern Australia, we're the ones cleaning up ghost nets, we're the ones recording and looking after the sea-grass areas. It's the people, the companies causing erosion from tree clearing, its flooding into the Gulf and other places and covering the sea-grass beds and the dugong are starving.

'We kill ten percent and people are so quick to jump on my people who use all the animal, we eat it all, we turn the fat into oil and medicines, and we only kill ten per cent, fifty percent is through degradation of the environment – dredging is a big one – pollution, all those chemicals coming out on the Great Barrier Reef, tourists, propellers, fishing, fishing nets, just last night thirty, forty dugongs would be caught in barra nets, rolled to the bottom of the sea and wasted. We'd be happy if we get five a week out here between 3,000 people and we share it out. Not all of the million odd Aboriginal people eat it, only about 200,000 of us across the north that hunt it, not for the fun of it, not for the party – it's quite hard and you don't always come back with it, we hunt to survive, we hunt because it's what keeps us healthy eating from all these different sources. If you're serious about protecting the animal why don't you look at the fifty percent?'

Yanner, critical of the Queensland Government's overreach of land clearing laws said: 'A lot of river banks are eroding away at a massive rate without the roots of the trees to hold them, and there are hundreds and hundreds of megalitres of extra silt getting washed out in the Wet season, covering the sea grass beds. That's a man-made industrial bloody thing, that's not us fellas.'

Hinch: 'To people who say if you don't do something, sea turtles will be extinct in forty years, what do you say to them?'

'I'd say, where they're rare, you're there. You come out to the Palm Island, you come out to Yarrabah, you come out to the Gulf, to Cape York, up to the Torres Strait, look at Arnhem Land, the Kimberley's, there's plenty of them, we look after them. We're not the ones who made them extinct. Where you fellas are, you have done that, there's no one out there hunting, we're all in prison. You've dredged, you've destroyed their grass beds, you've put out the shark nets, you've killed them left, right and centre, that's why you've got jellyfish everywhere.

'Introduced species like the horse and the cow have introduced weeds that the turtles can't dig below the roots, which prevent them laying their eggs. We've been wiping out brumbies in the lower Gulf, shot 13,000 in the last year. We've shot 130,000 pigs in the last three years with our ranger program, and the important thing about that, an autopsy on one of them spilled fifty baby turtles out of his guts. We're doing our part, what's the others doing? What are they doing about the pollution, what are they doing about the tree-clearing effect, the silting, the barramundi nets?

'We have healthy populations here because we regulate it very strictly. We don't need more rules against us, we need rules to allow us to look after our own things. My people alone have cut back on traditional hunting, but it's not because of our impacts, it's because we understand the white-man and industrialisation, fishing of barramundi, international fishermen, they're all killing them, and the dredging and the pollution running off into the Great Barrier Reef, all that stuff is having a big effect and we are still doing our little part.'

For me at the Stone celebration, growing up an avid conservationist, with a dash of anarchy and enviro-terrorism, it was hard to chow down on the dugong bone, but was my reaction due to only seeing one slice of the whole pie? Colonisation goes beyond the slash and burn of genocide and cultural decimation, but isn't this an example of us also colonising their kitchens, their family practices that don't fit nicely into our nuclear-family norms? Stop the Japanese killing thousands of whales commercially under the farcical banner of 'scientific research', yes – harpoon the whalers and feed them to the sharks. Same with the Chinese shark fin industry, fur pelt industry and the ivory peddlers. Kill 'em all and let God sort them out.

But there is a danger in equating traditional hunting with the effects of industry and the industrialised world – Indigenous hunting practices of these animals are a tradition, not an industry, that's the difference. After all, they've only been the custodians for millennia; maybe they look after their resources sustainably.

And if you think you are doing the world a favour eating your soya-based meat supplement, think again.

Marrying old ways with the modernity is something Indigenous people the world over must navigate with a foot in both worlds.

The councillor of the island community of Boigu, Dimas Toby, just before 2016 local government election, explained this paradox to me. Toby was driving me around his island, giving me the tour of his community. Outside was sweltering hot, and there were teenagers with nothing to do but throw their mobile phone up in the air, catch, then check the screen. Toby sees me notice. 'They're sending text messages to each other, they need to throw it in the air to get a signal.'

He turns and smiles at me as we crawl past the text-tossing teenagers. 'The problem with the democratic system that has been forced on us is that it divides our communities. We had a system of governing before the white man came. It was a tribal system, with a chief that was decided on by the community. This way united us, we all stood behind the one person. Now when we have two or more candidates running for the council of our community, it creates division within our community.'

About to stand for his second term, Toby said of his first term, 'I was like blindfolded when I started, it took me a year or so to listen to my community and understand their needs and issues. When a community is divided between more two or more candidates, the winner may spend his whole time trying to win over his enemies, and it means nothing gets done, and so therefore the community misses out. I think we should adopt the old ways of our system of governance again.'

However, to suggest that the use of cultural lore has not being without its problems and failings would be naive and disingenuous, and like people in every culture and community there are those who take advantage, like the councillor for the island community of Saibai, Ron Enosa, who was jailed for fraud after spending $316,000 intended for council that was mistakenly put in his account by the ATO, as well as pilfering some $30,000 from the community church at which he was a priest.

The presiding judge said it was arrogant of Enosa to spend money that was not his, and that others would be worse off by not having the benefit of the money. Enosa called me soon after

I published the story, saying he wanted to tell his side. I agreed but he never called back.

The PNG Nationals, or 'Paps' as they're called, scattered along the coast of PNG's Western Province coast, have family and cultural ties with the Top Western Torres Strait islands of Boigu, Dauan and Saibai stretching back millennia. These ties were in some ways severed with the ratifying of the *Torres Strait Treaty*, an agreement meant to protect this bond. All of a sudden the Paps became foreigners on land they have blood connection to, and today get treated as second-class citizens by many of their Torres Strait cousins.

It's easy to think of racism as being black and white, but hearing Islanders talk of Paps, just 4km north across a small body of water, as being 'dirty and untrustworthy', taking up time at the local medical clinics, and 'shitting in the mangroves', I'm reminded that prejudice is colour-blind.

The treaty also means a people struggling hand to mouth get busted by Border Force, in their massive $330M Cape Class vessels that look like the Deathstar, for taking more than the treaty's allowed traditional catch of six lobsters — costing them their banana boats, their only worldly possession and means of transport for hunting and survival, not to mention the hefty fine they can never pay and subsequent jail time.

PNG's Treaty Village Sibabadaru councillor Kebei Salee tells me: 'Many of us from the Treaty Villages feel that the arrangements of the Treaty are one-sided.

'Why does the boundary of the Protected Zone touch Sigabadaru and move along the coast west to Tais? Why is the line there?

These communities are not and never have been Torres Strait Islander communities, so why is it that line is there? It resulted in us losing most of our territorial waters and traditional hunting grounds.'

I've heard stories of under-age PNG 'house girls' caught up in bonds of sexual slavery, and seen PNG men working in yards, cutting the lawn with a machete for I'm told a measly few bucks a day, while there may be a whipper-sniper under the house – I'm told by one source it becomes a status symbol for some Islanders to have a PNG house servant around.

A man of PNG descent, who I will call Harry, personified the failings of an oral cultural and cultural lore.

A naturalised Australian citizen, Harry had spent his childhood and much of his adult life in one of the outer island communities in the Torres Strait. His father a PNG National had befriended a clan in the community who, according to Harry, had verbally bequeathed a small patch of land for his family. Years later Harry, in his fifties, was still living on the land in a beautifully maintained hut made from coconut fronds and bamboo with his PNG wife and young child, but with his dad long since passed he had no proof of the verbal agreement of his father and the clan.

Harry wanted to have mains power, sewerage and running water connected to his lean-to, and was happy to pay rates, but the council was not able to because the Prescribed Body Corporate (PBC) – the government recognised organisation of Traditional Owners – refused. The PBC said they had no record of the verbal agreement, and that the clan that Harry claimed gave the land to his father was not the clan that owned that patch of the island. The PBC said Harry had to go.

Harry suffers a lifelong mental illness, and medicos were concerned for his and his small family's well-being if he was forced off the land and, although a naturalised Australian, he was not eligible for government social housing as he's not considered a Torres Strait Islander Traditional Owner.

So if kicked off the land where he had spent most of his life, he would either have to go across to PNG, where he had family but was not a citizen, or down south to the mainland, hence severing his connection to his home and family ties. He had come to me to write a story about it, to hopefully cast a light on his situation, but after speaking with council I was told if I did, there was a good chance the PBC would kick him off the island, so I left it, leaving him in a limbo that at least prolonged his stay in what he considered his Country, a land and place that is all he has ever known.

Patty Mills can barely walk when he returns after midnight to the spartan council lodging where we are all bunked down. His uncles and village Elders had given him as thorough a workout as anything meted out by his NBA trainer, Steve Bekker.

'Steve was worried about all the days of training I've been missing coming up here, but when he saw me doing my dance practice and the workout my legs were getting, he said I'll be fine,' Patty says after knocking back a cold can of beer he had cadged off of me.

Steve grins in agreement.

Dance training had gone on the whole afternoon and after a traditional feasting of lobster, clam meat, turtle, pickled fish and yams cooked in coconut milk, Patty had to perform the sacred Beizam shark dance in front of the

Elders and the community. It's a dance rarely seen outside of Mer.

The shark mouth headdress worn during Beizam dance is a sacred emblem from the Malo Cult, the Meriam Mer belief system that pre-dated European arrival. The dance was once performed by the *Zogo le*, the powerful sorcerer of the village.

Today the dance is an important rite of passage for Meriam Mer men, and Mills had not performed it for over a decade.

After the dance Patty said in a speech to the community that returning to Mer and dancing in front of Elders was performing in front of his toughest critics, and he had to ensure he got it right.

'It gives me everything, it's who I am, it's who my family is – to be able to come here to take the time to see family, talk to family and refresh the lessons and the teachings that I was taught at such a young age, that were instilled in me, and be able to continue that, because this is a such a rich culture of customs and traditions,' he said.

'They (GOLDOC) didn't ask why I asked to come to Mer, and I'm glad they didn't. There are many people around the world who come to one of the Seven Wonders of the World to look at the Great Barrier Reef, so I wanted to take Tourism Queensland to look at where this world wonder starts. The Great Barrier Reef starts here at Mer, and Mer is the start of the culture that goes right through Australia. That is my role as ambassador, to be the connector between Aboriginal and Torres Strait Islander Australians, but also other places around the world – all the way to the middle of Texas.

'I've always been an ambassador for Australians, non-Indigenous Australians and Indigenous Australians. It's because of where I've been able to go on my sporting journey, I represent all of Australia. I let people know about who I am and that I'm not just a basketballer, I'm a person who comes from a very rich heritage.'

From the jungle encircling us, the symphony of insects fills the night. Patty, resting his arching legs and lithe six-foot frame, slouches in a deckchair and cadges a second beer off me.

'I have been instilled with culture from such a young age that I know who I am. And I know once sporting is out of the picture, I will have this to come back to and continue the customs and traditions that I've been taught,' he says. 'That's why its special to come back here and continue that on, and now I've just refuelled the culture tank for another year so I will be able to go and do what I do.'

As he downs the last of his beer, Patty listens to his father, Benny, explain the importance Meriam Mer culture.

'When you see Islander dancing it's important to understand its cultural significance, not only to Meriam Mer people but all people of Australia.

'This is not like doing the "bus stop" [dance moves], it's about a deeper level of understanding. It's not just part of Meriam culture, but part of Australian culture and something all Australians should have an understanding of – it's part of all of us, it's part of not just being an Islander, but of being an Australian.'

CHAPTER 20

ALL THE KING'S HORSES

(...and all the King's men, couldn't keep Torres News *away again) August 24, 2015*

'Who are you?' an irritable young woman with a pony tail demands. She has a distinct stuck up North Shore Sydney vibe about her.

'*Torres News* editor Aaron Smith,' I smile lackadaisically, 'And you are?'

'Michele Williams, from the Prime Minister's Office.'

Michele – not her real name, as I don't want to get sued – one of Tony Abbott's many media wranglers, looks flustered. The morning tropical heat on Mer is already starting to run her mascara and dark spots of perspiration spread from under her arms and across the small of her back. In fact, all the TV presenters are struggling to maintain their on-air make up and spotless grooming in the heat.

'Oh OK, I tried emailing and calling you multiple times to get a jersey to be on this junket, but you never responded,' I say.

Michele only noticed me at Eddie Mabo's grave when a group of kids came up to get high fives and ask: 'Hey *Torres News*, take our photo, *bala*.'

Trying to co-ordinate the gaggle of journos she hand-picked for Abbott's media stunt at Mabo's grave – part of his election commitment to spend a week a year in a remote Indigenous community – Michele turns on me.

'How did you get here?' she snarls.

'Mates,' I respond cryptically.

'And how are you getting around?'

'Other mates,' I grin with gritted teeth, starting to enjoy her frustration.

Since the community heard I'd been snubbed on the PM's visit to the Torres Strait, I've been snuck into empty seats on charter flights, driven around by locals on the ground and put up and fed by families, all of whom want their paper covering the spectacle.

Over the ensuing week, I am everywhere the PM is, usually before he arrives and sometimes where his vetted media aren't allowed.

Trying to assume a level authority over me Michele says: 'Well, all the journalists have to stand on this side of the grave to photograph the Prime Minister.'

'But I'm not in your media circus, mate, I didn't get one of those Government of Australia media badges.'

I walk off to set up on the opposite side of the grave she told me to, just to piss her off. We are on Meriam Mir land now, under their lore and there is not a damn thing she can do about it, just as *bala* Doug Passi told them on entering the shark's mouth at the airport.

The sense of loathing is instant and mutual between us.

Michael McKenna from The Australian, who was also snubbed from Michele's media entourage until he and half a dozen other journos chartered their own flight to Mer, says to me while waiting for Abbott to arrive that he thought the decision to try and muzzle local media is 'a disgrace ... always get the local media on side first.'

It's just before Abbott lays a wreath on Mabo's grave, describes him as a 'warrior' and remarks on Mabo's High Court battle to smash *terra nullius* by glibly saying: 'good on him for having a go.' Quite a turnaround from his 1994 comment that he thought the Mabo Case was 'dividing this nation.'

When Governor General Sir Peter Cosgrove laid a wreath on Mabo's grave three years later, the second Governor General to do so, he said: 'Let it be said, it might become – perhaps should become – a rite of passage, a necessary journey by every future prime minister, by every future governor-general.'

The failure of the Prime Minister's Office of excluding me from the visit is further sweetened by my front page story, that hit the news stand the day Abbott arrives in the Torres Strait, with a headline of: *PM's blackflip costs local business $tens and thousands,* 'blackflip' a typo nobody raised with me – it should have read backflip – that's how it goes with overworked staff that have to proofread their own copy.

For months before the visit, Canberra had been all through Thursday Island and outer islands, secret service spooks casing out potential sniper spots for terrorists, every hire car and hotel room booked out.

One of the three hotels on the island, the Jardine – named after Frank Jardine, the region's first magistrate who bragged of shooting more than fifty Aboriginals when 'pacifying' the Cape – was not happy when the Prime Minister and Cabinet (PMC) Office cancelled their blanket booking forty-eight hours before arrival. The Jardine has a policy that all cancellations made less than seventy-two hours before check in have to be paid in full. Abbott decided instead to muck in with the troops at Thursday Island's army barracks.

When owner Steve Mills confronted the PMC about the cancellation, at the height of the tourist season, he told me that they told him: 'We are the Prime Minister and Cabinet Office, what are you going to do about it?'

What he did was call me.

Once a popular hangout for the community, the Jardine Hotel is a shadow of its former glory, rooms are grubby, it feels faded and mole-holed. The meals often have sides of brown lettuce, tables are often not cleared by staff that turn over at an alarming rate, usually indolent backpackers or Indians on work visas happily suffering in the hope of permanent residency, the carrot of a better life dangled in front of them. I had multiple complaints sent to me from both staff and customers, and they've had a string of food safety violations. Once, taking my family there for lunch, my daughter discovered a massive turd in the pool, which the staff did nothing about when alerted of the floater.

When Steve called I insisted on checking his email trail. But it all checked out and he quite rightly had the PMC by the balls on this one, so I was happy to weigh in, and with much of the nation's media in town, the story went viral pretty quickly, both nationally and internationally.

After I broke the story Steve told *The Guardian:* 'I've been stiffed for a heck of a lot of money. If I'm not going to see it I want some sparks.'

Abbott first notices the story while been given a tour of the local supermarket on Mer, where a mother's working group is showing the PM firsthand the high cost fresh fruit and vegies. Abbott casually picks up the *Torres News*, glances at the headline and deftly places the paper back on the counter.

When one of the Mer mothers, Melora Noah, presents Abbott with a letter signed by sixty women, highlighting the high cost of living in the community, and the struggles families face with giving their kids a good education, where after Grade Six they are separated from families to go to boarding school on Thursday Island, or to better high schools further south on the mainland where they are even more disconnected with their Country and culture, Abbott only murmurs to Melora how it's one of the things they had to accept living there.

The comment is just months after his infamous 'Lifestyle choices' remark in Western Australia, after the State Government announced plans to close one hundred-and-fifty remote Indigenous communities: 'What we can't do is endlessly subsidise lifestyle choices if those lifestyle choices are not conducive to the kind of full participation in Australian society that everyone should have.'

Abbott assured Melora of a response to the letter within a fortnight.

The Mer mothers' letter, painstakingly crafted, was never responded to by Abbott, the self-proclaimed 'Prime Minister of Indigenous Affairs,' nor by his successor Malcolm Turnbull.

Melora's husband, Aven Noah, the TSRA representative of Mer, then gives me a lift down to the community centre where Justice Moynihan held the High Court in 1986 as part of the Mabo Case.

Flying in the afternoon before, I had mucked in with Aven and the rest of the community preparing for Abbott's visit. We clambered around the bush macheting palm fronds and banana leaves to decorate the school and Eddie Mabo's grave, joking over a couple of cans of beer, making light of the whole thing. But the community was genuinely excited about Abbott's noble gesture of being the first Prime Minister to visit Mer, and were hopeful that the symbolic visit to the birthplace of native title would be a platform to announce some grand plan of closing the gap, or of reaching the reconciliation and recognition First Nations people craved.

Unlike the day before when Aven and I were both stripped to the waist in footy shorts, sweaty and dirty, bouncing around in the back of a ute filled with pieces of jungle decoration, now Aven is dressed in a rich burgundy coloured silk kaftan that looks like he's just stepped off the Broadway show *The King and I*. Aven has a knack of dressing to the nines for these auspicious events on Mer, satin shirts with wide-brimmed Al Capone fedoras, or crisply-pressed loud Hawaiian shirts. Aven is always the showman, proud of his island home.

In an unusual moment of stillness, Aven, myself and Abbott stand together in silence at the beach just down from the community centre, waiting for Michele's media circus to arrive. Abbott's public appearance posture loosens, his fists unclench, his jaw stops grinding – he strikes me as a man never comfortable under the spotlight, unlike Aven.

Thinking this is my chance for a one-on-one, and to slam him with all my hard-hitting questions, I for some reason refrain. Instead we all three just gaze quietly at the three resident tiger sharks circling and lolling at the water's edge in front of us.

I feel almost sorry for the guy, the sharks circling in front of him maybe reminding him of the ones doing the same thing in the corridors of Canberra, Abbott staring out at sea, slowly nodding his head to his impeding fate. It's a fate

I'm terrified will hit before my next edition comes out a week later, potentially making me old news after we have printed and shipped. Luckily for me Abbott lasts a couple more weeks before he's knifed by Malcolm Turnbull and his faithfuls, including the region's local member Warren Entsch.

The stillness soon breaks when the tussle of the media scrum converge on us, and I am again in the pack elbowing my recorder in Abbott's face trying to get my two cents' worth of his time, where he ignores my question on whether he would address the region's high cost of living, instead answering questions on the economy and stopping the boats.

Standing there on the beach just down from where the High Court was held in 1986, under the shade of coconut trees – one of which was planted by Justice Moynihan and Traditional Owners back in 1986 as a gesture of reconciliation – seems the perfect place for Abbott to announce plans or policy to help close the widening gap, or strengthen the road to reconciliation and recognition, especially after he had just laid a wreath on Eddie Kioki Mabo's grave.

But none are made. In fact, no announcements of policy were made during his entire week spent in the Torres Strait and NPA.

However, Abbott provides one 'suppository of wisdom' on the beach on Mer, where he compares himself to former US President Richard Nixon, using how he pulled down barriers between the US and China in 1972 as an analogy for breaking down the racial barriers with First Australians: 'Just as Nixon went to China ... it may well take a conservative leader to bring about the ultimate form of symbolic reconciliation,' he says.

An unusual choice of analogy for an embattled Prime Minister with plummeting polls and a decisive by-election looming, especially after the recent 'Choppergate' scandal that saw Speaker Bronwyn Bishop's resignation after being busted charging the government for a chopper ride to a wedding. Considering the delicious wordplay on Watergate, the scandal that brought down President Nixon, I curse under my breath being a weekly paper, figuring I'd be the last journo in the country to pun the analogy. Turns out I am the only journo in the country to make the connection.

Choppergate, a source in the army tells me, is why the three Australian Army Blackhawk helicopters flown up from Townsville for the PM's visit were promptly sent back. I only chanced a glance of them at Horn Island Airport, returning from an outer island junket with Billy

Gordon, days before the PM's arrival. The PM and his contingent chartered Caravans and Islander small planes instead.

After the visit, media frenzied around the cost of Abbott's visit, originally pegged at $179,000, which was later raised to $216,000 once the $37,000 payout to the Jardine Hotel had been included.

With a running cost, my army source told me, of around $12,000 an hour each, and where the Townsville base is over six hours away, the cost of the three unused Blackhawks alone creates a dizzying set of numbers that dwarfs the official costing, not to mention all the extra army personnel and equipment shipped up during the lead up to the PM's road show. Senator Jan McLucas took my query to the senate's Estimate Committee but told me later those numbers had been buried in army operational costs.

During the senate estimates, McLucas also queried the PM's office over why I was excluded from the junket, which they denied being responsible for. The transcripts made entertaining reading:

McLucas: 'Did the department become aware that an oversight was made by the Prime Minister's office to not invite the *Torres News* to various events?'

Senator Nigel Scullion: 'I can recall the *Torres News* actually being present at almost every event. They were certainly there in Mer and at two other events. I can recall a representative of the *Torres News* being there ... I know the representative of the *Torres News*. He is quite a distinctive chap. I do know that he was present on Mer and I do know that he was present at a number of other events. I was just remarking that he was actually there at a number of places.'

Before leaving Mer, in front of the entire community at the primary school, and to the shock of students, teachers, parents and Elders, Abbott told them that while it's good the school had an above average attendance rate, '...not many of those kids would expect to go on to become doctors or lawyers.'

Later writing up the article I didn't believe my notes, and it wasn't until I checked Radio National's transcript, who recorded the speech, did I confirm it. Almost more disturbingly, I was the only journo in the country to make mention of the comment.

On leaving through the shark's mouth to fly back to TI from Mer, an Elder tells me that the gods were not happy with the visit this morning – an ill-wind blew up from nowhere just before his arrival.

It's an ill wind that returns for the last of Abbott's entourage, his team from PMC stranded on the runway, their plane with a mechanical failure. All clutching copies of the *Torres News* with my front page story that sticks it to them, their only option to get back to Thursday Island is to climb aboard my near-empty plane. Despite my friendly shit-eating grin and loud *G'day*, it's a very quiet flight back – there's a real stink on the plane, but nobody farted.

Maybe it's just an oversight, or maybe it's the reason I'm again snubbed, this time from the community welcome dinner for Abbott at Thursday Island's cultural centre that evening, something that when Warren Entsch discovers, invites me as his personal guest.

In the shadows on the sidelines, a flighty Michele can do nothing about my presence nestled in the amble bosom of Warren, right in the thick of it.

Warren, a few clarets in, bellows as he walks me up to introduce me officially to Abbott, 'Mate, credit where credit's due, he's the first Prime Minister to get out to the outer islands...'

'No, Fraser came out in the 70s to Yam Island, to negotiate the Torres Strait Treaty,' I say.

Without missing a beat Warren says as we reach Abbott, 'The first Prime Minister to ever visit Mer.'

A couple of days later, the TSRA has organised a meet-andgreet afternoon tea with Thursday Island's business owners. An underling's oversight sees me invited with a form letter, 'Dear business owner/manager.' When I arrive nice and early the TSRA rep at the door is surprised to see me, and with my track record of exposing their bureaucratic boondogglery, she's not at all keen to let me in.

Forcing a smile she says: 'Sorry, this is an invite only event.'

'Yes, I was invited.' Smiling back, I pass my invite letter.

'Oh, but you had to RSVP to be on the list.'

'I did.'

Checking through the list, 'So sorry, but your name is not here.'

Suspecting as much I say, 'That's ok, luckily I printed off my email reply, just in case this happened.'

I place the printout on the counter and walk in.

As Abbott works his way around the table shaking hands that includes a couple of Islander lobster fishermen, his eyes cast down to my hat sitting on the table.

Quite distinctive, my old straw cowboy hat from the high altitude salt plains of Northern Argentina and adorned with feathers, beads, alligator and piranha teeth, is from my years on the road before becoming a journo. It's an old friend that comes everywhere with me.

Abbott looks up from my hat to me, 'Oh, you're that journo.'

I just grin as we sit down. There's a room full of tables and he chooses mine.

Awkwardly Abbott asks the table, 'So tell me, are there any lobster in the region?'

Everyone not sure what to say just nods.

'...and does anyone fish the lobster.'

Again nodding.

'...and do any of the Indigenous people fish the lobster.'

The region's only real viable industry, it has been a hot bed of controversy for over a decade, where the Traditional Inhabitants have been battling the Government to gain a hundred percent control of the fishery, and requesting they remove the largely non-Indigenous commercial sector who they accuse of 'vacuuming the reef' of all fish, leaving locals with little more than leftovers.

Realising Abbott is burying himself right next to a journo, Michele rushes over and snaps at me: 'This is all off the record by the way.'

Closing my notebook, 'Not a problem, off the record from here on in, anyway I think I have what I need,' as I stand up and walk out. Already tipped off that Abbott will be going that afternoon to 'The Tip' – or *Pajinka*, as the local Indigenous population call the northernmost point of Cape York and of Australia – I have a boat to catch.

Abbott toured the five communities of the tip of Cape York, known as the Northern Peninsula Region, where he went out with the local rangers, posed with a shovel with members of the Community Development Project (CDP) – a euphemism for the inherently racist Work for the Dole scheme. An Abbott initiative, the CDP replaced the Community Development Employment Projects scheme (CDEP). Abbott in 2016 said: 'Abolishing CDEP was a well-intentioned mistake and CDP is our attempt to atone for it.'

The Government website describes CDP as something that: '...supports job seekers in remote Australia to build skills, address barriers and contribute to their communities through a range of flexible activities ... and is an essential part of the Australian Government's agenda for increasing employment and breaking the cycle of welfare dependency.'

Forcing welfare recipients to work for 25 hours a week, for a fraction of the minimum wage and less than the former CDEP, the CDP has been criticised for actually trapping people in perpetual unemployment, being bounced from one project to the next, being penalised for not participating, and where significant numbers become so disenfranchised that they drop off welfare completely.

Australian National University researcher Lisa Fowkes described it as being a 'very' racist scheme that is 'impoverishing Aboriginal communities.'

'This is part of a perfect storm of issues that are making life harder, more challenging, and also robbing people of a future in remote communities,' she told ABC online in 2018.

In the same year the UN Committee on the Elimination of Racial Discrimination asked the Australian Government how it will eliminate racial discrimination in the remote Work for the Dole program imposed on remote Aboriginal and Torres Strait Islander communities.

At an address to Abbott in the Northern Peninsula Area during his visit, the Northern Peninsula Area Regional Council Mayor Bernard Charlie says: 'We are suffering from policy designed elsewhere by others and which is not for our people.

'The data on what is happening to our people is appalling. The cost of living is high, and our life expectancy is low. We are lucky if we reach the age of fifty. We only have access to low skilled jobs and our communities suffer from high unemployment.

'We shouldn't be arguing about who is responsible, this problem is everyone's. We need to be united as one people and turn this unacceptable situation around. Prime Minister, this is an opportunity both personally and professionally for you to turn this around. The people of the NPA are strong and resilient and we need you to be our people's champion. I cannot witness another generation suffer. This is not about blaming, we just need the same social and economic advantages as any other citizen.'

Abbott responds: 'Indigenous Australians deserve to be first class citizens, with kids attending school and adults in work; we need to provide financial support, which should obviously not be spent on alcohol and drugs. You need to be given more responsibility for your own lives, and not just recognised in the constitution, but restore responsibility, respect, pride and self-respect. We need to flourish as one people. Indigenous people and settlers have to walk arm in arm into the future.'

Abbott's sentiment reflects his 2014 comment that: 'I guess our country owes its existence to a form of foreign investment by the British Government in the then unsettled or, um, scarcely settled, Great South Land.'

After Abbott's speech and as dinner is being served, the Inijinoo community dance team starts performing their 'Happy Dance' where they all shake a leg in good natured fun.

Michele rushes up to me and a couple of TV camera guys and says: 'Ok this is now closed to the media,' as she stands in front of the cameras.

Looking at me she says: 'We can give you a lift on the media bus to your hotel.'

'You haven't invited me on the bus before. Anyway, I'm staying in Community here in Injinoo.'

'But there's no hotel in Injinoo.' Flustered and at the end of her tether, Michele says: 'Well don't take photos of the Prime Minister eating.'

'I have enough photos of the Prime Minister; I'm here to take photos of the community.'

A Traditional Owner of Injinoo and one of the rangers that took me into Country camping a year or so earlier calls out from the crowd: 'Hey *Bala*, come take my photo with the Prime Minister!'

I walk off leaving Michele to stew, and join the throng of the community where I, while not an official guest for dinner and so told there's not enough food for me, sit down and share a lobster tail with another Injinoo resident, who isn't about to let someone go hungry, as nobody goes hungry at a feasting in Community.

Michele, on the other hand, winds up her visit to the region with a piss up, starting at the local tavern with a selfie, holding a tinnie with another prime ministerial staffer James Hart, posted on social media along with the caption: 'Sorry, I'm out having a bender with the locals!'

Staff of the Cape York Peninsula Lodge, where everyone was staying, confirmed that later that night dozens of members of the hand-picked press junket gathered there for 'off-the-record' drinks with the former Prime Minister and his staff. In a town that has been crippled by alcohol over many generations, and where heavy alcohol restrictions apply, this attitude was seen as offensive by some.

However, it seems hardly surprising, considering the wild party Abbott's office had after his leadership spill the following month, where it was rumoured Abbott was shirtless, and an Italian marble table was smashed by someone dancing on it, possibly Assistant

Infrastructure Minister Jamie Briggs, who was confined to a wheelchair the following day.

This is a man who admits in 2017 that in 2009 he had been too drunk to be in Parliament to vote on several important policies, while on a bender with fellow MPs Peter Costello and Kevin Andrews. 'I think quite a few bottles of wine were consumed by the three of us,' Abbott told ABC show, *The House*.

This is the Special Envoy for Indigenous Affairs created by happy-clapping Scott Morrison as a kickback in PM Turnbull's leadership spill that got Morrison the top job. This revolving door of Australian prime ministers made us an international laughing stock and the political coup capital of the democratic world, as the Mad Katter said at the time: '...more Prime Ministers than Pakistan.'

Abbott's appointment was received with condemnation and was seen as perpetuating the top-down patriarchy that leaves blackfellas out of the room. Indigenous Labor MP Linda Burney said of the appointment: 'They are making it up as they go along ... It is a major insult to Aboriginal people that can speak for themselves.'

Senator Patrick Dodson compared it to the Government's 2017 rejection of the *Uluru Statement of the Heart*, a carefully crafted document formed after months of consultations with 250 Indigenous leaders on how to reform the constitution and give them a voice in government. It asked for two reforms: 1) a First Nations Voice enshrined in the Constitution and 2) for the establishment of a 'Makarrata Commission' to supervise agreement-making and truth-telling between governments and Aboriginal and Torres Strait Islander peoples.

'The First Nations people have asked the Government for a voice, and we get Tony Abbott!'

CHAPTER 21

TRICK OR TREATY

Wee hours of June 4, 2017

With the swagger of a belly full of island *kai kai* and a few too many cans of XXXX Gold, I walk along the foreshore road on Mer away from the village. It's not dark and Mer's ethereal entities and bogeymen are not lurking in the shadows – no sense of foreboding tonight. The sea beside the road shimmers with the luminescence of the Milky Way, which was created by the eddies and currents kicked up by the cosmic shovel-nosed shark that lore says swam through the galaxy, scattering the stars into their constellations.

It's the end of the celebrations of the 25th anniversary of the handing down of the High Court's Mabo decision that set a world precedent for native title rights – and I had the privilege of being invited out to cover the occasion, and then kick back afterwards with Elders and community for a few brews and yarning. The community had been celebrating for the week leading up to Mabo Day, where dancing started early that morning and continued until evening feasting, and was still going strong when I left well after midnight. After the formal ceremonies and dancing concluded, the wail of the island chorus and thumping bass of the *warup*, the crack of the cooking oilcan used as a snare, and the rattle of the *kulap* (handheld seedpod shaker) constantly stir up people to dance to song after song. Various community members, young and old, man and woman, jumping up and joining in, as the *Akas* (elder women) walk behind the dancers spraying them with perfume and talcum powder, an informal sign of respect, while whooping and wolf whistles from the crowd egged them on.

The spring in my step comes from the gratitude of being included, especially when silver-haired Elder Ron Day says to me over the rim of his glasses: '*Bala* Aaron, when you going to dance?'

'But I'm a whitefella, Uncle.'

There is a pause between songs as the *warup* drummer massages wax into the taut snakeskin to keep it supple and sweeten its resonance. The drummer yells out a command in Language and the oil can snaps out a four count and it all crescendos again. Uncle Ron, squeezing my shoulder, chuckles, 'No, *Bala*. Tonight you are Miriam Mer man.'

I look to Billy Gordon, the State MP who gave me a lift out to Mer in his charter flight and say, 'I'll dance if Billy dances.'

Gordon shakes his head in horror: 'I can't dance!'

'Mate, if you don't dance here, on Mer, on 25th anniversary of Mabo Day, I promise it is something you will regret when you are lying on your death bed.'

'Fuck, Aaron, you bastard, don't do that to me.'

So finishing our cans of Dutch courage, we jump up and join the back row and thump our feet and shake our arms trying to keep in time and formation with the dance team, in a haze of perfumed talcum powder.

Even though I would always be an outsider to *Ailan Kastom,* the people of Mer over the years have given me the warmest of receptions. The community even took my wife and daughter under its wing – with my daughter adopted by one of the Akas and written into their family tree, after being invited to spend time feasting and celebrating at the end of year Grade Six graduation ceremonies of the local school. I even had my forty-ninth birthday on Mer and eventually wore a *lava lava.*

One of these times, while I helped the lads prep the *kupmurri* fire pit for the night's feasting, my six-year-old daughter dashes past, 'Going for a swim dad,' as she runs across the hot platinum white sand and jumps into the still water.

'Watch out for Uncle Beizam, mate,' I call after her.

Three bronze whaler sharks each around two metres long loll around in the shallows where she splashed and played. Completely without fear she yells, 'It's okay, they're my friends.'

Ten minutes later I hear blood-chilling scream: 'Dad help me!'

I turn around and see her chest deep in water circled by sharks. Pointing at the beach she hollers: 'I can't get out of the water, there's a crab, what if it bites me?!'

'It's the constitution, it's Mabo, it's justice, it's law, it's the vibe...' as the famous quote says from the iconic 1997 Australian film *The Castle*, about the great Australian dream of owning your home illustrates – 'Mabo' has become part of the lexicon of what's 'true blue'. The word Mabo even appears in the online Urban Dictionary defined as Australian slang that is: 'the act of taking something that isn't yours and claiming it as your own.'

But Mabo was a battle that was barely won, where the decision came down to a couple of disputed boundary lines of garden plots demarcated by stones. Greg MacIntyre, one of the *Mabo Case* lawyers, tells me their case was essentially saved by a filing cabinet they discovered in a back room of the Island Council. It was full of disputes of the boundaries of the garden beds dating back decades. It formed a strong part of their case, proving First Australians had a concrete sense of property. Without that record of decades of tribal clan bickering, the whole thing could have fallen over. MacIntryre and I talked about this over the din in Mer's 'wet canteen', the only licensed premises in the community open for only a few hours in the early evening each day. Unbeknown to me, I had walked in to the canteen with a moth sitting my shoulder, a totem of Meriam people which elicited quiet reverent nods of approval and a clear path to the bar – it just added to the layers of warm fuzzy joy the whole event imbued me with.

As significant as the Mabo decision was, it still falls short of reconciling the country's past, and in some ways, despite the symbolic significance of recognising First Australians in the highest court of the land, ironically almost continues to discriminate against them.

Anthropologist David Martin, who spent many years in Cape York, acknowledged while there is much to celebrate since the landmark Mabo case, there is also much to be critical of, especially the fact 'that not least, the inordinately complex, expensive, and for Indigenous people alienating processes through which native title is legally recognised.'

Not to mention the process can take so long that the generation that lodge the claim may not live to see its fruition, just as Eddie Mabo himself did not live to see the fruits of his labour.

In his 2015 paper, 'Does Native Title merely provide an entitlement to be native?', Martin suggests when it came to the provisions of the *Native Title Act 1993*, 'there is a false dichotomy between tradition and modernity in contemporary circumstances, and that Indigenous identities are better understood as "hybrid" in the sense that they involve a complex interpenetration of forms of identity and practice drawn from diverse domains.'

He fears native title claimants have to portray themselves in a conservative, reductionist and traditionalist way – that is, as a static culture, like something stuck in a glass cabinet at the British Museum.

He argues instead that any society or culture is fluid and ever-changing, and that claimants of native title engage with the wider society in personal, social, professional and economic ways.

There are, he further argues, multiple Indigenous modernities where Indigenous people embrace technology and the modern global village while still creating their own cultural space within that global village.

However, the Government's approach to Indigenous affairs, he asserts, does not take into account what constitutes contemporary Indigenous identity, expecting instead that Indigenous individuals should refashion themselves by rejecting their commitment to communalism and what is seen as social dysfunction, adopting instead modernism and individualism by entering the economic market by getting a job and buying property, even if that means leaving Country and the 'lifestyle choice' of living remotely – as Abbott put it in 2015 – by having to move to a metropolitan hub.

Martin also quotes Cape York Aboriginal intellectual and political activist Noel Pearson arguing, in a speech delivered at *The Earth Dialogue* at the 2006 Brisbane Festival, for what he describes as 'layered identities', defined as an individual having the 'capacity to be responsive to diverse cultural, emotional, ethical, pragmatic, economic, aesthetic and other affiliations across society, as well as within particular ethnic or cultural contexts.'

Brian Keon-Cohen, another of the Mabo Case lawyers, told me the day before I flew to Mer for the 25th anniversary celebrations that he acknowledged one of the failings of native title was that the burden of proof was very severe for Traditional Owners, because 'they have to demonstrate the continuing system of custom and tradition back to 1788, and a society that is essentially unaltered and the connections substantially unchanged since their ancestors occupied that land since 1788.'

He explained the need for urgent reform, stating that though substantial reforms to the problems were tabled in 2015, nothing had been done since.

Lawyer and senior adviser on constitutional reform for the Cape York Institute, Shireen Morris, wrote in her 2012 paper; *Re-evaluating Mabo: the Case for Native Title Reform to Remove Discrimination and Promote Economic Opportunity*, 'the legal construction of native title is in some important aspects discriminatory' for restricting claimants 'to the limited range of activities that can be proven by reference to traditional law and custom'. She argues that while Indigenous people may not be able to prove their ownership of their land as recognised by Australian law, these rights have never-the-less existed since well before the arrival of white men, and that while the Mabo Case did extinguish the fiction of *terra nullius* and recognise native title to land, it also failed to recognise the right of Indigenous people to own such land, and in doing so, led to a widening of the Gap.

As former Indigenous Affairs Minister Amanda Vanstone said in 2005, native title owners are 'land rich but dirt poor.'

With all its shortcomings, Mabo laid a foundation to build a better way, where some thirty-two percent of Australia's land mass is subject to native title determinations and some 2,000 ILUAs (Indigenous Land Use Agreements) have allowed successful negotiations about land use for Indigenous people. However, a quarter of a century on little more than the foundation has ever been built.

In 1996, the Wik people from Western Cape York Peninsula successfully made a native title claim to two pieces of pastoral land on their Country that the State Government was using. This threat of a native title claim to farmland cut close to the bone and went from the Federal Court to the High Court who determined that pastoralists did not have exclusive rights to the land and that the existence of a pastoral lease did not extinguish native title.

In response to the ruling, two years later the newly-elected Howard Government introduced the *Native Title Amendment Act 1998*, known as the 'Ten Point Plan' which led to the longest debate in the Australian Senate's history. The shrill hysteria of the white right, that the High Court had conducted 'judicial activism' threatening every Aussie battlers' backyard, resulted in a watering down of the *Native Title Act* by broadening powers of Federal and State governments to extinguish native title, and made the initiation of claims even more cumbersome as well as making urban areas a no-go zone. The *Ten Point Plan* keeps the door ajar for mining and farming interests, such as the highly criticised Adani Mine in Queensland, as one of the Plan's clauses states: 'governments are empowered to extinguish native title over crown lands for matters of 'national interest.'

It took sixteen years after the traditional custodians won their day in court in the *Wik vs. Queensland* case for the last parcel of land to be handed back to them in 2012.

The following year, the *Akiba vs Commonwealth* High Court case mentioned earlier where a group of Torres Straight Islanders applied for native title rights and interests in a major part of the sea area of Torres Strait, including a right to fish for sale and trade, provided yet another stone in the foundation of native title.

While somewhat of another hollow victory, Brian Keon-Cohen told me the importance of the *Akiba Sea Claim* was it proved, 'native title rights are not just for personal or domestic purposes but for commercial purposes,' and that 'large regional claims deliver a strong basis for claimant groups to negotiate, and perhaps in future to look at further negotiations in the nature of self-government, comprehensive agreements domestic treaties and the like.'

One of the precedents used to support the Akiba Case was what is known as the 'Crocodile Case' where Murrandoo Yanner, Aboriginal leader from Mornington Island in the Gulf, was prosecuted in 1994 for hunting two crocodiles. He was charged with contravening the *Queensland Fauna Conservation Act,* but argued that he was exercising his rights as a Gangalidda person as according to traditional laws and custom. The case went first to the Magistrate's Court in Mount Isa, where the magistrate upheld Yanner's defence, however the State government then appealed the decision to the Court of Appeal. Yanner then took the case to the High Court, where he won.

At a Native Title forum on Mer the day before 25th anniversary of Mabo Day, Yanner was a guest speaker. In his early forties, with a smoker's gravelly voice and a brawler's charm, he wooed the audience with his shooting-from-thehip, off-the-cuff speech, where he described native title as a 'bastardised, watered-down version of our sovereign rights – don't talk about native title – act.' Yanner called for protest and resistance. 'They can't lock us all up in prison. A house divided is a house defeated,' he said to grunts of approval from the crowd.

On 13 March 2019 another moral justice was served when the High Court ruled in favour a landmark Native Title case for the Traditional Owners of Northern Territory's Timber Creek, in what has been described as the most significant since Mabo. The ruling found that the Ngaliwurru and Nungali peoples should be financially compensated for the loss or diminishment of their native title and the spiritual and emotional hurt it caused. The Court stated: 'Each act put a hole in what could be likened to a single large painting – a single and coherent pattern of belief in relation to a far wider area of land. It was as if a series of holes was punched in separate parts of the one painting. The damage done was not to be measured by reference to the hole, or any one hole, but by reference to the entire work.' The Timber Creek case has implications of compensation in the billions across the country.

Also at the Native Title forum in 2017 on Mer, Billy Gordon said: 'This Mabo Day is a timely reminder of how far we've come but also how far we have yet to go.'

'There is still some unfinished business and I think this is a great opportunity for us to start talking about the next iteration of Mabo mark II, that would be to start talking about a treaty, a treaty I think will be the only way to go.

'We need to reconstruct the relationship black Australia has with white Australia, and I can't think of a better way to that than putting in place a treaty. A treaty isn't about us taking swaths of people's backyards, this is about a new relationship between black people and white people and particularly government and Indigenous people. I've always been critical of how government engage with Indigenous people and there's 30 years of policy failure in this area.

'Essentially the major discussion that's held around Indigenous people policy within the ALP and the LNP is by non-Indigenous people, we've got to be able to take that ground back.'

The talk of treaty and constitutional reform had reached a high tide mark with the *Uluru Statement of the Heart* released just days before the 25th anniversary of Mabo Day.

While there may well have been some mission creep in the original idea of discussing constitutional reform of making a provision for a First Nations Voice in the Australian Constitution, the fact that a historic statement from Indigenous representatives from across the country was flatly dismissed by the government left a bad taste in the mouths of many. A reform to the constitution would require a referendum, and despite the majority of Australians wanting to change the constitution to recognise Indigenous people, only eight of Australia's forty-four referendums have been successful. As well as including a preamble about First Australians in the constitution, it was also hoped constitutional reform would repeal two particularly racist parts, *Section 25* which contemplates a state disqualifying all members of a particular race from voting in a state election, and *Section 51 (xxvi)*, sometimes referred to as the 'races power', which provides the head of power for the Commonwealth to make laws for people of particular racial groups. It was amended at a referendum held in 1967 to repeal the qualification 'other than the Aboriginal race in any state'. This had the effect of enabling the Commonwealth to make laws relating to Aboriginal and Torres Strait Islander peoples.

Torres Strait Islander Kenny Bedford, a director of Reconciliation Australia, said two weeks prior to the creation of the *Uluru*

Statement of the Heart that: 'We want to ensure that through this opportunity for reform that we get substantive change of our constitution ... We absolutely reject symbolic words that say we are the First Nations People, we know that, that's obvious to us, we live with it every day.'

When it was rejected, Bedford described it as a 'king hit and kick in the guts.'

'It has undone years of progress and goodwill generated through a lengthy process of community engagement and reconciliation.

'This foul play has set us back years but I am guessing it will also highlight to many here and abroad the sort of barriers we face in Australian society.

'You cannot get a clearer example of "tell us what you want but we'll still do what we think is best for you".'

Noel Pearson said: 'I think Malcolm Turnbull has broken the First Nations hearts of this country, expressed in the *Uluru Statement from the Heart.*'

While the discussion around constitutional reform developed during the time leading up to and the subsequent rejection of the *Uluru Statement of the Heart,* there was dissent amongst the Indigenous Australians that constitutional reform was nothing more than symbolic recognition of Indigenous people in the Australian

Constitution, nothing more than a way of amending our national shame, and for white Australia to feel better for the past injustices. There was concern that a change in the constitution would be the death knell for getting a treaty or series of treaties between First Nations peoples and the government, and ending a decades-old fight.

As journalist Chris Graham said in 2013, calling constitutional reform a con that served to 'deny Aboriginal people the fundamental right to self-determination, but give them a warm fuzzy constitution and call that progress. Constitutional recognition is a poor man's treaty. It is another national apology, without compensation.'

The need for a treaty is legitimate, considering Aboriginal and Torres Strait Islander nations have never ceded sovereignty, and the nation we call Australia has been constructed over the top of existing nations.

But why not both? Yes, as a white Australian I find it incredibly embarrassing that our constitution does not recognise First Australians and has racist clauses within it, and I think we need a treaty with First Australians. I also agree with the then recently elected West Australian Senator Pat Dodson's comment in May 2016, that: 'We know treaty is a big discussion in the community, we know constitutional recognition is a big discussion in the community. They're not mutually exclusive matters.'

Around the same time of Senator Dodson's comments, Social Justice Commissioner Mick Gooda visited the Torres Strait as part of the push to get constitutional recognition on the board, where they had a boatload of constitutional legal eagles and Indigenous influencers set off from Thursday Island for outer island community dialogues on the subject.

He said at the start of the campaign in Thursday Island's ANZAC Park: 'The Recognise campaign is about making Australia a place where everyone can belong, where Aboriginal and Torres Strait Islander culture is Australian culture, thrown in with English, Scottish, Irish and all the other immigrants here today. The Sunday after the Saturday that this referendum occurs, we will wake up in a new country.'

When the Recognise boat finished its tour of the Torres Strait at Mer, I was there, again invited out by the community to cover the occasion, which was upbeat and full of promise. The boat was met with the young Beizam Dancers on the beach, with singing, wolf-whistling, cat calls and whoops of approval. Amongst the din Elder Alo Tapim, dressed in a red *lava lava* leans into my ear and whispers: 'Why aren't you wearing your *lava lava, Bala?*'

'I thought I had to live here at least thirty years before I was local enough to wear one, Uncle.'

'No son, you're *Ailan* man.' It took me three more years, but during a weekend on Mer where I celebrated my forty-ninth birthday, I finally donned my *Ailan* sarong.

When Mick Gooda finished his speech at the launch of Torres Strait leg of the Recognise Campaign in ANZAC Park, he closed with a poem by Aboriginal Poet Oodgeroo Noonuccal, called *Son of Mine:*
My son, your troubled eyes search mine,
Puzzled and hurt by colour line.
Your black skin as soft as velvet shine;
What can I tell you, son of mine?
I could tell you of heartbreak, hatred blind,
I could tell you of crimes that shame mankind,
Of brutal wrong and deeds malign,
Of rape and murder, son of mine;
But I'll tell you instead of brave and fine
When lives of black and white entwine,
And men in brotherhood combine—
This would I tell you, son of mine.

CHAPTER 22

WHERE THE WIND TURNS

April, 2014

Sultry, dark and brooding, water hangs in the air like a loaded gun. Mildew and moisture permeates everything, laundry never completely dries, flour and sugar cement in clumps, and the horizon disappears daily into grey which at times even swallows up the midday sun.

Sheets of rain rattle the windows of the community centre on Kirriri (Hammond Island), the outer edges of category five Cyclone Ita smiting the region. Starting in the Solomon Islands where it kills 23 people, Ita S-bends away from the Torres Strait on its path south where it later hammers Cairns.

My wife, daughter and I have been invited to the Community by the young up-and-coming artist Ceferino Sabatino, which everyone calls 'Nino', to attend his workshop on working with ghost nets, the discarded fishing nets that float through the world's oceans, creating indiscriminate death traps for countless marine life.

Slight in frame and stature, Nino's soft voice is barely audible over the driving rain on the tin roof, as he explains how to make one of his signature turtles from wire, string and ghost nets.

'We used to make traditional masks out of turtle shell, then the one day when I was fishing I found a ghost net floating with a trapped turtle, and so I now make turtles out of ghost nets,' Nino says.

It's the end of the Wet, the season of cyclones in the Far North where thick, black columns of monsoon clouds rumble and crackle lighting before dumping three quarters of the region's annual rainfall in a few weeks, in deluge after deluge. It's truly biblical. With the monsoons come the seasonal king tides, where the ocean reaches up to its highest mark each year, lapping at the back door of Islanders' homes, sometimes gushing flotsam and jetsam across the threshold or spitting sea spray over rooftops, while eating away precious inches of coastline that is their backyards.

It makes the swamp rats retreat from the foreshore rocks and claw into wall cavities of houses, as the king tides steal the beaches and submerge roads, their waters dark and foreboding as crocs in their rutting season become more brazen and lurk too close for comfort.

Tiny red ants invade houses, swarming around circuit boards of light switches and power points, drawn to their electrical warmth. The white ants chew deeper into the woodwork while the green ants retreat to their silky clumps of leaves in the mango trees. The particularly aggressive 'tiger mozzie' or 'BBQ stopper' swarm, spawning in the many pockets of rainwater trapped in refuse, puddles and kids' toys scattered around backyards.

Translucent geckos dart across the walls, their chirping, I'm told, are the voices of the dead talking. On the windows cling green tree frogs gorging on the smorgasbord of insect life.

Before the monsoonal trough forms over Indonesia around December and January and creeps west, before the first large globules of rain splatter down, the land is dusty, dry, desiccated and damn thirsty. Then the skies burst, cascading over guttering as waterfalls, turbulently foaming up out of storm water drains, swallowing streets and footpaths, transforming parks into swamps and creeping in under door sills. Everything that was dead comes to life, the landscape suddenly becomes a shock of bright greens.

An Elder tells me the rains wash away all the bad spirits and negative energy, allowing the islands to start the year anew.

After Nino's workshop, he drives us down to the waterfront of Kirriri as he explains the Islander relationship with the weather.

'There are four winds in the *Zenadth Kes* (Torres Strait), which are the seasons. Kuki is the Northwest that brings the monsoons (January to April) and Sager which is the Southeast wind of the Dry season (May until December). Then there is the Southerly Zay, which comes at any time and the Northerly Nay Gay which blows hot and humid (October to December),' Nino says.

Islanders have a totemic relationship with these winds, where everyone has both a clan totem animal and a wind. In fact their relationship and definition of the seasons are all based on these winds and on the migration and breeding times of birds, fish, turtle and dugong, the trees, flowers and fruit, and the changing positions of the stars at night.

Before Nino belts us across the narrow channel of the Strait that separates Kirriri from Thursday Island in his small open dinghy, he gives me some fishing tips: 'It's a new moon now. If it's pointing up like a cup it means the fishing will be good, and when the mangrove leaves around the bottom of the tree start to go yellow, it means stay away from the shark holes when spear fishing, and watch out for stonefish and stingers.'

The rain clears and as steam rises from the mangroves, we push off from Kirriri Beach and start to motor out. A large stingray jumps out of the water in front of us doing a flip before splashing down.

'If you see a ray jump out of the water like that and land on its back it means you will get sorry news,' Nino says. 'It also means bad weather is coming.'

In minutes Kuki whipped up the waves and as another monsoonal front hit us, we're drenched in seconds, but we're not cold, the warm rain clings our clothes to our bodies. Islanders' understanding of the Seawater Country runs deep – they can tell if a passing cargo ship is full or empty at night, just by the sound the waves chasing into it make. One time an Islander from Ugar, the smallest and most isolated Torres Strait community, headed off for home from Erub Island with only enough fuel for half of the trip. He knew he'd reach a certain current that would carry him the rest of the way home – and it did, washing him right on his island's beach, albeit ten hours late to a fretting wife.

In a few weeks Sager starts to blow, sending a sea breeze through our house that we haven't felt for months. It blows away the tiger mozzies and flies that have been tormenting us since Kuki blew and buffeted the other side of the island, leaving us in its lull. But with Sager blowing again, we can open the windows, turn off the aircon and hang the hammock back up in the backyard.

'Living where the wind turns' is a Brazilian expression for living somewhere that's far away from everywhere, apt really for the Torres Strait. It's also a sad analogy for how the winds are changing in regards to global climate, reflected starkly in the Torres Strait where, eighteen months after Nino's workshop, the worst ever El Nino, nicknamed Godzilla, hits the world hard at the end of 2015.

Nino never lived to see Godzilla ravage his beloved Torres Strait, his tragic untimely passing months earlier also meant he never lived to see the impact ghost net art was to later have on the world in advocating the plight of the oceans. Nino's funeral was a heart-wrenching experience with the whole community left in shock at his passing and dealing with the vacuum it left.

Although El Nino is a naturally occurring weather phenomenon where sea surface temperatures rise, which affect weather patterns that bring hotter and drier conditions for

Australia, the increased frequency and intensity has been correlated to human-induced climate change.

The Far North missed out completely on a wet season in 2016, bringing unprecedented water restrictions and questions of water security long term, where some outer island communities' water supply gets down to only a couple of days' supply.

The mangroves all across Northern Australia underwent an unprecedented die-back and with seawater temperatures rising above 32 degrees for weeks at a time, it caused the worst-ever coral bleaching episode in history. Aerial surveys of 520 coral reefs from Cairns to PNG revealed that ninety-five percent of that section of the Great Barrier Reef suffered bleaching, including most of the Torres Strait.

It was part of the third recorded global coral bleaching event, however the previous ones were less severe with around twenty percent bleaching in 2010 and sixteen percent in 1998.

Research on 400-year-old coral cores revealed major coral bleaching events have only occurred since 1998.

One of the world's most eminent coral scientists and convenor of the National Coral Bleaching Taskforce, Professor Terry Hughes, tells me over the phone after completing the aerial survey work: 'This has been the saddest research trip of my life.'

Hughes and other scientists involved in the survey are angry at the Government's inaction as well as its stance on climate change.

He said virtually all species of corals are being affected, including the most robust.

Reef scientist Justin Marshall tells ABC's *7:30 Report*: 'The prognosis just gets worse and worse as more of these global events occur. I guess what upsets me the most is that we are literally stealing the future from our children. I'm going to be dead within thirty years. I probably won't see the possible end of the Great Barrier Reef. But it's possible that my grandchildren will and that really upsets me.'

It's really driven home to me when we take a dingy out to dive on the reef at nearby Tuesday Island, a reef where I had taken my four-year-old daughter snorkelling only months before, where we explored an iridescent-coloured garden of soft corals. After the bleaching episode, they have all died and there is nothing left but bare rock. Much of the beautiful branch corals and bommies in the three bands of reef north of Thursday Island are also now ghost white or covered in a green slime.

The death of the reef, one of the most biodiverse ecosystems on the planet, is not only the loss of a natural wonder of the world and a national icon, but also threatens the existence of Islander way of life and customs, or *Ailan Kastom*. The reef is the part of their sea country that is not only referred to as their 'supermarket', but also the home and hunting grounds of their totems.

On the back of a terrible fishing season the year before, the lobster fishery suffers with the warmer waters of El Nino.

Jerome Kalwij, the manager of the local lobster packing factory, tells me: 'The stock that has been coming in this year is much smaller and of poorer quality than last year.

'The warmer water has not been good for us. The crays go deeper to find cooler water, and when they are brought to the surface and put in holding tanks, many die because the water is too warm, it's like a really slow cooker.

'Another problem with warmer water is that it holds less oxygen, which means we can hold fewer numbers in each tank.'

With ninety percent his market being live product, stock dying hits the bottom line for everyone in the industry.

'The divers are losing more stock from when they catch it to when we get it, we then lose more overnight in the holding tanks, Cairns loses some more, and yet more is lost by the time it gets to China. I think it would be around thirty percent all up, which is much higher than normal.'

Professor Hughes believes half of the bleached reef could die in the month following the bleaching, which actually later equates to more like sixty-seven percent die-back, and it would take a decade for the surviving reef to recover.

The following year the unthinkable happens when another major bleaching episode occurs, but this time without an El Nino to blame.

Hughes told me not as much of the Torres Strait was bleached this time, but it transpires to be a hollow victory: 'The reason bleaching in the Torres Strait is minor this year is because there isn't a lot of coral left. Even the big deep water bommies are showing signs of bleaching this year, and all the even more sensitive corals in the north have already been decimated.

'I'm not sure I have the moral fortitude to climb on the plane a third time, it's not easy to fly over reef after reef and record them as really badly bleached.'

Each bleaching episode takes around a decade for the coral to recover; in 2020, the Great Barrier Reef experienced another significant bleaching event, the third in five years.

The impacts of climate change, where the reef dies in the space of a couple of years, are only part of how living in the Torres Strait is being on the front-line of climate change. Sea-level rise is already impacting several of the island communities, inching away the edges of coastline, where the six most 'at risk' communities require significant seawalls, that cost in the millions.

Mayor Fred Gela told me that they lobbied for years trying to get federal funding, but it wasn't until they reframed the problem from one of climate change to problems with coastal inundation that they finally secured funding.

'There are a lot of sceptics when you talk about climate change, so in terms of accessing the funds needed, we have had to brand it under the banner of restoration of failing infrastructure,' Gela tells me after they finally secured seawall funding in 2014.

'It's been more than ten years in the making. Previously the branding was climate change and its impacts, but there are still non-believers in government as to whether or not climate change is real or not, so in order to get that $26 million through the door ... it was branding it as restoration of failing infrastructure.'

But the $26 million was only enough to build a seawall for the most at risk community of

Saibai, and little was left to address the other at risk communities.

At a summit for water security in the region in 2018, where once again the monsoons were not filling reservoirs enough to supply water for the dry season, Gela tells me: 'When we talk about climate change, we can see the changes, it is happening and for those that still choose not to believe it, it's harder to see it when you live in the densely populated metropolitan areas.'

'Temporary' mobile desalination units brought in to deal with the 2016 water shortages caused by El Nino Godzilla have not stopped pumping by the time Gela holds his 2018 water security summit, where again many of his communities are all but dry, and where daily water restrictions mean turning off the mains for several hours every day.

But just across a couple of kilometres north in PNG's Western Province people were doing it even tougher, where water refugees stream over daily desperate for drinking water.

Gela says: 'We all know when they feel it in the Western Province; our communities are a stone's throw away from them and we experience them coming over for water supplies we really can't afford.'

Councillor Kebai Salee from Western Province Treaty Village of Sigabadaru, the closest to the Torres Strait island of Saibai, tells me at the time: 'It's very, very dry now, many shrubs are on fire, drinking water levels and water for cooking is very low, our wells are nearly dry, it's a real problem. They are down to the last millimetres of water, and that's got to last for 900 people in Sigabadaru. All of our crops are dying and the bush is on fire, there are no more crops there.

'We are having to collect water from Saibai, but they are also having problems with water levels so they are putting restrictions on us as well.

'We will be in real trouble if this crisis continues. Mabadauan (another nearby PNG village) is also in the same sort of situation as are many of the other villages.

'This is not normal, as it is much drier than usual, the natural wells before would always have water in the dry season, but this year all the wells have dried out.

'We might lose our (banana) suckers for gardening as the roots are all burnt by the sun, so next year we won't have bananas.'

Gela says at the water summit that: 'It is entirely possible in the next 50 years that we become Australia's first refugees (from within Australian territory, due to climate change).'

While becoming climate refugees may soon become a reality for Torres Strait Islanders as the water ebbs forever upwards, the world's first extinction due to human-induced climate change, a small rodent, the Bramble Cay melomy, slips quietly into oblivion. The Great Barrier Reef's only endemic mammal that lived on the remote tiny island of Bramble Cay in the eastern Torres Strait has not been seen since 2009, and after an extensive search in 2014 is slated as extinct in 2019. In 1978 there were reports of hundreds of them on the island, but scientists blame sea level rise that since 1998 has decreased the island's area from four hectares to two-and-a-half hectares, taking with it ninety-seven percent of the little critter's habitat.

'Significantly, this probably represents the first recorded mammalian extinction due to anthropogenic climate change,' the researchers say in their report, quietly published on a Queensland government's website at the time with little media attention.

It's the tip of a melting iceberg, with other data suggesting anthropogenic climate change could result in extinction of one in six species of all life on the planet, compounding the sixth mass extinction the world is currently on the precipice of.

It enrages my inner greenie, as we are not without the means to change the way our species impacts the planet, just the will. As Stephen Hawking told Larry James in 2017, where he blamed human greed and stupidity for the impending climate disaster, 'We certainly have not become less greedy or less stupid.' Just before his death in 2018 he said humanity wouldn't survive the 21st century and would require a 'Planet B' to survive.

'We are close to the tipping point where global warming becomes irreversible. Trump's action could push the Earth over the brink, to become like Venus, with a temperature of two hundred and fifty degrees, and raining sulphuric acid,' he told *BBC News*.

David Attenborough reiterated Hawking's position later that year in December, while addressing 200 nations at an UN climate summit, where he said: 'Right now we are facing a man-made disaster of global scale, our greatest threat in thousands of years: climate change. If we don't take action, the collapse of our civilisations and the extinction of much of the natural world are on the horizon.'

The reason climate change has had to be rebranded to get federal funding in the Torres Strait is because of the old, white conservative men that dominated Canberra's giant Hills Hoist during this time, especially the Abbott/Turnbull/Morrison era, and their fear of the 'C'word – climate change.

These are men who uttered these 'suppositories of wisdom' (to coin Prime Minister Abbot's 2013 metaphor gaff) – Abbott in 2014: 'Coal is good for humanity...'; Treasurer Morrison in 2017: 'This is coal, don't be afraid, don't be scared,' bringing a lump of the black stuff into Parliament's Question Time for show and tell.

There is actually a large body of research that supports a hypothesis that conservative old white males are significantly more likely than other people to endorse denialist views on human-induced climate change. Professors McCright and Dunlap's 2011 paper titled, *Cool dudes: The denial of climate change among conservative white males in the United States*, drew upon ten years of data and other research to make this claim, and even suggested the rates of denial were even higher for those conservative white males who self-report understanding global warming very well.

This is also true for nearly all the tiny demographic of contrarian scientists who dismiss climate change and make up less than three percent of the scientific community on this subject.

This is despite the fact that nineteen of the hottest twenty years on record occurred in the last two decades, with 2020, at the time of this book going to print, to be in the top five. Queensland, in the summer of 2018, went into a state of emergency, from an unprecedented 190 bushfires burning out of control along the length of the state – which firies describe as a category five cyclone of fire – to the worst floods since the 1970s in a matter of weeks, all during record-breaking endless heatwaves.

Then only three months later the same part of Queensland won Morrison's Government a second term nobody saw coming, beating Labor's unlosable 'climate-change election' – revealing the redneck centre's short memory of the climate calamities.

By the end of 2019, Australia again broke its bushfire records with blazes described by many as 'hell on earth.'

Member for Leichhardt Warren Entsch, with his eighth election win under his belt, is made Special Envoy for the Great Barrier Reef. Two weeks after the election Entsch declared the World Heritage site doesn't need saving, while taking a swipe at climate change activists for 'indoctrinating' school students who were protesting the issue in Australia.

'They're frightening the living hell out of kids. It's like child abuse and I think they should be held accountable,' he told SBS News in 2019.

Contrary to Professor Terry Hughes' most recent and dire report of the state of the reef, Enstch said: 'We don't need to "save the reef" ... The reef is functioning well.'

The 'Cool Dude' paper builds on the established theory of 'white male effect,' or the atypically high levels of technological and environmental risk acceptance among white males. It quotes a 1994 paper by researchers Flynn, Slovic & Mertz titled 'Gender, race, and perception of environmental health risks which explains the white male effect', which states: 'Perhaps white males see less risk in the world because they create, manage, control, and benefit from so much of it. Perhaps women and nonwhite men see the world as more dangerous because in many ways they are more vulnerable, because they benefit less from many of its technologies and institutions, and because they have less power and control.'

Combining recent studies on the white-male effect in risk perception with those on the psychology of system-justification tendencies of political conservatives, the 'Cool Dude' paper concludes it is these perceptions and tendencies that lead political conservatives to defend the status quo and resist attempts to change it – what we call the 'conservative white male effect'.

They go on to say: 'conservative white males are likely to favour protection of the current industrial capitalist order which has historically served them well,' adding: 'heightened emotional and psychic investment in defending in-group claims may translate into misperceived understanding about problems like climate change that threaten the continued order of the system.'

The paper has been cited many times since its publication to explain the phenomena of these old white bastards because basically they have vested interests in the status quo, with their snouts deep in the fossil fuels, mining and associated stock investments trough. They are all up to their nuts in this shit and want to keep it that way.

Documents unearthed in 2018 revealed fossil fuel companies had secretly conducted research in the 1980s that showed their product would increase carbon dioxide in the atmosphere and cause apocalyptic ecological calamity by the early part of this century. The reports included predictions of sea level rise by five or six metres, ecosystems destruction, biblical floods, desertification, rising temperatures and water shortages. Despite these reports companies like Shell and Exxon continued to publicly deny the connection between burning fossil fuels and climate change, all the while raising the heights of their offshore oil rigs to accommodate sea level rise, strengthening helipads and pipelines and securing large areas of the Arctic that would become easier to exploit once climate change kicked in.

Comedian John Oliver summed it up most eloquently on his HBO show *Last Night Tonight* in 2017 when he said: 'We have been repeatedly asked: "Don't you want to leave a better Earth for your grandchildren?", and we've all collectively responded: "Ah, fuck 'em!".'

Feeling we may have already tipped past the point of no return, a conversation with the producer of the award winning kids TV show *Dirt Girl*, Cate McQuillan and her cast swayed me back slightly to hope. Sharing a punk rock past, Cate went bush when I stayed in the city – her show is all about sustainable living, inspiring the next generation to 'get grubby' in the garden.

I took Cate, Maree Lowes (Dirt Girl), Michael Balk (Scrap Boy) and Costa Georgiades (Costa the Garden Gnome) fishing around the back of Hammond Rock, the Kaurareg God Waubin that had turned to stone and whose blood protects the surrounding islands. While sharing the grandeur of the Kaurareg Dreaming with them, I shared my take on the nightmare we've created. We caught nothing, but Costa was delighted in the chunks of seaweed tangling up his line.

'Fucking beautiful compost,' he'd squealed in delight.

It was my only rule on the board: everyone had to swear like troopers — as they all worked in children's television and had been in character for days in the community, I figured it would help let their hair down.

'We've fucked it, I think there is no turning back,' I said as we drifted along in Waubin's current.

Cate, who had been working in partnership with Torres Shire Council to establish a community garden, said: 'Hope builds the future because lack of hope sure as hell doesn't. But it can't be blind faith or blind hope, it's about re-connecting to the profound and keeping people connected in a heart space — but hope's only half the story.

'There's three ways change happens — connect, understand, act. And if it doesn't happen in that order, it doesn't happen — you don't get profound behavioural change. Another way of saying it is love, know, do.

'But the problem is how people identify themselves, and being identified as a "greenie" has a taint for many people, and choosing to support the climate they feel like they are abandoning their political ideology, because being seen as an environmentalist is somehow fucked.

'So the expression I've been chucking around is social citizens, because no one bucks that, everyone gets it – we're raised to live in a community not an economy.'

On the flip side of the 'conservative white male effect' on climate change is what maybe should be called the 'Indigenous peoples effect.'

The UN Special Rapporteur on the Rights of Indigenous Peoples, Victoria Tauli-Corpuz, targeted Indigenous people the world over as those who could help provide solutions to alleviate and adapt to the effects of climate change. In her 2017 Address to the Human Rights Council, she stated:

Indigenous peoples are among those who have least contributed to the problem of climate change yet are the ones suffering from its worst impacts. They are disproportionately vulnerable to climate change because many of them depend on ecosystems that are particularly prone to the effects of climate change and extreme weather events such as floods, droughts, heat waves, wildfires and cyclones.

Some of the most affected regions are small islands, high altitudes, humid tropics, coastal regions, deserts and polar areas. Global warming increases disease risks, changes animal migration routes, reduces biodiversity, causes saltwater inundation of freshwater, destroys crops and results in food insecurity.

Indigenous peoples are not simply victims of climate change but have an important contribution to make to address climate change. Due to their close relationship with the environment, indigenous peoples are uniquely positioned to adapt to climate change. Indigenous peoples are repositories of learning and knowledge on successfully coping with local-level climate change and effectively responding to major environmental changes such as natural disasters.

They play a fundamental role in the conservation of biological diversity, protection of forests and other natural resources, and their traditional knowledge of the environment can substantively enrich scientific knowledge and adaptation activities when taking climate change-related actions.

Indigenous peoples can assist in providing solutions to mitigate and adapt to the effects of climate change.

The International Indigenous Peoples Forum on Climate Change and UNEP have noted that indigenous peoples can contribute to numerous potential adaptation activities by drawing on their traditional knowledge. Examples of such activities include documentation of traditional knowledge, climate monitoring and reporting, disaster preparedness, response and early warning systems, *rain water harvesting, traditional farming techniques and agriculture, coastal marine management, alternative energy development and the development of sustainable livelihoods.*

In a 2018 paper she co-authored, titled 'Cornered by Protected Areas', Tauli-Corpuz suggests;

...there is an urgent need to replace the fortress-conservation model (centrally controlled by government) with rights-based approaches to both improve conservation outcomes and end human rights abuses committed in the name of conservation.

...despite widespread poverty and insecure resource rights, evidence shows that Indigenous Peoples and local communities are nevertheless spending their limited resources on conservation efforts and achieving outcomes that are at least equivalent to those of government-funded protected areas.

...Indigenous Peoples and local communities are as diverse as their lands and resources, but many share an ethical interconnection with nature through their languages, beliefs, and practices, reflecting a commitment to respecting and caring for the natural world. In indigenous worldviews, people are seen largely as intrinsic parts of nature rather than as distinct and separate from it. Most Indigenous Peoples have a deep understanding of nature and adjust

their practices, institutions, and relationships to maintain an ecological balance.

...By denying the rights of Indigenous Peoples and local communities and destroying their long-enduring institutions—which have maintained ecosystem services over very long periods—traditional protected-area approaches often cause more problems than they solve.

...As the primary custodians of most of the world's remaining ... biodiversity hotspots, the essential role of Indigenous Peoples and local communities in managing terrestrial greenhouse gas sinks and biodiversity reservoirs needs to be globally recognized, promoted, and supported. Building on an emerging suite of approaches such as co-management, indigenous-managed protected areas, and indigenous territorial governance, community-led conservation initiatives should be leveraged to channel more conservation finance to traditional custodians to strengthen their management and improve conservation outcomes.

Dr Anne Poelina, a Yimardoowarra woman from Mardoowarra/Fitzroy River, who is an Adjunct Senior Research Fellow at the University of Notre Dame in Broome and council member of the Australian Conservation Foundation, echoed Ms Tauli-Corpuz's theory in 2018, urging scientists and researchers to incorporate Indigenous knowledge into mainstream practice in order for the world to have a chance of addressing climate change and planetary survival.

'The message for us scientists is to think beyond our own paradigms,' she told online news agency *Croakey*. 'We need collaboration with other scientists ... to recognise that traditional ecological knowledge is Indigenous science because it's thousands and thousands of years of observation, recording and transmission of knowledge over generations. Not only knowledge production but knowledge adaptation to complex and changing systems.

'So our voices need to be in there, they need to be valued, and they need to be part of the collaboration on how we right-size the planet and the wicked problems in the world we have created.'

Poelina also warns of the world entering a new era of colonisation where the rights of transnational corporations transcend those of humans and nature.

'We are being colonised by transnational companies,' she told *Croakey*. 'We're talking about divide and conquer, we're talking about manipulation, we're talking about cultural invasion and so on ... We are in a fight for the life of the planet and its people.'

In 2019, a week before Australia's climate-change election, eight Torres Strait

Islanders, with help of UK environmental advocacy group Client Earth, lodged a human rights complaint with the UN claiming the Australian Government has breached its human rights by not 'doing enough' about climate change.

One of the eight Islanders, Kabay Tamu from Warraber, said: 'This is ground-breaking and a world-first case that we are putting forward to the U.N.'

Warraber cops erosion all year round, on the south-east side when Sagar blows and the opposite end when Koki blows, then there's the impacts of the king tides. The current seawall built by the community twenty years ago is starting to succumb to the relentless pounding of the sea.

'Torres Strait Islanders are at risk of being the world's first climate-change refugees ... in our own country if Australia doesn't address the issue of climate change and its impacts and the causes of climate change,' Kabay tells me. 'It's the government's duty of care to look after our basic human rights, our basic right to live, our basic right to live the way we've lived for thousands of years, and we believe the government hasn't protected those rights or even helped us sustain our homes and our islands.'

Kabay, who has a nine-year-old son, is concerned for future generations of Torres Strait Islanders.

'Our children and our children's children will have to move and we don't want that.

'The problems with erosion is not just the loss of land but it's a social issue as well, because we will lose our connection with land and culture, to be able to participate in initiations.

'Having to move away is my biggest fear, leaving families behind in the cemetery. My house is one of the ones closest to the beach, so we live on the front-line.'

There have been times when the sea has eaten into the cemetery and families have had to pick up the bones of their loved ones off the beach.

'Things are not going to change unless we change, and we stop harming the earth and each year it seems to get worse.'

Two years after Nino's ghost net workshop of Kirriri, ghost net art from the Torres Strait starts to gain recognition nationally, then internationally, helping spread the messages of the ocean's plight from a uniquely Indigenous perspective.

A large installation of ghost net art and other works from the Torres Strait becomes an integral part of the 2016 *Taba Naba—Australia,*

Oceania, Arts of the Sea People exhibition at the Oceanographic Museum of Monaco, which later toured the world. One of the featured artists, Alick Tipoti from Badu, completed a huge 670 square metre mural on the rooftop of the museum, representing totemic images of turtles. At the opening, Alick got talking to the museum founder and key supporter of the exhibition, His Serene Highness Prince Albert II, and struck up an unlikely friendship. Known as 'The Green Prince' for his efforts to tackle climate change and his passion for saving the oceans, Prince Albert II accepted Tipoti's offer to come and see the climate-change coalface for himself.

Two years later the Prince comes out to Badu and stays with Tipoti in his beach shack. A far cry from the five star lifestyle of Monaco, Prince Albert II slums it with Tipoti in his lean-to lacking all the mod-cons on the beach, eating traditional food and diving off a dinghy on the reef to see firsthand the impacts of climate change and its impacts on the custodians of this patch of sea country.

He has to leave his private jet on the Horn Island runway, too big to land on Badu, instead flying in on Caravan, just like I do a few hours before him.

The Prince's minders are all hand-wringing at my presence as they are trying to control all media of the visit, but are unable to do diddly squat as I'm invited personally by Tipoti. Sweating in pastel polos, suffering the height of the Torres Strait Dry season, they can't guarantee me an interview with the Prince.

After he lands and is welcomed with flower wreaths, traditional songs, dance and blessings from Elders and Traditional Owners, I shove my palm into his with one hand, while I mic up his lapel with the other.

'G'day your Highness mate, welcome to the Torres Strait' – buggered if I'm waiting for his minders' approval.

He is amicable and the nicest (and only) billionaire I've ever gate crashed a handshake from, and a nice contrarian to the 'conservative white male effect.' He graciously gives me the sound byte I need to print my paper and sell a news grab to NITV.

'It's always important to not only see firsthand what the situation is in this region of the world but also to engage with the local communities, because every environmental challenge, especially when you look at oceans, it always has a human issue as well,' Prince Albert II says.

'You have to be able to maintain the livelihood of these communities, and they have traditions, of course, and they have a certain way of life, and we have to engage them in this and make sure they still have their livelihood.

'That's why it's important to have protected areas, to have protected species and to be able to find the best solution for the ocean and for different ecosystems but also to allow these communities to keep on thriving, now and in the future.'

The Prince is en route to a big conference in Townsville about how to save the reef, and had just come from Bali, where he attended a forum on how to deal with the plastic pollution choking the oceans. His visit hardly appears on the media radar, unlike the other royal visit of Harry and Meghan that's happening at the same time.

Over a bowl of two-minute noodles he cooks up before the Prince arrives, Tipoti and I talk while his family is a flurry of activity preparing for the royal guest: 'It's really happening, the impact of tidal waves, king tides, climate change,' he says, sitting on an old car seat in a garden of overgrown basil.

'I think we all know back in the 80s and 90s when we dived as kids with our uncles and older brothers and cousins, the reefs were rich and full of marine life. They still are but you can see their house, the reef, is falling apart. The corals are dying and it's impacting marine life, so it is happening and it's real but we're still here.'

While killing time for the Prince's arrival, TSIRC Councillor for Badu and Traditional Owner Laurie Nona takes me out to the back of the island to his shack, next door to Tipoti's, to show me how the sea is systematically eating away his platinum-white sandy beach-backyard.

Traditional Owners from nearly all the island communities have shown me similar sights where low tide marks were once coconut groves they played rugby on as kids, or stands of wongai plum trees now twisted dead and sun-bleached with their balls of roots reaching to the sky. Other islands have had graveyards inundated, exposing remains of ancestors, while others have to ride a dinghy down the main street in king tide season as the seawall are breached and eroded.

Laurie, a young leader and father of nine, built burly like a rugby fullback, is never one to mince words. I saw him tell Governor General Peter Cosgrove only a few weeks earlier, in no uncertain terms, the need for not only constitutional recognition for First Australians but also the need for Torres Strait Islanders to be recognised as a distinct race different from mainland Australia Aborigines.

'I really can't understand that there are some people still out there saying that climate change and global warming is not real. It's not a scam mate, it's fucking real,' Laurie tells me standing with his toes in the turquoise tide lapping away the high water mark just metres from his shack.

'This is my family campsite and as you can see it's happening, this is life to us, but this is happening right in front of us.

'Every year it's moving up at least a metre, a metre-and-a-half, the erosion, the inundation, we're on the coalface here.

'It's hard to explain to people how we feel, and how we want to work with Mother Nature to address that we human beings, we're the ones that's doing this, and we're the only ones who can stop this from happening. It won't happen straight away, but we've got to start somewhere and we've got to start now.

'This is where it's happening, we feel it, we see it, we experience it, we live it. It's very hard for people living in the urban centres to make that observation that there's something going on here and it's serious. They go from aircon shopping centres and offices to aircon homes so they don't really feel it.

'But we have birds not migrating on time, turtles not coming to lay eggs, fruits flowering at the wrong time, everything is happening out of whack. We get strange lice in the water we never had before, infections, even the turtle is starting to taste different.

'Mother Nature is confused at the moment – we're not working together with Mother Nature, we're not listening to Mother Nature.

'This is the time I feel that people of the globe, of Australia sitting in lounge rooms – hey we've got to do something about this, because I'm going to have grandchildren and us not doing anything about it, what are we saying to them, what are we saying to our generations to come, that we don't give fuck?'

CHAPTER 23

IN BLACK AND WHITE

18 June 2015

'I put a curse on you, a curse for the words that you write,' says the old man stepping out of the darkness and leaning in towards me, stabbing a bony finger into my chest. The old Islander is tall and thin but not frail, his malevolence palpable, his presence foreboding.

'Fuck you and fuck your black magic – I'm a whitefella, your *puri puri* curse can't touch me, that's not my culture,' I scream sitting up in bed, clammy in sweat. The grimy walls of my bedroom in the Crow's Nest Hotel pulsate slightly as I focus on the predawn hue filtering in through the window. Then the throb in my head kicks in, tongue dry and swollen – the last night of the Treaty Village tour with DFAT in PNG's Western Province ended up an early morning hell-raiser at the bar of the Crow's Nest.

Having woken myself with my own screaming voice, the thought of a curse placed on me, even as a dream, gives me a shudder, the dissociative of the drink waned enough to feel a wave of anxiety.

I swing my legs out of bed, cradling my head. It's been a restless couple of hours sleep. Rubbing my temples I remember another disturbing dream, where I was wading through dark swamp waters when a large croc rose out of a ripple, only its eye and nostril visible. It looked straight through me before sinking into the darkness from which it emerged. I remember an Elder telling me that *Koedal,* his totem of the salt water croc, was significant because their eyes could look forward and backwards, they could see both into the future and back into the past.

The night before started out with after-dinner drinks, then the second State of Origin rugby league bout between NSW and QLD on satellite TV kicked off a session of boozing that saw Ray from DFAT double-parked at the bar with a line of rum and cokes, as I and Kenny Bedford demolished the top shelf and worked our way through the bottom shelf – before memory blacked out to my sitting up in bed screaming.

Things had become hazy, I remember dancing the funky chicken to the live band with an old aunty – conversations bled together. I remember talking to the local police inspector, who had a jailhouse tattoo of a Ganga leaf on his forehead, who was very amiable but had a fierce reputation. When he was in town, all the Raskols hid in the bush. I was told that if he's chasing someone he goes to their humpy with a jerry can, douses it in fuel and lights a fag, telling the wife her husband had until he finished his smoke to show up. Otherwise he flicks the butt onto the hut.

Ray told me earlier, that day when he stopped me taking a photo of a dugong butchered into steaks for sale on a guy's front lawn just spitting distance for the police station, 'I heard this guy was confronted about selling dugong which is meant only for traditional and not commercial purposes and he just hacked him up with his machete and pushed into the gutter, and the police did nothing.'

But that night it was all back slaps and jokes about footy, and him carousing me that NSW had beaten Queensland in the State of Origin game we watched. Then in an awkward pause an Islander man who I had been drinking with turned to me, his ever-present grin dropped away.

'You whitefellas come here to our community, you stay and work and feel like you are one of us, but then you go, you fellas always go, get your promotions and leave. But we stay, we are still here, always have been, always will be.'

It wasn't aggressive, just an honesty loosened out of his lips by the drink – a discontent that always lies just below the surface.

A little later, a white Australian itinerant worker nuzzled my ear to share a joke.

'Why do crocs spin the blackfellas round in the water when they grab them from the river? To wash the dirt off them before they eat them.'

I didn't laugh, but nor did I berate him for his racist slur, or for assuming I would find it funny.

I remember the lifetime of racist jokes I had heard growing up in Australia, but never knew how to react, catatonic in how to express that I was not comfortable with it and thought it wrong. That classic Australian failing of our character of never wanting to be confrontational, where 'howz it goin' is always met with 'good.' A failing perhaps reflecting the unhealed wound of our unspoken past our country has been built on.

'How do you make an Abo woman pregnant? Come on her leg and let the flies do the rest,' I had heard at high school.

'A farmer driving in from his cattle station to town at night sees a blackfella hitchhiking on the road, swerves to run him over, five minutes later he sees another and swerves again. Then the farmer sees a priest with his thumb out so he pulls over to give him a lift. A few minutes later the farmer sees another blackfella on the side of the road, swerves but then remembers the priest in the car with him and swerves back to the road.

"'Sorry father", the farmer says.

"That's OK son, I got him with the door"', told to me not in some hick backwater truck-stop but in the enlightened hub of the metropolitan, at university.

'Do you know why black fellas are called boongs? Because that is the sound their heads make when they are shot.' That was told to me by Mayor Pedro Stephen one day recently – but it wasn't a joke, he was serious – he was shaking his head in disgust. The impact of hearing him use that derogatory description of his people made me squirm with guilt, despite never having shot a blackfella or never having used the word.

These jokes that today still pervade our national psyche reveal our racist underbelly.

But I am not racist, some of my best friends are black, I work with black people every day, I live in an Indigenous community, I have people of colour in my family, including my wife.

I tell myself these things, as do all liberal-minded progressives who like to think the racist is someone and something completely foreign and abhorrent to them, until my wife asks me to read American sociologist Robin DiAngelo's 2018 book *White Fragility, why it's so hard for white people to talk about racism*. Based on her decades of running racial awareness workshops, DiAngelo found, time and time again, white-liberals becoming defensive to the point of aggression in protest of their non-racial status, by vehemently listing off the memes I featured above.

DiAngelo suggests that 'white progressives cause the most daily damage to people of colour,' and that, 'the most effective adaptation of racism over time is the idea that racism is a conscious bias held by mean people.' Something she calls the 'good/bad binary,' positing a world of evil racists and compassionate non-racists, but her theory on white fragility delves into more subtle realms. She explores the idea that white is considered the racial default, from kids' beige coloured crayons called 'flesh-coloured' to descriptions of 'black' writers, or 'ethnic' writers – where a Caucasian author's ethnicity is never used as a descriptor. Not to mention that every institution and power structure in the world is predominately, if not completely, white, and usually male.

So I guess I have been 'blinded by the white,' wrapped up in my own douchebaggery of being born and raised on the privileged side of the racial divide, something I think nearly all of white Australia also suffers from. My blue-eyed-fair-skinned daughter, a minority in her classroom, struggles to navigate this terrain. Having been drilled not to distinguish differences in people based on colour, she resorts to saying they are 'b' people, her child-innocent racial coding for 'brown' people. While this gets an eye-roll from her brown-skinned mother, maybe the message here is for white Australia to accept that our beige perspective, the white dominant paradigm, will constantly raise unintended micro-aggressions of racism. And rather than deny them for fear of being reprimanded as a big bad racist, we should acknowledge it, become aware of it and try not to repeat it, one paper cut at a time, until we correct the ledger and carve out a better world.

A bookish school teacher, all prim and white privilege, told me once that the reason she had committed to a career of being a teacher in remote Indigenous communities was because of the unspoken shame she felt of her descendants, pastoralists who 'dispersed' the First Nations custodians off her family farm by 'bait or bullet'. She had dedicated close to a decade trying to wash the blood off her hands by quietly trying to help close the gap in her ordinary day to day life. That's a good start. We could all take heed from Uncle Koedal's crocodile eyes to see and own the evils in our collective past while doing what we can to put our best foot forward into the *bran nue dae*.

But as well as White Australia fronting up to its racial atonement, we also need to expand and understand what is Aboriginality, from Cook's noble savages to ideas of 'half castes' and its stolen generation and subsequent 2008 apology, from the '67 referendum to Mabo, right up to the Uluru *Statement of the Heart*. By my white racial default position, I am not qualified to talk about this, nor in fact perhaps to even write this book, so I will reflect on those more qualified.

Self-prescribed 'professional Aboriginal' Kerryn Pholi, in her 2012 article 'Why I burned my "Proof of Aboriginality"', said all her Aboriginal descent meant was, 'I could trace my ancestry back to a stone-age way of life more easily, with far fewer steps, than most readers.

'When I think about my Aboriginal ancestry, I feel gratitude. I feel gratitude because modernity has given me a life of ease, pleasure and privilege beyond anything an Aboriginal woman in pre-invasion Australia could possibly imagine. As a person of Aboriginal descent, and a female at that, I am grateful that I had the good fortune to be born here in Australia in 1975, and not here in say, 1775.

'Perhaps life for my Aboriginal ancestors (the Bundjalung people of what is now northern NSW) had its good points prior to invasion, just as European life around 5,000BC couldn't have been *all* bad ... though nobody seems to miss that particular lifestyle much or yearn to have it back.'

Having worked in Indigenous research and policy in various government agencies and NGOs, Pholi said she has previously used her Aboriginal identity to gain access to lucrative employment and built a 'career based on racism'.

'As a professional Aborigine, I could harangue a room full of people with real qualifications and decades of experience with whatever self-serving, uninformed drivel that happened to pop into my head. For this nonsense I would be rapturously applauded, never questioned, and paid well above my qualifications and experience.'

But a 'nagging sense of feeling like a complete fraud' led her to burn her documentation proving she was Aboriginal.

'To accept preferential treatment on the basis of one's race — in employment, academe, the arts, the media — is to participate in racism.

'It does not "close the gap", promote role-models or let you "challenge the system from within".

'To genuinely challenge racism we need to stop rationalising our individual self-interest, reject preferential treatment, compete in the open market for jobs, grants and audiences, and accept the financial and career consequences of refusing to be bought.'

Journalist Stan Grant, in his 2016 essay: *Can an Aborigine be a Smiths fan? I can be whatever I damn like*, says his Aboriginality is nothing more than a fact of birth: 'That is who I am but not all I am. The reality is more ambiguous, defying easy definition even as I may prefer to cloak it in a veil of certainty. To borrow from Franz Kafka, identity is a cage in search of a bird.'

While Grant described Pholi's article as 'a disgruntled employee who has slammed the door on the way out' and that she 'rejects her Aboriginality with the same zealotry as those who proselytise the moral superiority of Indigenous people,' he recognises that the rigid concept of Aboriginal identity has been corporatised and exploited for profit by some Aboriginal and non-Aboriginal people:

Aboriginal people are bound to a communal identity. This can impose a rigid conformity, accompanied sometimes by an intimidating lateral violence. Self-righteous Indigenous people take on the role of "identity police," deciding who is in or out. All the while, Aboriginal people face having to explain themselves to a wary, sceptical, ignorant – even hostile – Australian public ... Put simply: division breeds hate. Identity can be a source of warmth and richness, and it can add to a tapestry of difference that we can all share, or it can incite hatred, violence and terror.

Grant describes identity as a 'two way mirror'.

He said that while his Indigenous heritage forms a core part of his being, he is much if not more a product of his European heritage than of the Dreaming, as well as being 'a man who speaks some Chinese, enjoys Italian food, is fascinated by international affairs and politics, and is at home living in the world's great cities ... *I don't want to be put into any box; but rather, as Immanuel Kant said, to live free from "the ball and chain of an everlasting permanent minority."'*

Grant said he loves 'all things British: soft English rain, the green meadows, the barren moors: London with its lingering ghosts. English music has been the soundtrack of my life ... Can an Aborigine be a Smiths fan? I can be whatever I damn like.'

Grant's two way mirror may be a good place to reflect on Aboriginality and a sense of cultural identity, not just for First Nations people, which make up a fraction of our population, but for all Australians, 'black, white and brindle.' I, born an

Englishman, feel much more at home in Australia's vast and unforgiving landscapes, the brutal heat of the Red Centre with blood-coloured sunsets, to the chill of Tasmania's morning Bridgewater Jerry that rolls down Timtumili Minanya into D'Entrecasteaux Channel blanketing everything in white fog. I prefer dark skies that crackle with thunder and lightning that drowns out horizons in sheets of monsoonal rains in the Far North to Grant's soft English drizzle, and ACDC (the Bon Scott years) or early Oils and the Saints to the Smiths any day, but am I any less Australian?

And is Behrouz Boochani any less with his great Australian novel text messaged from the Nation's purgatory of Manus Island, or the Bird sisters, nieces of an Australian icon Nancy Walton-Bird, but themselves second-class citizens?

My sense of identity has only grown stronger with the privilege of editing the *Torres News* and all the doors into First Nations culture and life it has offered. While I have only skimmed the surface of the shared Dreaming, totems and how to read the landscape, it has left an indelible mark on me and my sense of who I am and where I live and call home. It provides that connection so many of us have lost or ultimately never had at a deeper level. I think if everyone was loud and proud of the country, culture and dreaming of the land on which they stood, such as the Kaurareg Country beneath the foundations of the *Torres News* office from where I write this – we would go a long way to healing our nation's wounds and slowing the planet's demise.

Beyond the success of Indigenous Ranger programs to care for Country, and the appreciation and valuing Indigenous art and culture, we now see the values of Indigenous Knowledge in aspects of science, from astrophysics to school curriculum, finally being developed in partnership with First Nations people and the Prime Minister and Cabinet Office. Yiman and Bidjara academic Professor Marcia Langton AM, Chair of the Curricula Project, is hoping this knowledge – with themes of fire, astronomy and water, using songlines, seasons and navigation to explore subjects of sustainability, trade and economics, livelihood, cultural expression, health and wellbeing, and social order – will become normalised cross-culture curriculum in our schools.

The Ngangkari healers, from the Ngaanyatjarra, Pitjantjatjara and Yankunytjatjara Nations in the central desert region of Australia, across the borders of the Northern Territory, South Australia and Western Australia, have been practising healing in mainstream hospitals as complementary medicine since 2013, and there has even been research into Indigenous Knowledge for applications in robotics and future technologies.

Cognitive neuroscientist Sheree Cairney, who conducted research with remote Aboriginal communities across Northern Australia, discovered that despite poverty and lack of opportunity, Aboriginal people there were happier than those in the cities, and that they were happier now than five years ago, and expected to be even happier in another five years. In her 2016 TEDx Talk, *What Aboriginal Knowledge can teach us about happiness*, Cairney said her research showed that their happiness came from a connection to culture and community and a sense of empowerment, and that culture is their identity. Her work is being used to marry Aboriginal culture, which is fundamentally based on stories, with that of Government, which is fundamentally based on numbers. Cairney ends her talk with a quote from her friend Trevor Gurruwiwi from Elcho Island in Arnhem Land, where he says: 'Walk with us, to share those knowledge from those two world views.'

I guess the concern is this may be seen by some as cultural appropriation, as US feminist writer Lorena Wallace wrote in her 2018 article *White people have no culture*, where she sees our culture as:

...that of colonization. Of genocide. Of taking. Of envy and of fear. The majority of white people can name no more than two generations back in their families. The majority of white people barely know where their grandparents were from, much less who their ancestors were. The majority of white people have no traditions, and the ones we have, are rooted in consumption and the superficial application of organized religion, both of which are steeped in histories of violence. Christmas is about a severed tree dropping dead needles on heaps of plastic crap, grinding the gears of our capitalist economy, a formerly pagan ritual that has been bastardized and twisted into a stressful display of wealth and excess. Easter is about disposable plastic balls full of processed sugar, many of which are left for years to mar the sterilized landscapes and rigidly decorated city parks and backyards. Valentine's Day was created exclusively by the greeting card industry to make you spend money on disappointing gifts and unhealthy treats for your unsatisfied monogamous partner.

The closest thing white people have to culture is our disturbingly fanatical obsession with sports ... The culture of white people is the culture of death. It is a culture of endless war, desensitization to human suffering, and the upholding of a brutal individualism fueled by greed ... So we take. We take the traditions, costumes, dances, songs, and agency of marginalized groups after we have decimated their populations and destroyed their homes, and we polish these items so the suffering cannot be seen.

We are truly heartless beasts, just like the Kaurareg said of Barbara Thompson, whom they rescued and adopted in 1844 in the Torres Strait from a shipwreck, when she didn't cry at the death of an Elder – she was told: 'Your people are like ghosts. They don't cry, they have no feeling. We are people, *garkigi*, we cry.'

However embracing a culture of connectivity and reciprocity – like that of Indigenous people the world over – that connects the brains of heart and gut to that of our heads, the space where Western reductionist, logic-driven thought is imprisoned, could be our saving grace, if grabbed with both hands now. We live in Paradise but don't have the time or means to enjoy it, and we need to wake up and smell the roses before Paradise is lost, we need to lose the hurry disease and live on Ailan time.

Edwardian amateur anthropologist Daisy Bates, nicknamed the 'White Queen of the Never-Never' said in her 1938 book, *The Passing of the Aborigines: A Lifetime Spent Among the Natives of Australia*, that she wanted to 'smooth the pillow of a dying race' and thought the Aboriginal people of Australia would become extinct. After living sixteen years in a tent on the Nullarbor Plain, this self-taught woman of science thought racial interbreeding a perversion of nature to be avoided at all costs.

I completely disagree with Bates, and think marrying Western thinking with Indigenous Knowledge and developing a universal sense of Aboriginality could go a long way to turn the world around. But in the remaining decade the UN says we have, with climate change Armageddon looming over us, the time for change is now. With the 2020's starting with Mother Gaia's spanking from Covid 19, systemic collapse seems well underway, so if we don't heed wisdom from the planet's Indigenous Knowledge, I fear we may well all be just smoothing the pillow of the dying human race. As the great Ephraim Bani said: *The past must exist, for the present to create the future.*

CHAPTER 24

THE ROCK

Sunrise, 23 December 2019, my last day in the Torres Strait

The detritus that the winds and currents deposit on Thursday Island fills me with both wonder and consternation. The endless pieces of micro plastic that we find in the food chain, bottle tops, plastic water bottles, shopping bags, toothbrushes, thongs, take-away food containers are now what make up the flotsam and jetsam of our era.

Over its 'settled' history, to coin a Tony Abbott-ism, TI has seen that detritus fall layer upon layer onto the sand of my beach backyard, which were slipways servicing the hundreds of pearling luggers that proliferated in the late 19th Century, right up until the 1970s.

Shards of Japanese rice bowls are still occasionally revealed by the shifting sands, from the many Japanese pearlers that inhabited the Island. Today all that remains of the slipways are calcified twists of rusty rail tracks, cogs and skeletons of old motors and the middens of broken beer bottles. So many shards of glass are scattered through the beaches, it is often referred as 'TI Coral'.

But today's flotsam swirls into the five oceanic gyres as perpetual islands of suspended plastic particles, scattered across every beach on the planet, serving as a reminder of our pandemic of consumer insanity and the arse-end of times we find ourselves in. In less than a lifetime there will be more plastic in the ocean than fish, the land barren from climate change and Monsanto's insect Armageddon, where crops will fail and everything raped and plundered for a short term gain at the expense of eternity, with nothing left but mould and mildew to chew away at our corpses. Maybe not even the hardy cockroach will prevail.

The disconnect that the transnational corporation model of global control has from the world around us is so starkly apparent when reflecting over the past two centuries of Australia's history, where our agriculture, fishing and mining are stripping Country of its vitality and ability to continue to be our cornucopia. If the forty-five million-year-history of the planet was twenty-four hours, humanity has only been around for the last minute, and the industrial revolution the last couple of milliseconds, but that's all we needed to turn the Garden of Eden into an overflowing ashtray. The last time atmospheric CO_2 passed 400 parts per million was the middle of the Pliocene some three million years ago, well before the first hominoids banged two rocks together to kick off the beginnings of the Stone Age and all that followed.

The view that early settlers of Australia had to subjugate and conquer the landscape and tame the wilds of the outback had not really been challenged in the mainstream until this century. Seminal works by historian Bill Gammage and Indigenous anthropologist Bruce Pascoe show that, rather than an unkept wilderness with marauding hunter-gatherer savages, the Australian continent may well have been a well-tended garden.

In his 2012 book, *The Biggest Estate on Earth: how Aborigines made Australia*, Gammage explored how, through complex land management using fire-stick farming, the life cycles of native plants, and natural water flow, First Nations people were able to create an endless food supply. Gammage drew his conclusions in part from how the pre-colonial landscape was reflected in early settler accounts of the land, including famous colonial painter John Glover who had for decades been critiqued and criticised for painting the Australian landscapes with English-garden sensibilities, where in fact he may have only been painting what he saw. Gammage argued that once

Aborigines were no longer able to tend to Country, it became overgrown and vulnerable to the hugely damaging bushfires the nation now endures.

Pascoe, accessing evidence from diaries of early explorers, took it a step further in his 2014 book *Dark Emu, Black Seeds: agriculture or accident*, challenging the colonial concept that First Nations people being primitive hunters and gatherers was just a convenient lie that made the invaders' theft of their lands more palatable for the nation's psyche. Pascoe explores theories that not only did Aboriginal people engage in land-management, from the Northern Territory to Tasmania, and from the west to the east coasts, including creating pastures, hunting corridors, dams and fish traps, but they also created terraced irrigated fields of yams and native grains, which were stored and traded in granaries, and milled into flour, as well as building permanent villages from stone and wood. He also explored the complex animal husbandry that drew their totemic relationships from fishing with dolphins and killer whales, to harvesting and sharing Bogong Moths in a culture of sustainability and reciprocity.

Pascoe rightly explains how, when the first sheep and cattle farmers pushed their herds into and across the interior of the country, the hard hoof of these ungulates compacted soil structures that explorers, only a few seasons earlier, had their horses sink 'up to the withers' as they laboured through rich pastures. Within a few years, those pastures and yams had been eaten close to extinction by livestock, creating the hard soil-dry interior of the wheat-belt we know as our iconic outback.

In a 2016 online interview with SBS, Pascoe, who has struggled to get academia to accept his ideas, said: 'I think it's very important for a people living in a country to know its history. I think it's very important for people to know world history and I think it would be very important for Australian students to learn the incredible social order that had been created.

'The ecological rules alone would make sure people got the water they needed, the food they needed, but if we also brought in the law then people would hopefully stop killing each other too.

'It doesn't mean we stop playing NRL or stop playing cricket, it just adds a real depth and a real age to the culture. Most world cultures don't last for two thousand years and here we are with a culture that is at least 60,000 years old.'

Engaging traditional oral knowledge into the contemporary Western mindset may go a long way to rebuild the way we interact with our environment. I always thought part of my role as a journalist was to get stuff down as a written record, as a way of preserving an oral culture that had been largely decimated by colonisation. I naively saw oral culture as both precious and fragile, and which needed to preserved in the written form, but it wasn't until talking with Torres Strait Islander artist, teacher and education content creator Tommy Pau that my preconception was turned on its head. Pau gave a talk at the launch of a program designed to bridge that divide of Traditional and Western knowledge systems and integrating them as a means of improving STEM (science, technology engineering and mathematics) subjects in both Indigenous and non-Indigenous primary school students.

Pau said mythology and Indigenous Astronomy were both Traditional Knowledge's pedagogy.

'This pedagogy was and is oral, visual and pragmatic, and that's science methodology.

'So Traditional Knowledge is scientific knowledge, it's based on scientific method, observation, recording and doing,' he said.

'This pedagogy uses eternal bodies to record this knowledge used as a means of visual record and recollection. Books can decay, recordings can be damaged, digital technology depends on magnetic energy, but the stars are their eternal compass, eternal library.

'My dad always taught us to observe, to look at things, take notice of things, look for signs, read nature, take notice of each other to see how we as a society are going.

'Take notice of place, the land, the environment, and look after place.'

Pau thinks Traditional Knowledge is relevant and applicable from preschool to higher education and scientific disciplines.

'I for one do not see a difference between Western science and Traditional Knowledge, both complement each other to use where they are applicable.

'Some people try to blame Western science for the environment, but we're all part of it because we all use mobile phones, we all drive cars, so we all have a responsibility to try and fix the environment, so we can't blame each other – we all contribute to the current state of global environment.

'Some people try to say this knowledge is better than this knowledge, but the two knowledges have to complement each other, it's all human knowledge.'

Professor Martin Nakata, the first Torres Strait Islander to gain a PhD, was behind the creation of the Indigenous Knowledge STEM program. He said: 'The sky has been a major part of all Indigenous people's lives and all our societies have looked at the skies and we have created origin stories, and explained the creation of significant geographical features, we've created moral stories about how to live in relation with each other, we've observed the relationship between the position of the sun, the moon, the stars and the seasons on the land and sea.

'We've used the position of the constellation seafood hunting and gardening and used the stars also for navigation and used the skies in many ways.

'What is coming out of the relationship is a very deep understanding of who we are as human beings and how we occupy the bigger environment that's beyond earth.

'Interestingly also is that they are so embedded in the ways we navigate our land, star maps work much like GPS works today.

'Star maps were also memory devices used to guide people, the pattern were then sung and these are based on actual songlines for all the trading routes across Australia, and these lines now parallel modern road systems, because Aboriginal people used those routes and that's how white people used them then built their bitumen roads on top of it.'

The memorising of star maps and songlines, which also tie in geographical features of the landscape, is based on the oldest known mnemonic strategy, called the method of loci. It is now thought to have been used in all oral cultures, where information is passed down through generations by song, dance and stories. The method of loci, which ties information to places or objects, is a technique also used by professional card counters in casinos around the world. Science writer Lynne Kelly wrote a PhD and her 2016 best-selling book *The Memory Code* about this, and believes this process of 'orality' was used to transfer knowledge in not just Australian Aboriginal culture, but early societies across Asia, the Americas and Europe, including the Celts. Kelly states it maintained a vast corpus of pragmatic information concerning animal behaviour, plant properties, navigation, astronomy, genealogies, laws and trade agreements and many other matters.

Kelly postulates that the mythology of Indigenous culture, such as Dreamtime stories, recorded by anthropologists have incorrectly led to assumptions of a primitive culture's way of defining the world. Kelly, however, suggests these stories were nothing more than nursery rhymes told to young children, as skeletal frameworks to build more and more information upon as an individual matured through various rites of passage, where only after becoming an Elder was the entire encyclopaedic bank of knowledge retained, which could be thousands of plant and animal species, seasonal and celestial changes and everything else in between.

Astronomer Duane Hamacher and mate of Martin Nakata expanded on the importance of Indigenous Astronomy and its contribution to modern science over a few brews and some spare ribs with Nakata, in his Aka's backyard on Thursday Island. Internationally acclaimed, Hamacher had spent several years researching the subject which involved in part consulting Elders on Mer.

'Traditional Knowledge and science work in a symbiotic relationship where there is knowledge sharing,' he said.

Hamacher had just co-authored a paper with Mer Elders about how the different ways a star can twinkle can predict the weather and seasonal change.

'Uncle Alo Tapim on Mer was telling me how, when the stars quiver blue, that tells you it's going to rain soon. As he's telling me this, in the back of my head I'm thinking this makes sense because at night as our eyes adapt to the dark, we don't see blue very well at all, but there are times when stars seem blue, when there is a light humidity in the air because humidity absorbed red and green light waves but not blue light waves.

'Then there are times when there are blue moon halos, which predict bad weather if the halo is clear but the stars are fuzzy that means it's going to rain very soon, but if the stars are really clear then you have a few days before it's going to happen.

'Halos are ice crystals in the atmosphere that cause light refraction and that always precedes a low front which brings rain.

'Researching other cultures, we find they had similar traditions. I've heard a bit about the twinkling stars in Melanesia which means the rain's coming. Twinkling stars represents turbulence in the atmosphere, you just got to know how to read it.

'A few years ago I was speaking at the Science Academy in Canberra at an astrophysics forum about Indigenous astronomy, and one of the physicists in the audience asked, "how's this going to help us in our astrophysics research?". I get asked this a lot and sometimes in a snarky way.

'There's a lot of ways this can do this, such as with super nova research, I told him, but taking all that aside if I take everyone in this room and drop you off in the frigging desert, let's see how long you live.

'Your knowledge of stellar formation, galactic dynamics or Big Bang cosmology doesn't mean a world of shit in that sort of environment.

'The Elders know how to read the stars in very great detail, how use them to get from point A to point B, how to get food, how to get shelter, when it's going to rain, they can read all that, without all the gizmos. The gizmos are ultimately not as accurate as they rely on one measurement of one thing, whereas they know how to read all the different things.'

Hamacher said during a break at a talk he presented in Townsville, some Aboriginal guys told him the story about how, 'one time they were sitting outside and it was a beautiful day in the middle of the afternoon, sunny, and an Uncle jumps up and says it's going to rain, and they all shake their head thinking he's losing it. Then eight minutes later, boom, it poured then stopped in about three minutes.

'They asked "how did you know that?" They didn't realise he wasn't looking up but rather at the ranges on the horizon, the clouds coming in, he knew how to read all of that. Then the flipside happened and they saw rain clouds coming and they say we better go inside and

Uncle said no, they're not going to hit us – and they didn't.'

As Nakata flipped the sizzling spare ribs on the BBQ, Hamacher looked out across the water where monsoon clouds were darkening the afternoon sky.

'We don't pay attention, we don't spend much time outside, and if we do, it's doing a planned activity, we don't really sit back and take stock and read the environment – it's a skill we all had at some point in time, but we get so obsessed with out frigging phones and Netflix and everything else that we never take time to connect with that – it happens across the board.

'One time when I was out at Mer talking to all the Elders, I went down to the beach at sunset to take some stock film of the sky and couple of kids were there playing.

'We got talking as Jupiter and Venus appeared high in the sky. And they were like, "oh do you know what that is?". I said "'I know what that is. Do you know what that is?", being a little bit smart on my own part, and the kids were like "oh yeah," and they proceeded to take the next two minutes pointing out all the different planets and stars, names both in Miriam Mir and English and what they mean.

'I thought *Jesus!* and I asked "Where'd you learn all this?" and they said their dads taught them. It was *beziam* season, and all the sardines were up on the shore, and they were telling me what I should do if I'm in the water with the sharks, and I thinking if this was in Melbourne or Sydney, where the parents are never more than ten metres away, but that evening there were no adults around and they were two metres away from the sharks, but they knew what to do. They were raised in this environment they have that connection, but we have lost that.'

Hamacher believes there's this idea that ancient cultures, Indigenous cultures aren't relevant because they don't have modern technology, 'but they have incredible banks of knowledge, but we trash it and disrespect it.

'Look at the Southern Cross which every second Aussie gets tattooed, but you can't even see the fourth and fifth stars of the Southern Cross in the cities, you can't see the Milky Way. How are you going to maintain that connection if you can't even see it?'

Our contemporary world, or *supermodernity*, is characterised by excess and the absence of place and the deep connection it imbues. We have undergone a transformation of our concepts of time, space, and the individual – where there is a sense of placelessness and disconnect. Places such as airports, highways, supermarkets, suburbs, shopping malls and even the internet are the geographies of nowhereness, where the rapid advancement of globalisation, communications and mobility have left spaces commodified and devoid of meaning, identity or community. This has created an existential crisis, a malaise of modernity at the heart of our communal demise.

TI, a.k.a. The Rock, an allegory for the planet, the third rock from the sun, is always making apparent the transience of everything. What the sea spray doesn't corrode or the isolation and remoteness drive insane, everything comes, and goes, here – buildings, dreams and people – it's a cosmic caravan park.

A dream within a dream, a manifestation appeared in an abandoned field a while back, smoke and mirrors – the Carnies came to town. Gilmore's Travelling Tropical Amusements to be more precise, an inter-generational family that endlessly traipses the country towns of outback Australia. An apparition of wonder for my young daughter, complete with ectoplasmic fairy floss, forbidden fruits of dagwood dogs, jumping castles, dodge'em cars and shooting galleries, all under the incandescent gloss of coloured lights, that for one night drowned out the night sky.

Matt Gilmore, proprietor of the show, said it was a hard life. 'Holus Bolus, I've lost everything I own on the road. Three times, caravans, boats, trucks, just smashed to pieces before my eyes. But I love coming to a new town and giving the kiddies this entertainment – but I could never stay somewhere for more than two weeks, I'd go crazy.' And with a puff of diesel smoke they were gone, again illuminating the allegory of life on the rock, which is a metaphor of the transience of existence on the whole.

So now on my last morning on TI, I go to the beach that is my backyard, I try to resist my bleeding liberal heart, urbane sensibilities and take in my time here as a complete whole, the good, the bad, the corrosion, the erosion and the detritus of my mind as it washes up against the flotsam and jetsam of the world at my backdoor.

Out of this detritus I have built a little Zen garden, all found objects donated by the tides over my years on TI. A turtle shell leans on the fence and dugong rib bones left over from feasts stuck into the fence posts. I rake the sand one last time, subjugate the weeds and absorb the particles into an expression of fleeting existence here and now.

We will take the morning flight to Cairns.

In a last-ditch effort of economic survival, *Torres News* merged with the company's sister publications in the closing weeks of 2019 to make the *Cape and Torres News*. It ended the sixty-three years of *Torres News'* masthead. It's the end of an era and the end of our time on TI which will wash away with morning tide. By April 2020, the *Cape and Torres News* will collapse, one of the many regional papers to succumb to Covid 19.

Ultimately, in the grander scheme of things, I guess we are all flotsam and jetsam, star dust scattered by the cosmic winds, temporarily manifested into a group of atoms bouncing around, making up the 'here and now' we all get so lost in. Mass extinctions, including our own, climate change, meteorites smashing into us and annihilating everything, all just grains of sand – stardust particles the lot of us.

ESSOS AND ACKNOWLEDGEMENTS

First and foremost, I acknowledge Traditional Owners and pay my respects to Elders, past, present and emerging on the Country of the Kaurareg people, where I wrote this book, the Countries of both the Gimuy Walubara Yidinji and Yirrganydji peoples, where I edited it, and the Country of the Wurundjeri Woi Wurrung and Bunurong peoples of the Kulin Nation, where Transit Lounge Publishing is based. I also acknowledge all of the Countries and its First Nations peoples on this island nation on which I have lived, worked and played over the past half century.

Secondly I say minha big esso to the communities of the Torres Strait and the Northern Peninsula Area of Cape York who shared their stories with me as the last editor of their paper, often the only voice for communities largely forgotten by the rest of the country.

I also thank the many in those communities that made myself, wife and daughter feel so welcome, our Ailan home of Zenadth Kes will forever be in our hearts.

I would like to thank my publisher Barry Scott at Transit Lounge and especially my invaluable editors Penelope Goodes and Dominique Wilson. And thank you to the Bousen family, Corey, Mark and Meg for the opportunity to be their barefoot editor.

Also big esso to; Lesley French, Pedro Napau Stephen AM, Cr Vonda Malone, Cr Phillemon Mosby, Fred Gela, Eddie Newman, Aven and Melora Noah, Jen Enosa, Sylvia Tabau, Milton Savage, Tapee Salee, Julie Laifoo, Vanessa Seekee, Liberty Seekee, Silva Seekee, Suki Seekee, Dr Martin Nakata, Kenny Bedford, Dr Gracelyn Smallwood, C'Zarke and Adana Maza, Frazier Nai, Melissa Martin, Bishop Saibo Mabo, Ned David, Dimas Toby, Ceferino Sabatino, Alick Tipoti, Laurie Nona, Daniel Takai, Phoebe Pilot, Gessa Pilot, Patty Mills, Patrick Mills, Daniel Gibuma, Timothy Gibuma, Aunty Wasi Tardent, Thomas Fujii, Kabay Tamu, Jared Noah, Daniel Charlie, Elsie Seriat, Glen Mackie, Gabriel Bani, Murrandoo Bulanyi Yanner, Kantesha Takai, Leo Akee, June Phineasa Mosby Bann, Hans Ahwang, Uncle Ron Day, Uncle Alo Tapim, Doug Passi, Charlz David, Torres Webb, Edmund Tamwoy, Leonora Adidi, Harold Matthew, Thaine Mills, Anthony Geagea, Romina Fujii, Aaron Fa'aoso, Cr Kebei Salee, Jeff Waia, Danny Morseu, Barry Williams, Alesha Savage, Bongo Sagigi, Leon

Filewood, Dian Lui, Aunty Betty Mabo, Uncle Bua Mabo, Sonia Mayor, Perci Misi, Harry Seriat, Ivy Trevellion, Rosie Ware, Uncle Frank Cook, Mavis Bani, Regina Turner, Marsat Ketchell, George Ernst, Dr Sam Jones, TI Kate Stewart, Cate McQuillen, Duane Hamacher, Annabelle Craft, Brian Randall, Kim Rubenstein, Shanil Nanayakkara, Nola Page, Jerome Kalwij, Farshan Fairoos, Bruce Ranga, Adam Delaney, Bruce Nelson, Gordon Fawcett, Al Harris, Bianca Barling-Seden, Brett Charles, Uncle Frankie, Raph Gushtaspi, Jade Stevens, Dangerous Dave Foster, the Favas, the Carrolls, Jon Wren, Larry James, Pooja Rana, Jeremy and Ruth, The Bird Sisters, Bob the Builder, Brian Millett, Phil Hughes, Jamie Horn, David Lacey, John Latham, JD Purdy, Heidi Gibson, Cynthia Lui, Billy Gordon, Warren Entsch, Shannon Fentiman, Senator Jan McLucas and everyone else I have forgotten to mention. Thank you also to my fellow newshounds for your comradery and support, in particular; Stefan Armbruster, Alf Wilson, Chris Roe, Jack Latimore, Rhanna Collins, Patrick Keneally, Rudi Maxwell, Ella Archibald-Binge, Lorena Allam, Chrissie Goldrick, Amy McQuire, Sam Davis, Derek Tipper, Tess Newtown Cain, Hillary Whiteman, Matt Nicholls, 'Trendy' Trev Tim, Kier Shorey, and Roger Bartlett.

Thanks also to my family, Vivi, Sassie, Mum, Dad, Celeste, Euclydes and Bella.

Lastly, I want to thank all the noisy Australians.

Those Australians who refuse to be quiet and compliant and accept injustice – those who are willing to go down swinging.

For all of you, do not go gentle into that good night.

BIBLIOGRAPHY

Australian Government, *Australian Citizenship Act 2007*, Commonwealth of Australia, compiled July 2016, http://www.legislation.gov.au/Details/C2016C00726

Australian Government, Department of Foreign Affairs, *Torres Strait Treaty (1978)*, Australian Treaty Series 1985 No 4, Australian Government Publishing Service, Canberra, 1995, http://www.austlii.edu.au/au/other/dfat/treaties/1985/4.html

Australian Government, *Immigration Restriction Act 1901*, Commonwealth of Australia, 1901, http://www.legislation.gov.au/Details/C1901A00017

Australian Government, *Native Title Amendment Act 1998*, Commonwealth of Australia, 1998, http://www.legislation.gov.au/Details/C2004A00354

Australian Government, *Northern Territory National Emergency Response Act 2007* (a.k.a. *The Intervention*), Commonwealth of Australia, 2007, http://www.legislation.gov.au/Details/C2011C00053

Australian Human Rights Commission, *Bringing them Home: Report of the National Inquiry into the Separation of Aboriginal and Torres Strait Islander Children from Their Families*, Australian

Government, Commonwealth of Australia, 1997, http://humanrights.gov.au/sites/default/files/content/pdf/social_justice/bringing_them_home_report.pdf

Bani E, *Cracks in the mask*, Frances Calvert (producer & director), Talking Pictures Icarus Films/SBS, 1997

Bates D, *The passing of the Aborigines: A Lifetime Spent Among the Natives of Australia*, John Murry, London, 1938

Beckett J, *Torres Strait Islanders: Custom and Colonialism*, Cambridge University Press: Sydney, 1987

Behrendt L, 'In Your Dreams, Cultural Appropriation, Popular Culture and Colonialism,' *Law Text and Culture 4, no.1*, 1998

Blainey G, 'Drawing up a Balance Sheet of Our History', *Quadrant vol.37 no.7-8*, July-August 1993

Bonwick J, *The Lost Tasmanian Race*, Fb&c Limited, 2017 (1884)

Bottoms T, *Conspiracy of Silence: Queensland's frontier killing times*, Allen & Unwin: AU, 2013

Cairney S, *What Aboriginal knowledge can teach us about happiness*, TEDx, St Kilda, 2016, http://www.youtube.com/watch?v=Cf-dK8HFP2c

Clements N, *The Black War: Fear, Sex and Resistance in Tasmania*, University of Queensland Press: AU, 2014

Connor J, *Australian Frontier Wars, 1788-1838*, UNSW Press: AU, 2003

Conrad J, *Heart of Darkness*, Penguin Classics, Penguin UK, 2008 (1902)

Cook J, *Made In H.M. Bark 'Endeavour' 1768-71: A Literal Transcription of the Original MSS*, Elliot Stock, London, 1893, http://gutenberg.net.au/ebooks/e00043.html#ch8

Council of Australian Governments, *The National Partnership Agreement for Remote Indigenous Housing*, Commonwealth of Australia, 2008, http://www.federalfinancialrelations.gov.au/content/npa/housing/national-partnership/past/remote_indigenous_housing_NP.pdf

Cowlishaw G, *The City's Outback*, University of New South Wales Press: Sydney, 2009

DiAngelo R, *White Fragility: why it's so hard for white people to talk about racism*, Beacon Press: Boston, MA, 2018

Durack M, *Kings In Grass Castles*, Corgi Books: UK, 1996 (1959)

Federal Court of Australia, *Members of the Yorta Yorta Aboriginal Community v Victoria & Ors [1998] FCA 1606 (18 December 1998)*, Commonwealth of Australia, 1998, http://www8.austlii.edu.au/cgibin/viewdoc/au/cases/cth/FCA/1998/1606.html

Fernandez E, Lee J-S, Blunden H, McNamara P, Kovacs S & Cornefert, P-A, *No Child Should*

Grow Up Like This: Identifying Long Term Outcomes of Forgotten Australians, Child Migrants and the Stolen Generations, University of New South Wales: Kensington, 2016, http://www.forgottenaustralians.unsw.edu.au/sites/default/files/uploads/LOW%20RES%2012859_UNSW_FASS_ForgottenAustralians_Report_Nov16_LR_FA.pdf

Gammage B, *The Biggest Estate on Earth: how Aborigines made Australia*, Allen & Unwin: AU, 2012

Grant S, 'Can an Aborigine be a Smiths fan? I can be whatever I damn like', *The Australian Dream: Blood, History and Becoming:Quarterly Essay 64*, 2016

Gray S, *The Northern Territory Intervention: An evaluation*, Monash University, 2011, http://www.monash.edu/__data/assets/pdf_file/0008/406943/Caitlin-edit-of-NT-Intervention-page-1.pdf

Haddon A C, Rivers W H R, Seligmann C G, Wilkin A, *Reports of the Cambridge anthropological expedition to Torres Straits, Volumes 1-6*, Johnson Reprint Corp., New York, 1971 (1901)

Haskins V & Maynard J, *Living with the Locals: Early Europeans' Experience of Indigenous Life*, National Library of Australia Publishing: ACT, 2016

High Court of Australia, *Mabo v Queensland (No 2) (a.k.a. 'Mabo case')* [1992] HCA 23; (1992)

175 CLR 1 (3 June 1992), Commonwealth of Australia, 1992, http://www6.austlii.edu.au/cgi-bin/viewdoc/au/cases/cth/HCA/1992/23.html

High Court of Australia, *Mabo v Queensland [1988] HCA 69; (1989) 166 CLR 186 (8 December 1988)*, Commonwealth of Australia, 1989, http://www6.austlii.edu.au/cgi-bin/viewdoc/au/cases/cth/HCA/1988/69.html

Hilder B, *The Voyage of Torres: The Discovery of the Southern Coastline of New Guinea and Torres Strait by Captain Luis Baez De Torres in 1606*, University of Queensland Press, 1980

Howard J, *Motion of Reconciliation*, Parliament of Australia, 1999, http://parlinfo.aph.gov.au/parlInfo/search/display/display.w3p;query=(Id:media/presrel/23e06);rec=0;

Howard J, *The Liberal Tradition: Sir Robert Menzies Lecture 1996: the Beliefs and Values Which Guide the Federal Government*, Department of the Prime Minister and Cabinet, 1996, http://pmtranscripts.pmc.gov.au/sites/default/files/original/00010171.pdf

Hudson S, *Mapping the Indigenous Program and Funding Maze*, The Centre for Independent Studies, 2016, http://www.cis.org.au/app/uploads/2016/08/rr18-Full-Report.pdf

Hughes R, *The Fatal Shore*, Vintage Publishing: UK, 2003

Hull H, *The experience of forty years in Tasmania*, Orger & Meryon: London, 1859

Idriess I, *The Wild White Man of Badu*, Angus & Robertson: Sydney, 1950

Idriess I, *Drums of Mer*, ETT Imprint: NSW, 2020 (1933)

Irvine L, *Castaway*, Victor Gollancz: London, 1983

Jahoda G, *Images of Savages: Ancient Roots of Modern Prejudice in Western Culture*, Routledge: UK, 1998

Jardine F L, *Narrative of the Overland Expedition of the Messrs. Jardine from Rockhampton to Cape York, Northern Queensland*, Alpha Editions, 2018 (1867)

Jode G de & C de, *Speculum orbis terrae*, be and Antverpiae, 1593, Stanford Libraries, http://exhibits.stanford.edu/renaissance-exploration/catalog/mb161sz2357

Keating P, *Redfern Speech – Transcript*, ANTaR, 1992, http://antar.org.au/sites/default/files/paul_keating_speech_transcript.pdf

Kelly L, *The Memory Code*, Allen & Unwin: AU, 2016

MacFarlane S, *Among the Cannibals of New Guinea: being the story of the New Guinea Mission of the London Missionary Society*, Presbyterian Board of Publication and Sabbath School Work, Philadelphia, 1888

Martin D F, 'Does Native Title merely provide an entitlement to be native? Indigenes, identities, and applied anthropological practice', *TAJA: The Australian Journal of Anthropology, Vol 26, Issue1,* 2015

Maugham W S, 'French Joe' (1926), *65 Short Stories,* Heinemann/Octopus, 1976

Maugham, W. S, 'German Harry'(1924), *Cosmopolitans,* Doran & Company: NY, 1937

McCright A M & Dunlap R E, 'Cool dudes: The denial of climate change among conservative white males in the United States', *Global Environ Change Vol 21 no.4,* Elsevier: Amsterdam, 2011, http://sciencepolicy.colorado.edu/students/envs_4800/mccright_dunlap_2011.pdf

Members of the First Nations National Constitutional Convention, *Uluru Statement of the Heart,* Uluru: Central Australia, May 2017, http://www.referendumcouncil.org.au/sites/default/files/2017-05/Uluru_Statement_From_The_Heart_0.PDF

Menzies G, *1421: The Year China Discovered The World,* Transworld Publishers Ltd: GB, 2003

Morris S, 2012, 'Re-evaluating Mabo: the Case for Native Title Reform to Remove Discrimination and Promote Economic Opportunity', *Land, Rights, Laws: Issues of Native Title, Vol 5, no.3,* Native Title Research Unit, AIATSIS, Canberra, 2012, http://aiatsis.gov.au/site

s/default/files/products/issues_paper/morris-ntip-v5n3-re-evaluatingmabo-native-title-reform_0.pdf

Northern Territory Government, *Ampe Akelyernemane Meke Mekarle 'Little Children are Sacred': Report of the Northern Territory Board of Inquiry into the Protection of Aboriginal Children from Sexual Abuse*, 2007, http://humanrights.gov.au/sites/default/files/57.4%20%E2%80%9CLittle%20Children%20are%20 Sacred%E2%80%9D%20report.pdf

Pascoe B, *Dark Emu, Black Seeds: agriculture or accident*, Magabala Books: AU, 2014

Paterson A B, 'Thirsty Island' (1902), *Three Elephant Power and Other Stories*, Dodo Press, 2007 (1917)

Pholi K, 'Why I burned my "Proof of Aboriginality"', *The Drum*, ABC: AU, 2012, http://www.abc.net.au/news/2012-09-27/pholiaboriginality/4281772

Queensland Government, *Aboriginal and Torres Strait Islander Land (Providing Freehold) and Other Legislation Amendment Act 2014* (a.k.a. *The Freehold Bill, the Freehold Act*), Commonwealth of Australia, 2014, http://www.legislation.qld.gov.au/view/pdf/asmade/act-2014-045

Queensland Government, *Aboriginal Cultural Heritage Act 2003*, Commonwealth of Australia, 2003, http://www.legislation.qld.gov.au/view/pdf/inforce/current/act-2003-079

Queensland Government, *An Act to Make Provision for the Government of the Native Inhabitants of the Islands of Torres Strait and their Descendants, and for other purposes* (a.k.a. *Torres Strait Islander Act 1939*), Commonwealth of Australia, 1939, http://www8.austlii.edu.au/cgi-bin/viewdb/au/legis/qld/hist_act/tsiao19393gvn7382/

Firth, R, 1932 in Reynolds, H. 2013, *Forgotten War*, New South Publishing, Sydney, pg.27

Reynolds H, *An indelible stain? The question of genocide in Australia's history*, Viking Press: USA, 2001

Robinson G A, Plomley N J B (Editor), *Friendly mission: the Tasmanian journals and papers of George Augustus Robinson, 1829-1834*, Quintus Publishing, Hobart: Tasmania, 2008.

Rousseau J-J, *Discourse on the Origins of Inequality Among Men*, Penguin Classic, 1985 (1754)

Rubenstein K, *Australian Citizenship Law 2e*, Law Book Co of Australasia: Pyrmont, 2016

Rudd K, *Apology to the Stolen Generations*, Department of Foreign Affairs & Trade, Australian Government, 2008, http://www.dfat.gov.au/people-to-people/public-diplomacy/programs-activities/Pages/text-of-the-apology-to-the-stolen-generations

Sharp N, *Footprints Along The Cape York Sand Beaches*, Aboriginal Studies Press: ACT, 2000

Tauli-Corpuz V, Alcorn J, Molnar A, *Cornered by Protected Areas: Replacing 'Forest' Conservation with Rights-based Approaches Helps Bring Justice for Indigenous Peoples and Local Communities, Reduces Conflict, and Enables Cost-effective Conservation and Climate Action,* Rights and Resources Organisation: U.S. & Canada, 2018, http://rightsandresources.org/wp-content/uploads/2018/06/Cornered-by-PAs-Brief_RRI_June-2018.pdf

United Nations Refugee Agency, *Convention on the Reduction of Statelessness,* United Nations, 1961, http://www.unhcr.org/protection/statelessness/3bbb286d8/convention-reduction-statelessness.html

United Nations, *United Nations Declaration on the Rights of Indigenous People,* United Nations, 2007, http://www.un.org/development/desa/indigenouspeoples/wp-content/uploads/sites/19/2018/11/UNDRIP_E_web.pdf

United Nations, *Universal Declaration of Human Rights,* 1948, http://www.un.org/en/universal-declaration-human-rights/index.html

Verne J, *Twenty Thousand Leagues Under the Sea,* Wordsworth Editions Ltd: Hertfordshire, 1995 (1870)

Wallace L, 'White people have no culture', *terra incognita media,* 2018, http://www.terraincognitamedia.com/features/white-peoplehave-no-culture2018

West J, *The History of Tasmania*, CreateSpace Independent Publishing Platform, 2016 (1852)

Wharton W J L, *Captain Cook's Journal During His First Voyage Round The World*, Elliot Stock: London, 1893

Wills K H, 'Reminiscence', *Brandon Papers*, OM 75/75/3, John Oxley Memorial Library, Brisbane

www.ingramcontent.com/pod-product-compliance
Lightning Source LLC
Chambersburg PA
CBHW011141290426
44108CB00021B/2705